W9-ARY-966

BORN TO RUN
the Bruce Springsteen story

By Dave Marsh

A Delilah Book

Dolphin Books

Doubleday & Company, Inc.

Garden City, New York

1979

Copyright©1979 by Dave Marsh
ISBN: 0-385-15443-7
Library of Congress Catalog Card Number 79-52514
Dolphin Books
Doubleday & Company Inc.
All Rights Reserved
Printed in the United States of America

A Delilah Book

Cover Design And Book Design By Ernie Thormahlen
And Mick Rock For T.R.A. Studios Inc.

"It's My Life" written by Roger Atkins and Carl D'Errico, copyright © 1965 Screen Gems-EMI Music, Inc.

Used by permission; all rights reserved.

All other songs written by Bruce Springsteen. "Blinded By The Light," "Growin' Up," "If I Was The Priest,"

"It's Hard To Be A Saint in the City," copyright © 1972, Bruce Springsteen/Laurel Canyon Music, Ltd.; "The E Street Shuffle,"

"Fourth Of July, Asbury Park (Sandy)," "Incident On Fifty-Seventh Street," "New York City Serenade," "Rosalita," copyright © 1974,

Bruce Springsteen/Laurel Canyon Music, Ltd.; "Born to Run," Backstreets," "Jungleland," "Thunder Road," copyright © 1975,

Bruce Springsteen/Laurel Canyon Music, Ltd.; "Adam Raised A Cain," "Badlands," "Darkness On The Edge Of Town," "Factory,"

"The Promised Land," "Racing In The Street," copyright © 1978, Bruce Springsteen; "Independence Day," "The Promise,"

copyright © 1979, Bruce Springsteen Used by permission; all rights reserved.

For Barbara —And All The Tramps Like Us.

TABLE OF CONTENTS

Independence Day

"Me and the boys got some work to do. You wanna come along? It ain't like the old days . . . but it'll do."
Edmond O'Brien, *The Wild Bunch*

This book was first written in 1976. Flush with the newness of Springsteen's success, it was shorter, breezier, I guess happier. But that version never appeared, because Mike Appel (who then controlled Bruce Springsteen's song publishing rights) at the last moment withdrew his permission to quote from the lyrics. Perhaps it was fortuitous: I now realize that, back then, the story was far too fresh for me to appreciate it fully.

At any rate, the manuscript moldered in my desk until last summer, when I finally asked Bruce what he thought about my updating it. My reasons had nothing to do with permission—this isn't an authorized biography. But I felt Bruce, having already suffered enough at the hands of people with typewriters, was owed a veto. Fortunately, he accepted the idea.

My reasons for writing the book go beyond its role in rationalizing my Springsteen fanaticism (which justifies itself). As did Jon Landau, when I saw Bruce Springsteen, I saw my personal rock history flash before my eyes—the dreams and hopes of what might have been were suddenly restored. For me, this is not a story about just Bruce Springsteen. It is also a chronicle of rock in the Sixties—and in the Seventies, as its innocence curdled into cynicism.

For that reason, the hardest part of writing *Born to Run* was leaving my own voice out of it. Without such distance, there's no question that the book would have been merely a zealot's rant. And while I wanted to write a fan's book—indeed, while I knew how to write no other kind—I also wanted Bruce Springsteen's story to speak to everyone who cares about the music and about what's happened to the people who make it and love it. But now it's time to let down my guard.

I believe that rock and roll has saved lives, because I know that it was instrumental in shaping my own.

When Bruce speaks of rock reaching down into homes without culture to tell kids that there is another way to live, I understand it personally. That is exactly what happened in my house. If this book succeeds, it's because it takes the measure of the life of a bus driver's son (like Bruce Springsteen)—or a railroad brakeman's son (like myself) or perhaps your own life—and spells out something of what rock and roll has given to them. We had nothing; rock lent us a sense that we could have it all.

But over the past decade, rock has betrayed itself. It gnaws at my marrow to recall a hundred sellouts, from the rock opera movies that were all glamour and no heart, to the photos of rock celebrities with international jet-set fugitives. The inevitable result was records that were made not with feeling but because there was a market demanding product, and concerts performed with an eye only toward the profit margin. Rock became just another hierarchical system in which consumers took what was offered without question. Asking who was fake and who was for real used to be half the joy of the thing. Losing that option was our own fault, of course, but that doesn't make it hurt less. Rock saved my life. It also broke my heart.

So then the advent of Bruce Springsteen, who made rock and roll a matter of life and death again, seemed nothing short of a miracle to me. Not because it shifted the trend toward sounds I preferred but because it proved that one man could make a difference; because it said that it was every man's responsibility to root out the corruption that had seeped into rock.

I remember four days in Los Angeles during the summer of 1978. On the first night Bruce climbed atop a six-story building to paint a mustache on the billboard advertising his album on Sunset Strip; "artistic improvement" he called it. The next night he played the Forum, the area's largest arena; it was sold-out, but the show was as intimate as any with fifteen thousand participants could be. The night after that, performing with as much intensity as he had at the Forum, Springsteen played with an unknown band from Oklahoma in a roadhouse out in Callabasas that couldn't have held more than fifty people. And on the final evening, Bruce played the Roxy in Los Angeles, before a live audience of five hundred and to thousands of radio listeners. There had been some confusion about tickets, and not everyone who had stood in line all night got them. Springsteen apologized, live on the radio, then played as forcefully as anyone I have ever heard.

Every day now, new rock and rollers appear, fierce with determination not to compromise. "Punks," they often call themselves, and though I'm not yet thirty, they make me feel old. For I know that rock can never be for them what it was for me and my friends—itself a means of avoiding compromise. I recognize that some of what I have written here seems overstated. There was no helping it. For Bruce Springsteen is the last of rock's

great innocents. There can never be another quite like him.

But as long as weeks like that one in Los Angeles are still possible, even the betrayals seem worth it. If his admirers sometimes treat Bruce Springsteen as a messiah, don't blame them. Only understand what it meant to us for the great promise of rock and roll to be fulfilled at last.

So this book was written to remind myself that these things really happened, as much as to share the story with others. And at the end, what I remember is not one of the happy songs, but one of the saddest. When Bruce sang it that night at the Roxy, he dedicated it to his father. It made me think of mine, and how desperately I've always wanted to communicate to him what's happened in a world he will never know. But tonight, that song also brings back to me the whole story of rock

and roll itself. It is called "Independence Day."

Poppa go to bed now, it's getting late
Nothing we can say can change anything now
Because there's different people comin' down here
  now
And they see things in different ways
And soon everything we've known will just be
  swept away
So say goodbye, it's Independence Day
Poppa now I know the things you wanted that you
  could not say
Say goodbye it's Independence Day
I swear I never meant to take those things away

New York City
April 24, 1979

1

The E Street Shuffle

August 15, 1975

On this hot night in Greenwich Village, two hundred kids huddle in dank humidity at the corner of Mercer and West Fourth Streets. Their faces alternate between hope and despair. Some have come from as far away as Philadelphia to see the rock show across the street.

The club is the Bottom Line, the showcase nightclub of the Manhattan music industry. Its fluorescent marquee reads:

Aug. 13–17
Bruce Springsteen
& the E Street Band
Sold Out

Tonight is the middle night of the stand. The crowd

is waiting on a chance at standing-room tickets—fifty per show, all that are left to buy—an opportunity to do nothing but elbow up to the bar or crowd around the coat-check room. They may not see much, but at least they'll be there.

Selling out the Bottom Line for five nights (ten shows) isn't terribly difficult. The club seats only five hundred. But Springsteen is playing here out of conviction. His new album, *Born to Run*, is about to be released; it is the most rabidly anticipated LP in years. Springsteen hasn't had a new record in nearly two years, but in that time his cult has trebled. A tape of the title song is already an underground hit in Boston, Cleveland, Austin and Phoenix. In New York, Springsteen's following is sufficient for WNEW-FM, the city's leading FM rock station, to broadcast tonight's first set live. From the Jersey coast to Connecticut, cassette recorders are hooked to radio receivers.

Springsteen is prepared. Wednesday's opening sets were rocky in all the wrong ways—ragged and nervous. But Thursday's performances turned the corner. Bruce regained his keen edge. Unlike almost every other contemporary rock star, he has earned his following not with records but with stagecraft: charismatic, intense and intimate two-and-one-half-hour shows. By the end, he is drained and so is the crowd. <u>Few leave unconvinced.</u>

Last night's second set ended well after two A.M., with the crowd on its chairs and the band rocking the final encore, "Twist and Shout." Not counting an hour off while the Bottom Line staff cleared the first show customers and let the second group inside, the band had been onstage for more than six hours. And unlike the similar marathons of the Grateful Dead, this was not laid-back hippie music; this was street-level, kick-ass rock and roll and rhythm and blues, music to dance to, conjure with, and be overpowered by.

Tonight, passing WNEW's emcee Dick Neer, Springsteen delivers a spiel patterned after Muhammad Ali's heavyweight title fight boasts. Tonight, he's out to prove that he's the champ. He says this into an open mike, and when it reaches the radio listeners milliseconds later, a few are bemused. Of course he's the champ—the only problem is that, at this point, rock has few other contenders for the title.

Still, it requires more than the usual amount of arrogance to make this claim. Since the beginning of the summer, the group has played only in the studio. The four previous Bottom Line sets are the only ones that have included Miami Steve Van Zandt, the new guitarist. But the band lives up to every boast. Van Zandt is ready; he looks a gunslinger, relaxed but coiled for action. Drummer Max Weinberg is smashing a few practice shots into his kit. Clarence Clemons, the big saxman, thunders scattered notes from his tenor horn; he glowers, white-suited and very black, at the virtually all-white audience, as enticing as he is threatening. Pianist Roy Bittan and organist Danny Federici finger their keyboards, itching to start. Garry Tallent, the implacable bassist, stares past his beard at his shoes, absently plucking his heavy strings.

Suddenly, Bruce hits the stage. A white spot hits him; from the first note, it's clear that Springsteen sees something unusual at stake tonight. Maybe he's thinking of that long line of radio-linked tape recorders rolling from Asbury Park to way up in Westchester, and on out across Long Island. Instead of the solo number he has been opening with, Springsteen grabs the mike and flails his arm like a man falling off a bicycle as the band crashes into "Tenth Avenue Freeze-Out," the story of the band and one of the songs from *Born to Run*.

The band charges into "Spirit in the Night," dedicated "to all the folks down by the Shore, down at Greasy Lake." In the middle, Springsteen crawls onto one of the front tables, prompting squeals of delight from the patrons, to sing a verse up close. He leaps back onstage and finishes the song, then dives into the magic world of the Crystals' "Then She Kissed Me." The beauty of the arrangement has Springsteen almost breathless; he sings as if the song were new to him, as if he really *had* just mustered up the nerve to go up and ask that dream-date if she wanted to dance. His twelve-string guitar notes fall into the night and travel those airwaves like a message home.

Through his comic autobiography, "Growin' Up," its delight balanced between the devilish and the angelic, and into the searing "[It's Hard to Be A] Saint in the City," which resolves the issue in favor of both sides, the roar of the crowd grows louder. Then the stage goes black. Weinberg begins to snap rimshots like a tired metronome. All at once, a blue spotlight hits Bruce squarely and Bittan strikes some beautiful rolling chords on the piano. The organ slips underneath for a couple of bars, and Miami Steve's wailing guitar cries out. Then Springsteen brings his arm up, and snaps it down.

"Bam!" he cries, leaping into the air. The music rises with him, and as his feet hit the boards, the music falls back.

"It was, uh, about three, four years ago—four years ago, about this time of the year, around August," he begins, his voice raspy. "I was working in this bar down on the Shore. I worked there for three, maybe four months, place called the Student Prince." A cheer. Springsteen has made the bars of Asbury Park—his home turf—nearly as famous as he is. And tonight, there is a large element in the audience which has been following him long enough to remember those clubs.

"So it was me," he continues, the rhythm ticking away, "and it was Steve here and Garry. Garry was in the band then. And Southside Johnny.

"Do you folks get down to the Shore much?" He's answered with maniacal cheers. The mention is a set-up; Bruce has accomplished the virtually impossible feat of making New Jersey fashionable. The shouts of

affirmation come even from fans whose summers are spent on the rooftop tar beaches of the city. "Well you gotta go see Southside Johnny's band, yeah, the Jukes." He croaks this, giggling, half little boy, half adult.

"Anyway, this is about three, four years ago, me and Steve and Garry are working in this bar down there. And we were feelin' like, like real discouraged at the time," he says, as though this is now unbelievable. "Because no one would give us a gig or nothin'. We went into this bar—the only way we got this job was this guy had just bought the bar and we went in there about midnight on a Saturday night. You know, there should be a few folks in there, right? Went into this place, the darkest, dingiest, dampest place you ever seen and there was nobody in there. Right?

"So we walk up to this guy and say we'll play for the door. You know, we'll charge a dollar at the door and we'll play for that. So we had a seven-piece band at the time, a big band. And we brought the band in the first week and we made, hell, we musta made..."

"Thirteen seventy-five," interjects Miami Steve, with a flat air of doom.

"Yeah, we split $13.75 between us," Springsteen goes on, chuckling a bit. "And a few guys quit, you know. The next week I was there with a six-piece band. Threw some cat out—five-piece band. This went on for a few weeks until we got it down to ... You get down to your boys when you're starvin'.

"We was playin' this joint and we was always figurin', like, these people was trying to set us up. Like, 'Man, I got the manager from the Byrds comin' down here tonight to check you guys out. So you dudes better be good.' Right? So we would play like mad dogs all night. And about three in the mornin' we'd all be sittin' at this damn little table, sayin' 'Where is the cat? You know? What happened to the joker? Where is the dude?

"And Steve, Steve was known then for practicin' his guitar, day in and day out, night and day, all the time. Every time I'd see him, he would practice, practice, practice. He always had his guitar with him, everywhere he went, you know. See him on the boardwalk, he's always got his guitar with him. Practice, practice, practice.

"So one night after the gig, we was all feelin' down in the dumps and you know, you're sittin' there sayin' 'Man, we're better than them cats and they got *two* records out. How come we ain't got no record out?' Right? You do all that kind of stuff, you know. Me and Steve was feelin' really, really drug out, and we figured we were gonna walk home. Figured we'd walk north along the boardwalk.

"So we got out there and it was a nasty night. It was rainin' and the club was flooded because some bikers come along and ripped off the front door. Really," he says when the crowd begins to laugh. "They just ripped the sucker off and brought it home with 'em or somethin'. I don't know what they did with it." As though the door, not the flood, were amazing. "They are that thing. *Right.*"

"So we was walkin' down the boardwalk this time of night. It was late—musta been four in the mornin'. Steve had his guitar with him. He was practicin'. And we was just walkin' down the boardwalk, figurin' we wanted to get home." The music continues its slow but inexorable pace, Federici's organ joining the melody every few bars. But Miami Steve has dropped out; he is too engrossed in the story. Springsteen swings over to his side of the stage and they pretend to peer into the distance.

"All of a sudden, we see somethin' comin'. I said, "Steve, you see somethin' comin' down there?'"

"Umm huh," Van Zandt answers.

"He says yeah. I said, 'I don't know *what* that is.' But we don't want to take no chances, like, we just wanted to get home. We don't wanna fool around. So we ducked in this doorway, you know [they lean back]. And he told me to peek out. And I peek out.

"Whatever it was was comin' in the rain. The wind was blowin', it was in this big mist. And it was dressed all in white."

Clarence Clemons jumps into the spotlight, facing Bruce and Miami Steve. He begins to swing his arms and slowly walk in place, as though approaching them. His size, and their cowering figures, make the saxman seem truly a force of nature.

"Dressed all in white with a walkin' stick. Walkin' like there ain't no rain, no wind. I said, 'Steven! Are you ... am I crazy or is that dude carryin' a *saxophone*?'" Now the crowd catches on. It roars with joy.

"So we figured," Bruce says, as Steven nods in terrified agreement, "any dude walkin' in the rain at four A.M., dressed all in white, walkin' like there's no rain, with a saxophone is not to be messed with! Let the sucker walk on by, right?

"So we huddled in the doorway, and we were sorta scared. [Steve hides his face, ducks behind Bruce, peers over the singer's shoulder.] We were a little scared. We were thinkin' we didn't want to get messed around or nothin'. I thought, that's all I need—come home with $3.50 and a messed-up face tonight.

"We heard his footsteps comin' closer. [Steve pantomimes the steps, banging on his guitar strings.] And they came closer [banging] and closer. They came even closer than that [final bang]. Now we figured this is no time to look like we were scared. We figured this guy is gonna come along, so we better at least look like

we're bad. So here the cat's comin' and we're startin' to get ready." Steve pushes Bruce toward Clarence. Bruce drags his heels, but edges a little nearer. "And this cat comes up and he turned and he faced off right in front of us in the doorway and I just jumped back like this [falls into Steve's arms, as the music continues to swell].

"The first thing we did was, we throw all our money down. Threw *all* the damn money down. Then I still didn't know where the cat was at. He didn't move, he didn't do nothin'. He just stood there. And he held out the saxophone. So I took out my sneakers—I wasn't goin' to take no chances—and I threw them down. I figured he might want me to do that.

"But all he did was ... put out his hand. [Clarence's hand edges into the spotlight, which is still fixed on Bruce]. So me and Steve leaned back and we got just ... a little ... closer. And then when we touched, it was like:

Sparks! fly on E Street
When the boy-prophets walk it handsome and hot
All the little girls' souls grow weak
When the manchild hits 'em with a double shot
The schoolboy pops pull out all the stops
On a Friday night ...

And suddenly the band and the crowd sing with Bruce, in a moment of unity and passion:

The teenage tramps in skin tight pants do the
E Street dance
And it's all right

In that moment, it is a good deal better than all right.

Bruce atop the piano at the Bottom Line during his 1975 broadcast.

2

It's My Life

Bruce Springsteen has made Asbury Park, New Jersey, famous. But that's not really his hometown. He grew up fifteen miles inland, in Freehold, a small town of the sort that has almost disappeared since the freeways re-routed traffic. It isn't a place of suburban ranch homes and half-acre lots. It's the kind of community familiar to Americans who grew up before World War II—more than a bedroom to its residents, but without the pretensions of a city. There are a couple of factories—the largest makes Nescafe instant coffee—and the seat of Monmouth County; small shops rather than shopping malls. Towns like this have been sliding downhill for years; in today's world, the very concept of such places is outmoded. Still, there is something

secure about a town like Freehold; it has a feeling of stability tract housing can never create.

Bruce was born in Freehold on September 23, 1949, the first child of Adele and Douglas Springsteen. (He would later acquire a pair of sisters, Ginny and Pam.) Their surname is Dutch, (not Jewish as is commonly supposed), but Douglas Springsteen's ancestry is mostly Irish; his wife is Italian. Bruce apparently acquired his talent for tale-spinning from his maternal Grandfather Zirilli.

A story Bruce used to tell about his youthful life in Freehold sums up the place, and the time. It is, of course, considerably mythologized, but those who were around in the old days say that almost every word is true.

"I lived eighteen years of my life in a small town in New Jersey, next door to a gas station—Ducky Slattery's Sinclair Station. That was the guy's name, Ducky Slattery. He was an older guy. And I lived next door.

"You know how in a small town, the place where the people hang out these days is down at the gas station. Everybody comes in and sits around at the gas station. Some guy comes in, somebody goes out, pumps the gas, comes back in. Ducky Slattery and this guy Bill who was kinda . . . This cat had a pink Cadillac. It was a sight! Got drunk, smashed it up.

"Ducky Slattery had this one line he ripped off the Marx Brothers. Anybody'd come in, he'd say, 'Wanna buy a duck?' That was his big line—not too original, but it worked. 'Wanna buy a duck?' Whaddya gonna do with a duck?

"I had a duck . . . my father killed a duck for Thanksgiving once. Helped me get out of the draft. Went down to the Army, told 'em ever since I seen my father kill that duck, I go crazy every time I see a duck. Told 'em, if I was out there on the battlefield in Vietnam, and I seen a duck, I might do anything—start killin' generals or something'. I could do anything—I don't know what I do when I see a duck."

(Bruce actually beat the draft in the classic Sixties fashion. "They gave me the forms and I checked everything. Even said I was a homo and all that. Then this guy calls me into his office, talks to me for about three minutes and tells me to go home.")

Douglas Springsteen had a variety of jobs, ranging from factory worker to prison guard. But mostly he drove a bus. "My father was a driver," Bruce recalls. "He liked to get in the car and just drive. He got everybody else in the car, too, and he made *us* drive. He made us all drive." It's a trait Bruce retains to this day; he likes the feeling of being in an automobile, behind the wheel or riding shotgun, cruising slowly or careening recklessly. His fascination with highway imagery in his songs is not an idle one.

Springsteen attended parochial schools, not the best environment for a headstrong, idealistic kid who refused to learn his place. "I lived half of my first thirteen years in a trance," he has said. "People thought I was weird because I always went around with this look on my face. I was thinking of things, but I was always on the outside looking in.''

Bruce was far from the most popular kid in school. Nuns seemed to single him out for harassment. ''In the third grade a nun stuffed me in a garbage can under her desk because, she said, that's where I belonged. I also had the distinction of being the only altar boy knocked down by a priest during Mass. The old priest got mad. My mother wanted me to serve Mass, but I didn't know what I was doin' so I was tryin' to fake it.''

Some of the trouble may have been self-inflicted. Bruce is by nature reserved; he does not reveal much of himself with any ease. Coupled with an equally strong streak of self-reliance often misinterpreted (even in his adult life) as arrogance, this spelled problems. Once, in fifth or sixth grade, he was sent to a first-grade classroom, as punishment. ''I got down there and I was still actin' up. So the nun says to one of the little kids in class, 'Jimmy, I want you to show Bruce how we deal with people who act like that down here.' And this little kid gets up, walks over and slaps me in the face.''

He might have hated school anyway, but parochial school, with its emphasis on discipline and social restraint, was poorly suited to anyone rebellious by nature. ''I was there eight years,'' Bruce says. ''That's a long time. I still remember a lot of things about it. But I don't remember anything nice about it, so I guess I didn't enjoy it. It has nothing to do with me. I'm not involved in it. I'm here to play music; I'm in a rock band. Some people pray, some people play music.'' He attended a public high school.

Conflict was not unknown at home, either. The Springsteens were much less than affluent—from time to time, they lived with his maternal grandparents—and because Douglas was often out of work, the problems were even more severe than for most poor kids. Both Bruce and Douglas are headstrong, volatile personalities, without much use for superfluous rules. In such circumstances, a son with vision and ambition can seem less than a blessing. Bruce's memories of his early life are a mixture of the hilarious and the bitter. "We had a bathroom with a big gaping hole in it," he told an early interviewer, "and it looked right into this convent. I used to tell the other kids that during the war an airplane crashed into it—to save face, y'know?" (The story has a germ of truth: the bathroom window was broken).

The family was typical American working class; culture was television and the daily paper. "I wasn't brought up in a house where there was a lot of reading and stuff. I was brought up on TV," Bruce says. "Who was William Burroughs? They never brought him up in high school in the Sixties—unless you hung around with that kind of crowd. And I didn't hang around with no crowd that was talking about William Burroughs."

The crowd he did hang around with was trouble enough as far as his father was concerned. Although he now speaks of his father with both affectionate humor and a kind of intense identification, there was a time when the mixture of love and hate all adolescents feel for their parents was seriously unbalanced. Introducing an old Animals song, Bruce used to tell this story: "I grew up in this small town about twenty miles inland. I remember it was in this dumpy, two-story, two-family house, next door to this gas station. And my mom, she was a secretary and she worked downtown. She married my pop as soon as he got out of the Army; they got married and she took that job. And my father, he worked a lotta different places, worked in a rug mill for a while, drove a cab for a while, and he was a guard down at the jail for a while. I can remember when he worked down there, he used to always come home real pissed off, drunk, sit in the kitchen.

"At night, about nine o'clock, he used to shut off all the lights, every light in the house. And he used to get real pissed off if me or my sister turned any of 'em on.

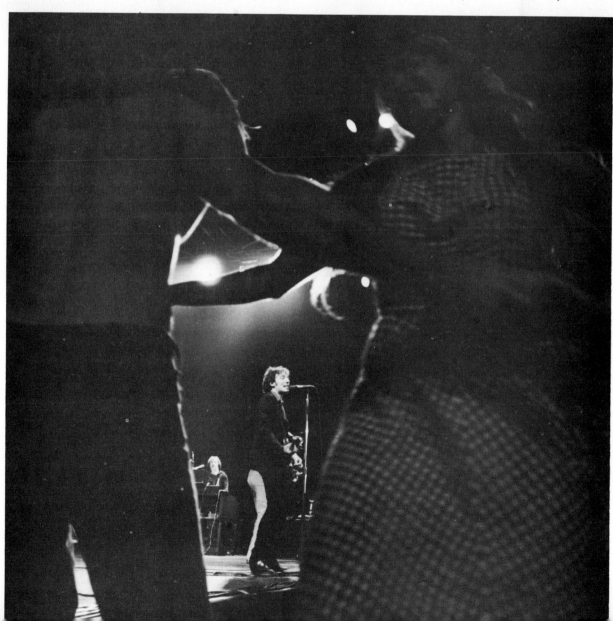

And he'd sit in the kitchen with a six pack and a cigarette. My mom, she'd set her hair and she would come downstairs and just turn on the TV and sit in the chair and watch TV till she fell asleep. And she'd get up the next morning and go to work again.

"My pop, sometimes he went to bed, sometimes he didn't. Sometimes he got up. Sometimes he didn't get up. And I used to sleep upstairs. In the summertime, when the weather got hot, I used to drag my mattress out the window and sleep on the roof next door to the gas station. And I watched these different guys—the station closed at one and these guys, they'd be pullin' in and pullin' out all night long. They'd be meetin' people there. They'd be rippin' off down the highway.

"As soon as I got sixteen, me and my buddy, we got this car and we started takin' off. We used to take off down to the beach, sleep on top of the beach houses. We used to spin up to the city, just walk around the streets all night long 'til the cops would catch us in the Port Authority and call our pops. My pop, he'd never come and get me. I remember he always sent my mother. Everytime I got in trouble, my mother would always come and she'd always say, 'Your father, he don't even wanna come.'

"I used to always have to go back home. And I'd stand there in that driveway, afraid to go in the house, and I could see the screen door, I could see the light of my pop's cigarette. And I remember I just couldn't wait until I was old enough to take him out once.

"I used to slick my hair back real tight so he couldn't tell how long it was gettin'. And try to sneak through the kitchen. But the old man he'd catch me every night and he'd drag me back into that kitchen. He'd make me sit down at the table in the dark, and he would sit there tellin' me. And in the wintertime, he used to turn on the gas stove and close all the doors so it got real hot in there. And I can remember just sittin' there in the dark, him tellin' me ... tellin' me, tellin' me, tellin' me. And I could always hear that voice, no matter how long I sat there. But I could never, ever see his face."

Throughout this recitation, the music has kept up an ominous, unresolved figure. The drums rumble, the electric glockenspiel rings remorselessly, bass and guitar mumble the same phrase over and over. But now that phrase resolves itself, swells into something beautiful but aching; the soprano sax squawks in confusion, but through this maze there is a route to freedom. The sound, halfway to cacophony, builds to peak volume, and when Bruce resumes his story, he has to shout to make himself heard.

"We'd start talkin' about nothin' much. How I was doin'. Pretty soon he'd ask me what I thought I was doin' with myself, and we'd always end up screamin' at each other. My mother she'd always end up runnin' in from the front room, cryin' and tryin' to pull him off me, try to keep us from fightin' with each other. And I'd always, I'd always end up runnin' out the back door, pullin' away from him, runnin' down the driveway, screamin' at him, tellin' him, tellin' him, tellin' him how it was my life and I was gonna do what I wanted to do."

And the music swells a final time as Bruce sings the famous opening lines:

It's a hard world to get a break in
All the good things have been taken
But I know there's ways
To make certain these days
Though I come dressed in rags
I will wear sable some day
Hear what I say!
[Shouted] Man I'm gonna make for certain . . .
ain't gonna be no more of my time spent . . .
sweatin' rent . . . Hear my command! I'm cuttin'
loose . . . it ain't no use . . . tryin' to hold me down
. . . stickin' 'round
Cause baby [Baby!]
Remember [Remember!]
It's my life and I do what I want
It's my mind and I think what I want
Show me I'm wrong
Hurt me sometime
But someday I'll treat you real fine

"It's My Life" is the perfect story-song for Springsteen. The situation he describes in the introduction is dramatized but still recognizable; it hits so hard because, despite its personal (and apparently authentic) details, it is also a universal story of what happened to fathers and sons in the Sixties . . . perhaps what happens to parents and children eternally. As a result, watching Bruce go through that epic onstage can be confusing: Should one weep, or dance in joy at his release? Exhilaration is the victor; through music, Springsteen triumphs, leaving the prison of small-time life behind him. It's corny all right—you can see the same sort of scene acted out in the classic John Garfield boxing film, *Body and Soul*—but, like sports and the movies, rock and roll represents for many working-class kids the only prospect of surmounting the despair of their inheritance. As Bruce would later realize, the real miracle was that he and his father had the same goal—both wanted more for Bruce than Douglas had ever been able to have. "What they didn't understand," Bruce would say in 1978, "is that I wanted it *all*." From the beginning, rock and roll was the medium for obtaining it.

It's appropriate that Bruce's first exposure to rock and roll was Elvis Presley on *The Ed Sullivan Show*. Like Bruce, Elvis came from a background that offered neither financial support nor much hope. "Man, when I was nine, I couldn't imagine anyone *not* wanting to be Elvis Presley," Springsteen remembered years later. He was so worked up over the experience that his mother bought him a guitar. "But my hand was too small to get into it. Besides, guitar lessons at the time were like a coma, buzzing on the B-string. I *knew* that wasn't the way Elvis did it." For five years, he put down the guitar. But he still listened, and dreamed.

In 1963, even before the advent of the Beatles, lightning struck. "I was dead until I was thirteen," Bruce says, and he means it. "I didn't have any way of getting my feelings out. Then I found this thing. I was a drummer, but I wasn't working enough to buy a set of drums. So I bought a guitar." With it came an identity: "When I got the guitar, I wasn't getting out of myself. I was already out of myself. I knew myself, and I did not dig me. I was getting into myself."

This guitar came from a pawnshop, for $18. "It was one of the most beautiful sights I'd ever seen in my life. It was a magic scene. There it is: The Guitar. It was real and it stood for something: 'Now *you're* real.' I had found a way to do everything I wanted to do." His cousin Frankie taught him his first few chords. The thrill was immediate. Since the day he began, Springsteen says, "Rock and roll has been everything to me. The first day I can remember looking in a mirror and being able to stand what I was seeing was the day I had a guitar in my hand."

His parents were appalled at this obsession. Springsteen not only believed that rock was all that counted—he acted like it. But no amount of pressure could make him stop. Just playing on his own was sufficient to lend him a joy he'd never known before.

The radio was an encyclopedia of music. He bought few records except those he wanted to learn to play, but his instincts, while idiosyncratic, were excellent. "I've always listened to what I loved, and watched what I loved. I play the records that I like. But I hate to study anything. The main reason I started doing my own arrangements and writing my own songs was because I hated to pick them up off the records. I didn't have the patience to sit down and listen to them, figure out the notes and stuff. So it's all just assimilation. I've been playing for eleven years and you just assimilate all these things," Bruce said in 1974. "It goes through something in you and it comes out with something of what you've been watching."

He loved the classic artists: Elvis, Chuck Berry, the Beatles, the Rolling Stones. And the second line of the British Invasion: Eric Burdon and the Animals before they went psychedelic, Manfred Mann's early records with Paul Jones as lead vocalist, the Byrds' folk-rock, the Who's power-mad singles. But the radio was full of dense mystery in those years, from the orchestrated paranoia of Phil Spector and Roy Orbison to the odd, crude, supremely energized Gary "U.S." Bonds. Bruce stored away limitless treasures: "Mountain of Love," by Harold Dorman, Claudine Clark's "Party Lights," soul hits by Sam Cooke, Martha and the Vandellas and the rest of Motown, Sam and Dave, Eddie Floyd and other (Stax) artists, Mitch Ryder's and the Rascals' neat twists on white rhythm and blues. It was perfect music for dance bands; there was no folk music, no Chicago blues (except the numbers the Stones and Animals converted), just rock and soul.

Until early 1965, Bruce simply woodshedded, just another high school kid with a guitar. In another part of Freehold, though, a gang of fifteen-year-olds were carrying the fantasy further, setting up a band of sorts—guitar, bass, drums, voice—in one-half of a three-story duplex. In the other half lived a thirty-two-year-old factory worker, ''Tex'' Vinyard, and his wife, Marion. Tex was, and is, a big, blustering fellow with a booming voice, a salty tongue and a genuine love for kids. But the sound pounded through the walls, driving Marion to distraction. Finally, she convinced Tex to go next door and tell the kids to knock it off.

A few days later, George Theiss, the rhythm guitarist, came by to apologize. Along the way, he suggested that Tex—who was on strike from his factory job—might be interested in managing the Castiles (as the band called themselves, after the soap George used to wash his hair). Marion was not enthusiastic, but where kids are concerned her heart is as soft as her husband's. The dining room furniture was pushed aside, and rehearsals began. When some of the band failed to show up for practice regularly, Tex fired them, and the deposed lead guitarist took with him the band's only microphone and its only amplifier. But Tex soon found a twenty-five-year-old bass player named Frank who owned an amplifier and who was interested in filling in as lead guitarist. Practice resumed. ''We were soundin' better,'' Tex remembers, ''but we weren't exactly gettin' anywhere.''

Then, on a night when, to use Tex's words, ''It was rainin' like a cow pissin' on a flat rock,'' a kid from a few blocks away knocked on the screen door. ''Hi,'' he said, looking up at the tall, rangy Tex. ''My name's Bruce Springsteen. I hear you're lookin' for a guitar player.''

''George had told me about this kid in school named Bruce for two or three weeks,'' Tex says. ''And he kept saying, 'I'll ask him.' But really, George kinda had eyes for Bruce's sister, Ginny. So apparently he'd just go over there and get Ginny and forget about Bruce.''

Bruce had an old Kent guitar that he'd borrowed. Tex asked if he knew any songs; he didn't really know much, beyond a few chords and snatches of a few guitar parts from songs on the radio. ''But I'm quick to learn,'' he said.

''The kid just had something about him,'' Tex recalls. ''Just like I could see it with George. There was something there. They wanted the band, their heart was set on it. So I said to Frank, 'You teach him.''' Now there were three guitars—Frank switched back to bass, in the end—running through a simple amp.

At the end of the rehearsal, Bruce looked up to Tex. ''Am I in the band?'' he asked. Tex said he wasn't sure. Why didn't Bruce come back when he'd learned, say, four or five songs.

''The next night ...'' Tex laughs. ''The *next* night, it must have been about eleven o'clock, there was a rap on the door. 'Hi,' he says. 'I'm Bruce Springsteen. Remember me?' I said, 'Yeah. I remember ya.' He says, 'Well I learned a little. You gonna let me play for ya?' I said, 'Yeah.'

"Well, this damn kid sat down and knocked out five songs that would blow your *ears*. Five. Leads. No amplifier but five leads. He said, 'Oh, by the way, I learned a couple more.'" Tex says, rolling his eyes in remembrance of his amazement.

"Frank teach ya?" Tex asked, playing it cool.

"No," Bruce replied innocently. "I listened on the radio."

"He knocked out a couple more," Tex says, "and I'm sittin' there with my ears goin' WHAT?!? WHAT?!? WHAT?!? I couldn't believe it.!"

Tex arranged a special rehearsal two days later for Bruce's audition. The other boys arrived, George feeling especially cocky with a school chum on trial. Tex hadn't let on about the extent of Bruce's new-found repertoire. He still recalls the scene.

"Bruce is standing there with his ass out of his jeans, his damn old boots all run over, always in a T-shirt, pimples all over his face. So George says, 'Bruce, why don't you show us what you learned?'"

Bruce asked Frank to loan him the guitar the older player was using. He then proceeded to tune it, much to Frank's amazement. Then he plugged it in, and knocked out the songs. "Well, Bruce cut loose with those damn things," says Tex, "and you shoulda seen the look on George's face. The drummer dropped his sticks. Bruce is real cool. He says, 'How did I do? All right?' He's serious!

"Well, George just turned around to me and said, 'Hey Tex, I'm still lead singer, ain't I?'" Vinyard throws back his head and roars. "Bruce says, 'Well, am I gonna make it in the band?' I said, 'Son, as far as I'm concerned, you're in the band.'"

Tex remained on strike, and, with only $21 per week in benefits from the union, he was rapidly falling into debt. But he spent as much time as possible with the boys, and he and Marion soon became deeply attached to them. The boys responded, and so did many of the other kids in the neighborhood. If the other kids weren't allowed inside while the band was rehearsing, they'd pull milk crates up to the window and press their faces against the pane to watch and listen. After forty-five days of rehearsal—steady, two or three times a week, as soon as homework and household chores were done—Tex decided the Castiles were ready for their first gig, a dance at the West Haven Swim Club.

With the big engagement coming up, the Castiles grew nervous, not about their lack of experience but about their impoverished equipment. "The amp was beginning to rattle," Tex remembers. "Now, across the street from us was a music store, next to the pool hall. Here comes the thrill: The boys were all sweet to me and Marion for a week straight. I know they're leadin' up to somethin' but I don't know what.

"All this time, remember, we ain't even got a microphone. We're just singing, without a mike. So they give me this look. 'Tex, have you looked over at Ralph's yet, in the window? Boy they got a new amp over there.

It's the latest and it's a beauty.' Which it was. Detached amp—had a separate head, which in those days was a big deal.

"Well, it was about nine o'clock at night and the store was already closed. 'Tex,' they said, 'let's go take a look at it.' And the owner drove up just then and he says, 'Hey, Texas, what's up?' I said, 'Ah, the boys just want to look at the amp.' He opened the store and let us have a look.

"They went, *Look!* It's got three inputs!' It was a Danelectro 310, made right over here in Neptune City; biggest amp on the market at the time, except for the Vox Super-Beatle. And it had full reverb—nobody had *reverb*. Bruce coulda played with that thing and got his en-joys.

"I said, 'I'd like to have it. How much is it?' Well, it was a little over $300. Might as well have been three thousand as far as I was concerned. But they had to have it, they just had to have it. Then they had to have two or three microphones, which meant I had to go out and buy a fifty-watt Bogen amp for the PA. The boys got together and found a couple of old amps and glued the speakers together and that was our PA. But the amp was a beautiful thing, and I went into hock for it. I think I gave him $5 down for it and it was $11 bucks a month—for about three years."

The West Haven gig went well; the Castiles closed the show with a favorite of Tex's, Glenn Miller's "In the Mood," rearranged by Bruce. Proudly, they took their $35 and insisted that Vinyard accept his $3.50 commission. "Next day they came over and I bought 'em about $8 worth of picks and about $12 worth of strings."

Tex Vinyard likes to paint himself as crusty and crafty, but the feeling doesn't hold. His delight in dealing with the Castiles remains something special, and one of his fondest memories is the night a couple of years ago that he and Marion were introduced at a local nitery as "the Mom and Pop of rock on the Jersey shore." The appellation was earned. Although the Vinyards have no children of their own, they have helped put about a dozen through college, and not only musicians. In time, Bruce's sister, Ginny, became as frequent a visitor in their home as Bruce himself. Young musicians in the Shore region still often turn to Tex for advice, and he can still tell you what each of them likes to eat for dinner. During the Sixties, the Vinyard home was a genuine extended family, far more real than any of the hippie communes of the day. Marion's private photo albums are filled with smiling teenage faces eating pizza, listening to records— simpler pleasures out of a time that elsewhere seemed complicated in vicious and unnecessary ways. For the Shore musicians, Tex and Marion's home must have seemed a refuge. In the sixties, finding a sympathetic adult who liked rock was like striking a seam of pure gold.

Of all the kids that Tex worked with (he would later

manage and book twenty-one bands) the Castiles remained the most special, and Bruce and Ginny (along with George) the most special of the Castiles. "I never loved two kids more in my life," Tex says today. "Many a night they'd sleep over. And many a night Bruce would fall asleep curled up with his guitar." For his part, Bruce played eloquent homage when he delivered a heart-felt dedication to Tex and Marion at his 1978 Madison Square Garden debut.

From the beginning, Marion Vinyard kept scrapbooks, and she has continued them, not only through Bruce's rise to fame, but for the other boys as well. Through these books, one gets a feeling of the time, which was marvelous for rock bands, even young, naive ones. Dances were held at a variety of places: teen clubs, high schools and junior highs, roller rinks, swim and country clubs, Hi Y canteens and CYOs. One Castiles show took place at the grand opening of a

Shoprite Supermarket; another time, they played the local drive-in, as openers for *The Russians are Coming, The Russians are Coming.* There were charity shows hosted by disc jockeys, with a few top-flight local bands opening for acts like Lenny Welch, Dion and the Belmonts, Anthony and the Imperials. There were battles of the bands, held at Keyport Rollerdrome. Tex remembers one where a young girl slipped the results into his pocket a few minutes before the show even began. (The paper is in the scrapbook.) It was a nothing scene. Everywhere, a beginning act like the Castiles was worth $35 per date; top attractions like the Motifs (the biggest local act at the time), $125. Half-hour sets, four or five a night. No original material, just the latest rock hits and perhaps an oldie or two, like "Twist and Shout."

It didn't take long for the Castiles to move up in class. George Theiss was (and is) a first-rate vocalist;

Bruce was immediately recognized as an outstanding guitarist. But Springsteen was not allowed to sing; Tex felt his voice wasn't good enough. He took lead vocals on only two songs, Van Morrison's (Them) classic "Mystic Eye" and the Who's anthemic feedback orgy, "My Generation." In the summer of '65 those songs were adventurous stuff, notable mainly for anarchic energy. Tex felt that Springsteen's raw vocal projection fit the bill.

By early 1966, the Castiles were riding a crest. They developed an original song, "Sidewalk," which achieved such popularity that, in the scrapbooks, there is a petition from fans begging for a recording. But the band lacked the resources and the savvy to find a record label, and the boys were far too young anyway. (Frank left the group after a teen club proprietor said that kids didn't want to see a twenty-five-year-old on stage; Bart joined the Army and was killed in Viet Nam.)

On May 22nd, 1966, the Castiles took matters into their own hands. There was a small recording studio in the nearby Brick Mall Shopping Center in Bricktown and on this rainy Sunday, the band piled into Tex's '61

Mercury and went over to cut a couple of sides. Bruce and George wrote the songs in the back of the car on the way over: "That's What You Get" and "Baby I." The record was never released, not even locally, but Tex still has acetate copies. The songs are so crudely recorded that they don't reveal too much, but it is interesting to hear this fresh-faced, effervescent music, with strong melody and propulsive rhythm. On "Baby I," Bruce's guitar cuts through enough to discern a simple but strong style developing. The playing is more remarkable because, during the recording of the first side, Bruce's E-string broke. There was no replacement and no time to go out and buy one. The Castiles had one hour of recording time which cost $50; they settled for what they could get. Maybe the experience left its mark.

At this time, the teenage world was divided into two camps. In the Shore area, they were known as Surfers and Greasers, which was not quite the same as wimps and hard guys. Surfers were relatively clean cut and listened to white rock; Greasers wore leather and denim and preferred soul music—what was sometimes disparagingly referred to as "boogaloo" by the other side. It was a simple and long-standing division among kids; in England it took the form of Rockers and Mods, while in parts of America farther from the beach, Surfers were called Continentals or Frats, Greasers were sometimes known as Hitters. Whatever, the essence of the matter was the same. Surfers had prospects, some hope of a future; Greasers often had none. (It was a while yet before the hippie movement then blossoming in cities like New York and San Francisco would penetrate to places like Freehold.)

The Castiles were a hybrid band, and as a result, Bruce remembers that they "took a lot of heat from both sides." Freehold was located equidistant between Route 35, the highway near the Shore which was the main strip for surf clubs, and Route 9, the inland highway where the greaser clubs were located. It was a period of transition for both surfers and greasers—musically, this was reflected in the development of bands that played more than instrumentals. Before the Castiles only about two other Jersey bands had vocalists; everyone else played instrumentals, either the greasers' soul funk, or the surfers' twangy beat ("Night Train" versus "Pipeline," as it were). But at grease clubs, the Castiles had problems because they were too adventurous, splicing songs from the early albums of the Animals and Who into their Motown repertoire. At surf clubs, the British rock was all right—although the smoke bombs the Castiles used were a little *outré*—but the band's looks didn't make it. The Castiles not only wore semi-greaser uniforms (frilly shirts, snakeskin-style vests, black pants and socks, Beatle boots), but they had long hair. No one had long hair. Greasers still lingered in duck-tail fashion; surfers cropped theirs tight to the skull. At the greaser bars, the Castiles sometimes came close to brawling with the customers. At the surf clubs,

particularly the Sea and Surf in Sea Bright (which Bruce remembers as "the surfer stronghold"), the group was spit at, attacked with thrown pennies and generally reviled. "But there was always a minority that dug it," recalls Bruce. That might have had something to do with the Castiles' innovations, which included dragging a life guard tower indoors, on to which Bruce could climb up to start the set.

Such strokes of innovation were all that separated the Castiles from ten thousand other bands that blossomed in the years following the Beatles. "There were three hundred bands for every job," Tex says, and he's not exaggerating. While it would not be fair to say that all of them sounded the same, it would be accurate to say that almost all of them tried to emulate one of the half-dozen major British bands: Beatles, Stones, Who, Kinks, Animals, Yardbirds. (Judging from the acetates, the Castiles were very influenced by the Beatles.) This music was unschooled but utterly stylized, ground out in garages and back-rooms, occasionally making it to the same kind of tiny two-track studios that the Castiles used. Once in a while, such groups would get lucky and score a hit: the McCoys, from Ohio, with "Hang On, Sloopy," the Swinging Medallions, from the South, with the soul-influenced "Double Shot," the Five Americans, from Oklahoma, with "I See the Light," Count Five, from California, with "Psychotic Reaction," one of many rip-offs of the Yardbirds' "I'm a Man." More often, the records had confined regional success, as was the case with Bob Seger's "Gloria"-like "East Side Story" and Dylan-influenced "Persecution Smith." Sometimes, the musicians would go on to bigger things—John Fogerty's Blue Velvets became Creedence Clearwater—but the music wasn't the sole purpose anyway. As E Street Band drummer Max Weinberg remembers, "When I was fourteen, the band was it. It was your identity."

In later years, such grass-roots music became known as punk rock, mostly because it was simple, ragged and raw, but emotionally honest, in contrast to the constricted, self-conscious music the bigger names in rock had begun to toy with. Were these musicians punks? Not exactly—they didn't have gangs that swiped cars and hubcaps or go around looking for fights, although there was sometimes no avoiding it. Punk rock, and its audience, was more concerned with style, a certain posture and attitude that encapsulated their view of life. In a way, this perspective was not dissimilar from hippie ideology: It was equally cynical (if not more so) about jobs, schools, the Army and other institutions.

But the Surfers, Frats, Continentals, Greasers and Hitters of the mid-Sixties—lump them together as punks, if you will—were different from the hippies in more important ways. For one thing, they did not espouse isolation from the rest of the society the way the hippies did. The punks genuinely regarded the adult world as irrelevant, but in their secret hearts, most have known that this moment was just a teenage dalliance, part of the natural adolescent transition between child-hood and maturity.

Punks did not owe much to the beatnik bohemian tradition. They belonged to an older strain in American culture, one with roots that went back to Billy the Kid. Before Elvis Presley, this outlaw punk tradition was mostly expressed through young male movie stars—James Cagney, John Garfield, Humphrey Bogart, Marlon Brando and James Dean—who established the punk perspective: bitter, alienated, tough, somewhat sentimental, cynical but also committed to values that seemed forever to be slipping out of reach or fading into oblivion. In *Rebel Without a Cause* and *On the Waterfront,* Dean and Brando established the look for the contemporary rocker version of the punk. The kids in *West Side Story* were a remarkably sweet-tempered version of it, and that film was (despite its inauthentic music) heavily influential, especially on the gang-oriented East Coast.

As Weinberg says, the rock band was another kind of gang, where guitars replaced zip-guns. The beatnik/hippie concepts—largely derived from European and Oriental culture—were never terribly accessible to most Americans, except as a fad. Levis make more sense for people who ride in cars than flowing robes do. Rowdy music has greater resonance for people who spend their life numbed by factory and shopclerk work and to whom modal expressions of serenity are meaningless. Drinking overshadowed other drugs for the Sixties punk, and when drugs came onto the scene, they were approached with the same frivolous zest as alcohol, not with the pretensions of enlightenment the hippies claimed for them.

Philosophically, the difference was simple but crucial: For hippies, Western society had disintegrated to the point where it deserved to be mocked and abandoned. For punks, that society's disintegration meant something more various, confused and economically immediate: rebellion was imperative but so was respect, as if an instinctive, atavistic memory of earlier values remained. Perhaps that is the reason that the hippie ethos was so easily corrupted and merchandised, while in the late Seventies, an attempt to revive and extend the hard-edge spirit of punk was doomed to commercial failure.

It was Bruce Springsteen's fate to become the key figure in the transition from hippie music and back toward a more naturalistic rock style. Springsteen writes of cars and girls, the key icons of this macho movement, the way the hippie writers wrote of drugs and universal peace/love—with commitment and passion. (The tragedy of seventies punk was that too much of it had all the commitment and sneered at the passion.) In Springsteen's songs, a questing, romantic spirit is inevitably scorned and banished; he is torn between his own abandonment of the traditional values and his desire to seek them as a refuge. He is not a drop-out; he is an outlaw, in line with what Norman Mailer had

written in 1960: ''There was a message returned to us by our frontier that the outlaw is worth more than the sheriff.'' America had eclipsed its frontiers—Vietnam was a disastrous attempt to find a new one, the moon-shot was a clownish one—but in Springsteen's songs that frontier made a reappearance, both everywhere and nowhere. It was the only thing worth seeking and an impossible goal, simultaneously a chimera and the most potent force in the world. The answer was personal; it had to do with style, give that style whatever name you will. In ''Backstreets,'' Springsteen stated it concisely and perfectly:

Remember all the movies, Terry, we'd go see
Trying to learn to walk like the heroes
We thought we had to be. . . .

Musically, this outlaw spirit gave punk music (in its original Sixties incarnation, anyway) a connection with black popular music—soul, not jazz—that the hippies lacked. Hippies attempted to fuse rock with folk, jazz, classical, Indian, Native American, Middle Eastern and twelve-tone elements; punk-rock retained the basics, elaborating upon them only slightly, never willing to abandon the basic beat.

But because the punks are rarely articulate, because they more often come from the American underclasses (one reason punks don't drop out is because they can't afford to), mainstream rock went into decline. As the Beatles became baroque and the West Coast bands seemed unable to come up with anything visceral, only a few standard-bearers of the old sound remained: Even the Rolling Stones fiddled with sitars, while the Who toyed with rock opera. John Fogerty of Creedence Clearwater Revival sometimes seemed the last man in the world capable of writing straightforward rock songs —or at least the only one willing to do so. Most of the real heirs of the early rock tradition wound up playing in local bars, struggling to make ends meet— though once Springsteen revived the sensibility, it was surprising how many people seemed to have been waiting to follow suit.

But that was all in the future. For their time, the Castiles were successful. Bruce was developing a style, learning licks (it was said that, hearing a new chord or technique, he could master it in twenty minutes and

play it back better than the person who taught it to him), writing songs. He had been writing since he joined the band, even though not much of his material could be included in the stage show. He was in public school now—the switch came in ninth grade—but still on the outside of its social life. "Music became my purpose in life," Bruce told Robert Hilburn of the The Los Angeles *Times*. "Before that, I didn't have any purpose. I tried to play football and baseball and all those things. I checked out all the normal alleys and I just didn't fit. I was running through a maze. Music gave me something. It was never just a hobby—it was a reason to live."

Kit Rachlis of the Boston *Phoenix* remembers interviewing Southside Johnny and the Asbury Jukes. Each of the band members told Rachlis the story of how he had come to a crisis point, where a decision finally had to be made whether to pursue music as a career or give it up. "Did everyone you know go through that?" asked Rachlis. "Everyone but Bruce," Southside replied. "Bruce always knew. There was never any question about it as far as he was concerned."

The passion was all-consuming. "One time, George and Skibotts [the drummer who replaced Bart] came to me and said they got a job," Tex remembers. "So I said to Bruce, why don't you go out and get a job and go to work? He went into the living room and jumped into Marion's lap and said, 'Tex is screamin' at me.' She said, 'What's the matter?' He said, 'He told me a dirty word. He told me to *work*.'" Apparently, Bruce viewed outside jobs as a trap, designed to keep him from developing his talent for rock.

He saw sex similarly. There was a time for girls, but they never came first. When one friend got married, Bruce told him flatly, "You ain't never gonna go no further in your music career now." No one was going to trap Bruce Springsteen into a house, kids and a nine-to-five future. In any event, sex would not have been easy for a small-town Catholic boy. "You weren't asking a girl, 'Do you want to dance?'" he remembers. "You were asking her, 'Do you *wanna*? My life is in your hands.' We're not talking about a dance; we're talking about survival." Still, if girls were secondary, they were definitely far ahead of whatever came third.

Drugs weren't even on the list. Although many people thought that Springsteen's twitchy, itchy stage mannerisms meant he must be on *something,* in fact he always abhorred anything stronger than beer. "People take drugs because their friends do it," he said. "At the time, I didn't have many friends. I had a guy I'd see once in a while, and a girl, but outside of that, there was nobody. I wasn't in that circle. Consequently, I was oblivious to a lotta social pressures and stuff within the scene, 'cause I was on the outside, lookin' in—until I

The photos here and on page 25 are from Tex Vinyard's Castiles scrapbook. On the opposite page, Bruce is second from the right. Above, Springsteen (far right) wears a pair of boots whose style defines the era: sharp, pointed and glossy. That's George Theiss in the center.

started to play. Then people came closer. But by then it was too late. I was totally involved in what I was doing, and I had no need for anything else, or for anybody. I was there, and that was it, for me."

Springsteen is a loner by nature. Even today, he is the sort of person whose favorite moments often involve being alone: speeding down a highway, or just soaking up the atmosphere at four A.M. on a deserted street. This came naturally to him (his father apparently shared it), but in the late Sixties, threatened by the draft on one side and school on the other, Bruce became even more determined to find a way out. And it would be his *own* way—that more than anything was the purpose of his music.

The Castiles were beginning to feel a bit frustrated simply playing the surf bars in New Jersey. They suggested that Tex attempt to find them bookings in New York, in Greenwich Village. Tex, somewhat reluctantly, agreed. "Shit, there were ten thousand bands in New Yawk," Vinyard says. "But the boys said, 'Aw, Tex, you gotta try for us.' Finally, I called the Cafe Wha— that was on the same street with the Night Owl, where the Lovin' Spoonful were getting started, the Mothers of Invention and the Fugs. Anyway, I called for an audition. 'Naw,' they said, 'we ain't auditioning nobody, we got a hunnert bands to audition, and we only got thirty nights open for the rest of the winter.' But finally

I convinced them to at least hear us.

"So we got up there, and everybody's real nervous. But Bruce, he says to Curt, the bass player, 'I want some good lead bass. Not plunk, plunk, but lead— with a pick.' He came out with 'My Generation' and I hate to say this, but we got twenty-nine out of the thirty bookings." It was January 1967, a real triumph in a Village scene that was about to explode nationally, with the Spoonful and other groups. But the Castiles, perhaps because their name was not hip, perhaps because their music was a little behind the trend (although in New Jersey, their surf/grease hybrid was called "psychedelic"), were offered no recording contract during the stay in New York.

And by summer, high school would be over for the Castiles. The band had offered an early start, and some madhouse moments. They once played the local asylum. "We were terrified. This guy in a suit got up and introduced us for twenty minutes, saying we were greater than the Beatles," Bruce would remember years later. "Then the doctors came up and took him away." But the innocence was draining out of the rock scene, and, with it, the time for high school bands like the Castiles. "Bruce was getting ready and wanted to go on further with music," Tex remembers. "The other boys wanted college or marriage. But we stayed close, and I went with Bruce to gigs many, many times."

3

Greetings from Asbury Park New Jersey

It was a summer of massive changes, the year of the hippie and the anti-war movement. The Summer of Love. But in Freehold, it was something different. Bruce took off for New York the night of his high school graduation, which didn't do much for the party his parents had planned. He came back in the middle of the night, but his father made sure he went to the school the next day to get his diploma. Other changes were brewing as well.

The Castiles were over, and Bruce was working with Earth, the first in a series of other bands. Influenced by the recent emergence of Cream, with a power trio "heavy metal" sound, Earth played lengthy guitar based songs, heavily influenced by the Doors and Tim Buckley. And Bruce had discovered in nearby Asbury Park a haven for young musicians like himself. Miami Steve remembers Bruce riding into town with a new Les Paul model Gibson guitar, "the fastest guy on the scene." "The concept of taste had not yet entered my thinking," adds Bruce. "I just wanted to play as fast as possible." So he became a sort of Alvin Lee-by-the-sea.

Asbury Park is a small-time beach town, dismal by most standards. Downtown is nearly empty, devastated by municipal default in the Thirties, urban renewal in the Fifties, a race riot in 1970. Cross the railroad tracks driving east toward the beach and life picks up, but only a little. White wooden beach hotels sit next to greasy spoon restaurants. On the boardwalk, there's Madam Marie's, the fortune-telling shack that later turned up in Bruce's "Sandy," and a couple dozen arcades. But the width of the boardwalk nearly exceeds that of the tiny beach which has eroded as much as the man-made landscape around it.

The ferris wheel is much smaller than those at the resorts farther south. Instead of Atlantic City's Steel Pier, here, at either end of the boardwalk, there are the musty, chipped-paint Casino and the Convention Hall. Even on Fourth of July weekends, the place is only three-quarters occupied. Right next door, only a few feet south of the Casino, begins Ocean Grove, a Methodist camp town where you can't drive on Sunday or drink any day of the week. Farther down the beach, the teen dream lights of Point Pleasant and Seaside, with their more prosperous boardwalks, can be seen on clear nights. This is no idyllic Big Sur landscape, but for someone with a taste for tackiness, for connoisseurs of junk-food Americana, Asbury still scores points as paradise.

Residential Asbury is tough. The beach homes and some of the old hotels used to be luxurious; the year-round homes were never anything more than humble bungalows. In the winter, people hustle, hoping for a summer drought; rain can spell disaster to the tourist trade.

The real attraction of Asbury had nothing to do with the beach. The draw for musicians was a club called the Upstage, which had two sessions on weekends, one from eight to midnight and another from one to five

A.M. Bruce remembered the place in his liner notes for the first Southside Johnny and the Asbury Jukes' album, *I Don't Want To Go Home*. "There were a lotta musicians there, 'cause the bands that came down from North Jersey and New York to play in the Top Forty clubs along the shore would usually end up there after their regular gig, along with a lotta different guys from the local areas. Everybody went there 'cause it was open later than the regular clubs and because between one and five in the morning, you could play pretty much whatever you wanted, and if you were good enough, you could choose the guys you wanted to play with.

"The Upstage was run by this beat-type guy named Tom Potter who plastered the walls with black light and pin-ups and showed '50s smokers to the kids in between the bands . . . It was a great place. He'd slip you five or ten bucks to sit in and you could work it so you'd never have to go home, 'cause by the time you got out of there it was dawn and you could just flop on the beach all day, or you could run home before it got too light, nail the blankets over the windows of your

room and just sleep straight through till the night.

"There were these guys . . . Mad Dog Lopez, Big Danny, Fast Eddie Larachi, his brother Little John, Margaret and the Distractions (house band), Black Tiny, White Tiny, Miami Steve and assorted E Streeters plus the heaviest drummer of them all, in terms of both poundage and sheer sonic impact, Biiiiig Baaaaad Bobby Williams, badass king of hearts, so tough he'd go the limit for you every time, all night. You will never see most of these names on another record besides this one, but nonetheless, they're names that should be spoken in reverence at least once, not 'cause they were great musicians [truth is, some of them couldn't play nothin' at all] but because they were each in their own way a living spirit of what, to me, rock and roll is all about. It was music as survival and they lived it down in their souls, night after night. These guys were their own heroes and they never forgot."

Garry Tallent, the E Street Band's bassist, also remembers the Upstage. "I think that club was what was special about Asbury," Garry says. "There weren't many other areas that had places like that. Like I never sat down with a record—I just learned from playing with other people."

Earth was short-lived, but Bruce soon had the next band together. As the Shore's hottest guitarist, he had his pick of associates. For Child, which played the same sort of heavy-metal blues, he teamed up with Vini "Mad Dog" Lopez (no relation to the big-band leader), Danny Federici (who was from up north, around Passaic) on keyboards, and a guy named Vinny Roslyn (who had earlier played with the Castiles' main rival, the Motifs) on bass.

Springsteen recalls his first meeting with Vini. They were at the Upstage when Bruce was approached by "this real short-haired guy, real short hair, shorter than Charlie Watts has now. It was 'Mad Dog' Lopez, just out of jail. He told me about that, says he's looking for a guitarist, 'cause I was the hottest guitar player then, and did I want to join his new band? Funky [Tallent] I met because he used to pull a damned chair out in the middle of the floor and stare at me, until finally we just started talking after a show one night. But we didn't play together for a long time after that. Danny Federici I met in Tom Potter's office; he was wearing a three-quarter-length black leather jacket, very greaser, and his wife, Flo, had on a blonde wig."

Sringsteen soon found out that there was already a rock band named Child somewhere nearby. So the group's name was changed to Steel Mill. By most accounts, this was the premiere band of Springsteen's youth. It would eventually enhance his reputation, spreading it over the mid-Atlantic coast as far south as Virginia. The band was enormously popular with beach kids everywhere; there are still tapes floating around from that era.

What they reveal is illuminating. Steel Mill has always been described as playing "heavy metal" music, which usually means blues based, instrumental-oriented rock with a leaden beat. Steel Mill had the blues base—Springsteen's guitar style was obviously patterned after the B.B. King-influenced single-note playing of Eric Clapton, Jeff Beck, Mike Bloomfield and Danny Kalb—but it had a more driving and flexible rhythm foundation. The material was quite remarkable—"Resurrection" was a scathing look at Catholicism, with lines like: "Take me to church on Friday/And we confess our sins/Special low price on three Hail Marys/My soul is clean again." The mockery, the underlying spirituality and the sound add up to an approach that is pure *Live At Leeds* Who. Steel Mill did other kinds of material—a version of Martha and the Vandellas' "Dancing In The Streets," for instance—but all of it was tough, aggressive and overpowering. It is far from what Bruce would later do, but it is also some of the best heavy-metal music ever played. Steel Mill deserves its legend.

Actually, Steel Mill was formed while Bruce was in Ocean County Community College. College didn't last long (although Bruce did manage to have a couple of poems—not good ones—published in the school literary magazine). Springsteen has a natural instinct for drawing the wrong kinds of attention from authorities. But at college, he was roundly disliked by his fellow students as well as by the faculty. "The times were weird, the students were weird, and the school was weird," he says. The conversation concluding his academic career came after a number of other students had petitioned for his dismissal. He was called in by a counselor.

"Look, you've got problems at home, right?"

"No, things are great. I feel fine."

"Then why do you . . . *look* like that?"

"What are you talking about?"

"There are some students who have . . . complained about you."

"That's their problem."

But Bruce stayed in school a while longer. He finally left after meeting a record producer in New York, who promised him that he'd have a deal in no time. "Quit school," he said, "you won't have any trouble with the draft." Since Bruce was not exactly in the market for a degree, he left the college—but he never heard from the producer again. Still, he quite easily stayed out of the Army.

In early 1969, Douglas Springsteen decided to seek work in California. Bruce was determined not to go along; he remained in Freehold, living in the family's home until he was finally evicted, after which he moved around, staying with Tex, Miami Steve and other musicians, and for a time in a house with some surfers. ("Surfing was the only thing besides cars and music that I could relate to at that time," he said.) It was a perfect time and place to learn rock and roll, even though New Jersey is a national joke. "When I was eighteen and playing in this bar in California," Bruce recalls, "people would come up to us and say, 'Hey I really dig you guys! Where ya from?' And I'd say New Jersey and they'd just go, 'Yech! Ech!' "

But the isolation of the Jersey Shore, where there was nothing to live up to, was also an advantage. Free to develop a style without pressure of trends and false criteria about what was hip, Springsteen was able to concentrate on music that elsewhere was forgotten: Paul Jones, Manfred Mann's lead singer, became a decisive influence on his vocal style; soul music helped shape his rhythm style. Bruce has most often been compared musically to Bob Dylan and Van Morrison, but the Dylan influence is mostly expressed lyrically, not instrumentally, and what he shares with Morrison, beyond a vague similarity of voice, is mostly a common affection for soul rhythm. As critic-producer Jon Landau has put it, "For twelve years, Bruce had the time to learn to play every kind of rock and roll. He has far more depth than most rock artists because he really had roots in a place—coastal Jersey, where no record company scouts ever went." Absorbing styles and influences that were too quickly forgotten in the music industry centers, Springsteen became not so much a human jukebox as a human synthesizer, with an enormous repertoire of songs, influences, bits and pieces picked up from almost anything on the radio. He built his songs on guitar lines and hit records of vague memory, which gave his most original songs an immediately familiar quality. It's part of the rock dream that even the briefest, most minor hit single might have some eternal quality; Bruce Springsteen distilled the essence of that quality, and shaped it with a genuinely original vision.

That summer, Bruce and Steel Mill headed for California. It was the thing for a rock band to do that year. Bruce drove out, but since he didn't know how to shift the car's manual transmission, he had to have a friend change gears for him. In California, Steel Mill's first gig

At his first-ever show in Memphis, in 1976, Bruce visits backstage with Eddie Floyd, the soul singer who sang "Knock On Wood" with him that night.

was at Esalen, the original spa of the self-awareness movement. ''I'd never been outta Jersey in my life,'' Bruce said. ''Suddenly, I get to Esalen and see all these people walking around in sheets. I see some guys playin' bongos in the woods. It turns out to be this guy who grew up around the corner from me.'' Later, at a date at the Matrix, the Berkeley club founded by the Jefferson Airplane's Marty Balin, Steel Mill drew a rave review from the San Francisco *Examiner*'s Philip Elwood.

Elwood called the band's ninety-minute show ''one of the most memorable evenings of rock in a long time,'' and he added, ''I have never been so overwhelmed by an unknown band . . . [Springsteen] is a most impressive composer . . . 'American Song' [has] political-military observations, ranging from Concord Bridge to the present, and there is one called 'Lady Walkin' Down by the River' that is a fascinating juxtaposition of stop-time solos, interesting lyrics and a heavy, heavy ending.

''The band is currently splitting hot dogs four ways to keep things together while delving into the local music scene. They deserve and demand attention.'' The review drew enough attention to get the band invited to audition night at Bill Graham's Fillmore West, and to be given a chance to cut a demo for Graham's Fillmore Records. Steel Mill was offered a contract but apparently turned it down because the advance money was too small.

Steel Mill returned to New Jersey, a little dejected but certainly just as popular. Miami Steve Van Zandt was soon added as bassist, replacing Vinny Roslyn. Managed by a surf board shop owner named Tinker West, Steel Mill became sufficiently popular to earn up to $3,000 a show at local colleges. But Bruce grew tired of Steel Mill's approach, and in early 1971, he let the band fold up, deciding to form a much larger group: ten pieces, with horns and girl singers. While rehearsing that band, Bruce decided to put together a group composed of everyone who wasn't already in another band.

That was Dr. Zoom and the Sonic Boom. It played three dates, one of which was an opening for the Allman Brothers. The membership changed nightly: ''Somebody'd take a solo and we'd all fall down laughing,'' Springsteen says. The group even featured a Monopoly table set up in the middle of the stage. ''That was to give the people who didn't play anything a chance to be in the band,'' Bruce recalls with a laugh. ''You know, so they could say, 'Yeah, I'm in Dr. Zoom. I play Monopoly.' '' ''Everybody made about five dollars each,'' Vini Lopez adds.

Later that summer, Asbury Park went to the ground, in a fire from the race riot. ''We went right down with it,'' Miami Steve says. They lived on a dollar or two a day, developing a series of arcane rituals. Pinball was a passion; Springsteen was the best at that. Monopoly was more complicated. Their version of the game included

special cards that assured that the less scrupulous players would win. Springsteen was supposedly Boss here, too, except when Van Zandt showed up. Even then, Bruce had an edge. He'd come well supplied with snacks, and, eventually, he could trade them for property and other considerations. In this kind of community, the musicians who stuck with it developed special bonds. Insulated from the big time, they knew they were prey for small-time hustlers. As a result, they came to trust no one easily, except one another. Nicknames proliferated (''Southside'' for Lyon, the blues fan; ''Miami'' for Van Zandt, who hated the winter weather; ''Big Man'' for Clemons, because he was). There was a kind of code, the sort of thing that Western movies propose for outlaws. Loyalty was its first tenet. To this day, the original Asbury Park musicians have bonds unfathomed—and unbreakable—by outsiders.

But Dr. Zoom was meant as nothing more than a stopgap until the ten-piece band was prepared for its debut. Miami Steve, for one, contends that the ten-piece group—the first known as the Bruce Springsteen Band—far outstripped Steel Mill in ability and concep-

tion. "Musically, it all kinda ties in with the Jukes and everything, because this was our first experience with horns," said Van Zandt. "We spent six months getting the guys. That was the first time that we ever found out that—forget rock and roll—there's no such thing as rhythm and blues horn players. At least in our area, with white guys; they all wanted to do jazz." But in the process, Springsteen found musicians who would stick with him for years: pianist and guitarist David Sancious, bassist Garry Tallent, Miami Steve (now switched back to guitar), Lopez and Federici were the core of the ten-piece band.

"But after six months, we finally got the band together," Steve continued. "And we played two gigs, and broke up." The ostensible reason was a lack of jobs—promoters simply weren't prepared to deal with such a large band. The horns went after the first gig, which was held in Richmond, Virginia, where the band had planned to move. But soon the gang was back in New Jersey, and playing as a five-piece, as described in

the E Street Shuffle story in Chapter One. (Indeed, that story is very close to the truth, Clarence Clemons has since revealed. He was playing down the street from the five piece Bruce Springsteen Band back in Asbury Park, when he encountered Bruce and Steve, standing on the street during a between sets break.)

The rest of the band still had day jobs. Van Zandt had joined the construction union, using a jackhammer on highway repair. Falling into debt, Steven went out on tour with the Dovells, the Philadelphia act that had hits with "You Can't Sit Down" and "The Bristol Stomp" in the early Sixties. Tallent gave guitar lessons. Clemons did social work with young kids. Only Bruce refused to have any part of a non-musical job. The problem for everyone else was that there just wasn't enough work—nor enough money. Bruce might occasionally slip off to the Village to play solo dates, but the rest didn't have such options. Under this financial pressure, Bruce eventually had to let the band break up. He would try it as a solo act for a while.

4

The Punk Meets the Godfather

"You see they didn't know what to do with me at first. I was strictly a rock and roller. But they heard these songs and the first record came out sounding like some folk music album."

—Bruce Springsteen

Somehow, Tinker West met a pair of songwriters named Mike Appel and Jim Cretecos. Appel and Cretecos had been aspiring performers and producers—actually producing a Mercury Records LP by a heavy metal band called Sir Lord Baltimore—but in order to make a living, the pair had taken jobs as writers in Wes Farrell's songwriting mill, where they had written a hit for the Partridge Family, the era's quintessential teeny-bopper group.

Springsteen's audition was a smash. "He sang as if his life depended on it," Appel remembered years later. The song was about a "deaf, dumb, and blind kid who 'danced to a silent band.'" Appel and Cretecos recognized Bruce's talent immediately. "Look, there was never any doubt in my mind that he was one of the greatest. Onstage in that leather jacket . . . like Elvis. We all want a piece of that leather."

But Appel and Springsteen lost touch. Bruce went out to California; this time, he said, he wasn't planning to come back. But the experience was horribly frustrating. "I didn't know anybody out there, and I wound up playing with these fourteen-year-old kids in garages," he recalled. And when he got back, Appel had forgotten the name; Bruce had to pressure Mike's secretary to take the call. Finally, it dawned on the songwriters that this was the same kid who'd auditioned for them. They got Bruce to write a batch of songs for them simply by asking him to come by the office. He had the first one finished by the time the bus hit the Lincoln Tunnel.

Prolific Bruce may have been. Shrewd he was not. He signed a long-term management contract only a few days later, on an automobile hood in the unlighted parking lot of a bar.

In early 1972, Springsteen was living in an apartment over a drug store in Asbury. Although Bruce rarely bothered with books, he did pick up a copy of Tony Scaduto's just-published biography of Bob Dylan. Paging through the book, he came upon the story of Dylan's signing to Columbia Records: Apparently the young folksinger had simply auditioned for a man named John Hammond, who seemed to be some sort of legendary music business figure. In *The Benny Goodman Story*, Bruce remembered, Hammond had been portrayed by Dennis the Menace's father. So when Appel called to tell Springsteen that he had arranged an appointment with Hammond, at least Bruce knew what Mike was talking about. (Actually, Appel had been trying to reach Clive Davis, the president of Columbia Records. But Davis was out of town, so Appel "settled" for the most famous talent scout in recording history.)

In fact, John Hammond had had a hand in some of the greatest events in American musical history. The scion of a branch of the wealthy Vanderbilt family, Hammond developed a passion for jazz and blues while still in his teens. In the early Thirties, he rediscovered Bessie Smith and recorded her best sides. A little later, he was responsible for signing Billie Holiday to

Columbia. In 1938, Hammond organized the famous Spirituals To Swing concert, which first brought homegrown American music to Carnegie Hall. In the Fifties, he had recorded the great Aretha Franklin. In the Sixties, he had been among the first to spot Dylan's budding genius. If there is a popular music aristocracy in this country, John Hammond is both its most elegant and most venerated figure. But in 1972, Hammond was some years between major discoveries. His position at Columbia was secure thanks to his past contributions, but many felt that, as a talent scout, he was finished.

Hammond was less than desperate to find a new hit act. That had never been his philosophy in the first place; when he signed Dylan, the cracked-voice singer was known to CBS executives as ''Hammond's folly.'' Unlike most other record company employees, Hammond did his job out of passion, not for personal wealth. After all, he was born with the latter. But when Appel called, Hammond's secretary, also operating on instinct, made an appointment. Hammond recalls: ''She said, 'I think you might do this. He came on very strong.' I said, 'OK. I have fifteen minutes.' ''

Springsteen and Appel entered in a rush of enthusiasm. Appel, who has rarely been described as charming, opened the conversation on the boldest possible note. ''You're the guy who discovered Bob Dylan, huh?'' Mike snapped. ''Well we want to find out if that was just luck or if you really have ears.'' To Hammond, whose gentility is almost old-world, this gratuitous abuse came as a shock. ''Stop!'' he said, ''You're making me hate you!''

For his part, Bruce remembers the occasion with comic trepidation. ''I went into a state of shock as soon as I walked in. Then Mike starts screamin' and yellin' about me—before I ever played a note, the hype began. I'm shrivellin' up and thinkin', 'Mike, please, give me a break. Let me play a damn song.' ''

Hammond scowled as Appel's tirade continued. Finally, he said, ''Bruce, why don't you sing something

for me.'' Springsteen got out his guitar and did ''It's Hard To Be A Saint In The City.'' Longer and less rocking than his usual style, it was almost a folk song. But its impact, lyrically and musically, was impressive.

''I couldn't believe it,'' Hammond recalls. ''I reacted with a force I've felt maybe three times in my life. I knew at once that he would last a generation.'' Hammond wondered whether Bruce had ever worked as a single. Springsteen replied that mostly he'd played in bands. Hammond called Sam Hood, who was running the Gaslight, a tiny club in the Village, and quickly arranged an audition performance for that very night. Then he called in a few other CBS colleagues. ''The initial reaction was, 'Well, he looks so much like Dylan, he must be a copy of him,'' Hammond says. ''But he's not, not even remotely.''

At the Gaslight that night, Bruce sang for a crowd of about a dozen people, including Hammond. The talent scout's ears hadn't lied. He arranged an audition recording session for a few days later, to be produced by himself. Appel was requested to make himself scarce.

At the audition, Bruce played piano; while he is not nearly as adept on that instrument as he is on guitar, he is usually not so clumsy as he was that day. The pressure showed as he hammered at keys, striking them with far more force than was necessary—or effective. But there was a simple strength to the music, and the imagery in many of the songs was prolific and exciting. He did about half the songs from what eventually became his

first album, *Greetings From Asbury Park, New Jersey.* But the song that impressed Hammond most was a fluke: He asked Springsteen if there were any song he had written but would never perform live, and Bruce responded by playing "If I Was The Priest." The demo is rough, like all the others, but Hammond was knocked flat by the lyrics:

Well now if Jesus was the sheriff and I was the priest
If my lady was an heiress and my mama was a thief
Oh and papa rode shotgun for the Fargo line
There's still too many outlaws tryin' to work the same
    line

Anti-Catholic imagery ran rampant: Virgin Mary runs the Holy Grail Saloon; the Holy Ghost runs the burlesque show. It ends with Bruce refusing Sheriff Jesus's request to come up to Dodge City.

The song also cleared up another point for Hammond. "It seemed unlikely that he was Jewish," he laughs today. "But when he sang that song, I knew he could only be Catholic." Indeed.

Hammond took the audition demo tape to Clive Davis. Davis has an autocratic reputation, and Hammond knew an eager reception was far from guaranteed. "You know, I've brought a few stiffs as well as some good people to Columbia," Hammond says. "But Clive loved what he heard on the tape. He said, 'You know, John, he's very amusing, isn't he?' I said, 'He's more than that, Clive. He's fantastic.'"

Hammond asked an attorney—not one who works for CBS—to take a look at Bruce's contract with Appel. "It's a slavery deal," the lawyer reportedly said. Nonetheless, Bruce's faith in Mike was complete. So, on June

9, 1972, Springsteen was signed to CBS Records.

But Springsteen was not signed directly to CBS. In May, he had signed a management agreement—for one year with four one year options—and another agreement giving Laurel Canyon (the Appel/Cretecos production company) exclusive right to his recordings for the same length of time. The recording agreement provided for a royalty of three per cent of the retail selling price, and that Bruce would make five albums for Laurel Canyon.

The Laurel Canyon/CBS agreement, however, provided that Bruce would make a total of *ten* albums, and that Laurel Canyon would receive a royalty of eighteen per cent of the wholesale price—about nine per cent of the retail price, or approximately three times what Bruce would receive. Naively, Bruce never bothered to have these provisions explained to him by an attorney; he would later pay the price for his cavalier attitude toward money.

For the moment, it seemed more important that CBS was advancing him $25,000 in a lump sum (to be charged against royalty revenue, of course), and that the contract provided a $40,000 recording budget. Springsteen could finally make an LP. He quickly called together his Asbury Park cronies, and began prepara-

tions for re-forming the Bruce Springsteen Band with Tallent, Federici, Sancious, Clemons and Lopez.

The record company, Appel and Cretecos were stunned. They saw Springsteen as a solo act in the Bob Dylan/James Taylor bracket, and rock was the farthest thing from their minds. At the time, the trend was toward solo writer-performers like Taylor, Carly Simon, Joni Mitchell and Carole King, who recorded with studio musicians and made understated, tasteful pop recordings. Bruce had accurately described his musical history—eight years in rock groups, two months on his own—but, as he would later remark: "They forgot about the eight years and went with the two months."

CBS and the managers gave in only partly. Hammond has steadfastly maintained for years that Bruce is always at his best as a solo writer-performer, and he still seems to cherish the idea that Springsteen will make a "pure" album in that style. Appel and Cretecos came around more easily; rock and roll was their past, too, although they still wanted a record that would fit the commercial mainstream.

In any event, Bruce had no intention of letting down the boys back home now that his chance had finally come. He found the notion of recording with session musicians—who he felt played for the bucks alone—

repugnant. The rest of the group was playing a gig down in Richmond when the contract was signed, and they quickly headed back for rehearsals in Jersey. Only Miami Steve was missing, and even he showed up in time to play a minor role, punching an amplifier head to produce a blast of feedback on "Lost In The Flood."

It was a band of archetypes. Drummer Vini Lopez was a wild man who lived as hard as he played, in the great spirit of Keith Moon. Lopez had a reputation as a barroom brawler—he earned his nickname, "Mad Dog," by giving his own trumpet player a sock in the lip (according to the ever-veracious Miami Steve).

The other half of the rhythm anchor, Garry Tallent, also fit the pattern of rock band personalities. Originally a guitarist, he was intimidated into becoming a bassist by the recorded prowess of master guitar player Jimi Hendrix. Shy and steady, Tallent was like the Rolling Stones' Bill Wyman and the Who's John Entwistle in preferring the back of the stage to the front. Like Entwistle and Wyman, Garry's bass playing is as firm and unobtrusive as his persona; but he has a certain deadpan wit, and he is a passionate rockabilly fan with a record collection—jointly held with Southside Johnny—of immense quantity and quality. Tallent, in fact, claims to have burst into tears after first hearing Roy Orbison's "Running Scared," a song of no little consequence in the Asbury pantheon.

Clarence Clemons is another story. At six foot four, he stands a head taller than anyone else in the band. He is also several years older. Clemons played football at Maryland Eastern Shore University (with Emerson

Left to right: Clarence Clemons, David Sancious and Danny Federici at the beach in 1973.

Boozer of the NY Jets), and he had tryouts with the Dallas Cowboys and Cleveland Browns before a knee injury ended his hopes of an NFL career. He is alternately quiet and boisterous, (on road trips, his room parties loudest and longest), with a piercing laugh and the sense of humor to go with it. A genuine eccentric known for his generosity, Clarence plays perfectly off Bruce onstage—the relationship has made him a favorite in his own right.

David Sancious is also tall and black, but he is Clemons' opposite in almost every other way. Slender, with the long fingers and huge reach of the keyboard player, he is also a red-hot guitarist, although he rarely had the opportunity to play that instrument with Bruce. (He would later play guitar with Stanley Clarke, the jazz bassist.) Temperamentally, Sancious was unlike the rest. Introspective rather than simply shy like Tallent, Sancious had studied classical music, and jazz as well. His playing added an exotic dimension to the band: He would drop in quotes from Monk during his breaks, or open a set with a selection from Mozart.

The group was completed by Danny Federici, "The Phantom." Federici grew up in Passaic, in North Jersey, far from the rest of the gang, but he fit in neatly. His tough exterior and "dese" and "dose" enunciation hid a softer spirit that came out in the songs; his organ playing, when given free reign, has a warmth and strength that is genuinely soulful.

With Springsteen as lead guitarist, plus session bassist Richard Davis and pianist Harold Wheeler on a couple of tracks, this was the band with which Springsteen went into the recording studio that June.

Appel and Cretecos were the "producers," although they quickly discovered that it was an arduous task to convince Bruce to change any of his musical ideas once his heart was set on them. Of the two, Cretecos seems to have been the more important factor in the studio (until he was cashiered following the second album).

Appel later admitted that he was at first against the band concept. "Perhaps I was too caught up in his lyrics. When Bruce came in and played me 'Spirit In The Night' on guitar, I liked the song, but I didn't extend the tune into the band backing. Bruce said, 'It's just because you listened to it on guitar. You can't tell exactly how it will sound.'"

When the time came to overdub electric guitar on the tracks, Appel was adamant. "Look," he said, "this is supposed to be a folk record and *that* is a rock and roll instrument." Springsteen held out. It was his music, and it would be played his way. ("When I painted houses," as he puts it, "I'd paint any color you wanted. But now I'm playing music, and I do it my way.") But Springsteen's victory was only partial. The production, was not sympathetic to rock, and as a consequence, Springsteen—already acquiring a reputation as a forceful showman on stage—had a record that made his rock and roll sound tentative, an aberration coming from some sort of "street poet."

Part of the problem with *Greetings From Asbury Park, New Jersey* was that it was finished in only three weeks. "Bruce had a lot of ideas," Appel later said. "But he wasn't knowledgeable about the studio. He had definite ideas, so many that he didn't know which one to pursue. He had so many ways of expressing the same song."

But it was precisely the job of the producer to help Bruce decide on what ideas to use before he entered the studio and began to spend costly studio hours on such

decisions. It is a measure of Appel and Cretecos's lack of ability in this area that the album as finally released reveals that those key artistic decisions about arrangements were *still* unresolved.

Not that three weeks is an exceptionally long time in which to make a record, anyway. Had Bruce been recording in an expensive, top-flight Manhattan studio, the excuse offered might have been that time and money simply ran out. But he was working at tiny 914 Studios, in suburban Blauvelt, NY. And the only reason to record there, besides a sympathetic engineer named Louis Lahav, was to save money. (It certainly wasn't convenient, for Bruce and the band, who lived in New Jersey, or for Appel and Cretecos, who lived in Brooklyn.) CBS would advance the full $40,000, regardless of how much was actually spent making the album. By scrimping in the studio, by recording in a cheap but technically inadequate facility and cutting down on mixing and mastering time, Laurel Canyon could save some money to keep the organization going. This practice is not uncommon among under-capitalized rock organizations, but it is, of course, terribly short-sighted. The meals Appel could buy with his savings are long since forgotten, but the album is still around—in that sense, to haunt.

The album might have been completed even more quickly and cheaply, but when Appel first delivered it to CBS, the company sent them back into the studio. "There's no single here," they said. So Bruce recorded "Blinded by the Light" and "Spirit in the Night" for release as the album's potential hits. Some of the band had gone back to Virginia, so the songs were recorded with Bruce playing bass, guitar and piano, and Harold Wheeler adding the other keyboard on those tracks.

Whatever its flaws, *Greetings From Asbury Park, New Jersey* is one of the most ambitious debut albums of the Seventies. The problems are conceptual and technical; Springsteen's writing and performance are outstanding. There is no denying the compelling melodies of "For You" and "Spirit In The Night," the passion of "Blinded By The Light" and "It's Hard To Be A Saint In The City," or the effervescent good humor of "Growin' Up" and "Does This Bus Stop At 82nd Street?"

It was the lyrics that brought Springsteen the most attention and no wonder. The opening lines of the album —from "Blinded By The Light"—represent his tumble of images perfectly:

Madman drummer bummers and Indians in the
summer with a teenage diplomat
In the dumps with the mumps as the adolescent
pumps his way into his hat

The song continues that way for four verses—pure excess, and pure rock and roll. *Greetings* has ten songs, and, while none of them has the barrage of images of "Blinded By The Light," none of them is streamlined, either. On occasion, such verbose lyrics become cumbersome. "Mary Queen Of Arkansas," with its sexually ambiguous lover, demands more focused writing than this style can give it, and "The Angel," despite the fact that Springsteen praised it at the time as his most "sophisticated" number, now seems little more than the most pretentious song ever written about an outlaw motorcyclist. More than anything, however, these songs typify the conceptual inadequacy of the singer-songwriter approach: Rather than writing about motorcyclists as observed, Springsteen wandered off into a rather unremarkable fantasy about them. On the other hand, while equally indulging in fantasy, "For You," "Growin' Up" and "It's Hard To Be A Saint in The City," are more tightly focused, minutely observed; onstage, they've become rock classics.

There were reasons for the excess verbiage. "I let out an incredible number of things at once," Springsteen said of that group of songs. "A million things in each song. They were written in half-hour, fifteen-minute bursts. I don't know *where* they came from. A few of them I worked on for a week or so, but most of them were just jets, a real energy situation." As far as Bruce knew, this might be his only chance to make a record. It is typical of his obsessive drive that he determined to put everything he knew or could imagine on the first album.

At their best, these scattershot lyrics are remarkably effective, flinging epigrams like artillery. The final lines of "Blinded" still stand as the test of Springsteen's ambition and motivation: "Mama always told me not to look into the sights of the sun/Oh, but Mama, that's where the fun is." When such phrases strike home full-force, they can freeze a moment or an attitude forever. Like Rod Stewart's "Every Picture Tells A Story," "Growin' Up" offers a marvelous capsule of that moment in adolescence when attitude and style are everything:

I stood stone-like at midnight, suspended in my
masquerade
I combed my hair 'til it was just right
And commanded the night brigade

As a whole, the song goes much further than Stewart's image of hair-combing and mirror-posing, which is soon dropped for a depiction of sexual exploits. "Growin' Up" is the ideal vernacular portrait of the young rebel outsider, lost in the crowd with an improbable vision:

Well, my feet they finally took root in the earth
But I got me a nice little place in the stars

And I swear I found the key to the universe
In the engine of an old parked car

Springsteen says that he has never read many books—Scaduto's *Bob Dylan* and Mario Puzo's *The Godfather* are among the few—but some remarkably sophisticated ideas leap from his songs. Many better educated men have sought futilely to capture the magic of the teenage dream; Springsteen gets it all in a line. And he refuses to stop there. Most great rock writers are miniaturists, but Bruce reaches for the largest canvas of all—he wants to portray nothing less than existence itself, as seen at a certain time, from a certain perspective. In songs like "Growin' Up," he goes a long way toward achieving that goal, and in the process lends a voice to a group of people that generally go unheard.

Springsteen's concerns, from the beginning, have been with moral, ethical and spiritual dilemmas. "For You," for instance, is about suicide. (Oddly, it is also the one song on *Greetings* that heralds the style and concerns of Springsteen's later work.) It is among the best of his love songs, and, as a contemplation of death, Jimi Hendrix's "I Don't Live Today," Jackson Browne's "For A Dancer" and Paul Simon's "Mother And Child Reunion" are the only rock songs that can match it. But Browne, Simon and even Hendrix view death philosophically; Springsteen, while offering some philosophy, concentrates on the very human narrative. By any standards other than rock and roll's, "For You" might be overwrought, but the sheer emotionalism of the performance sweeps such objections aside. (Greg Kihn's later version does not come close to the sweep of Springsteen's, because his much cooler reading is more descriptive than felt.) The story is pure melodrama—the singer is in an ambulance with his girlfriend, who is fading fast—like every corny rock death number since "Tell Laura I Love Her" and "The Leader Of The Pack." As life ebbs, we come to know both of them with a startling degree of intimacy, and to grasp the dimensions of their relationship. In the end, "For You" manages to bring the rock death song cliches to life.

As in "For You," the best of Springsteen's imagery is action and character oriented, rather than abstract. We care about the suicide victim not because she is a symbol of death—though we may come to care about the symbol too—but because the singer cares so completely about their lives together. "The point in a lot of my stuff is that they're like scenarios, they're like plays," Bruce has said. "And the power is not so much in the immediate imagery or the immediate physical picture that's presented as it is in a certain battle being waged between just whatever forces are in the songs. So generally, I write things on a bigger-than-life scale in a certain way.

"Plus, I write about moments. I don't write about the everyday ... I write a lot about action moments, moments when people are pushed to take a certain action, to do something, to do anything to get out of their present situation or circumstances or predicament—to step out, to get out of that boring thing, to break loose. And I think there's a certain romanticism and a certain kind of everyday heroism that is inherent in this. It's something that is very real to me.''

The best rock songwriting—songs by people like Chuck Berry, Bob Dylan, John Fogerty, Peter Townshend—has always been heavily populated. In the space of a few lines, subtle characters live full lives. (By this, I don't mean extravaganzas like Dylan's ''Sad-Eyed Lady Of The Lowlands'' or Townshend's *Tommy*. Better examples are found in brief, three stanza rockers like Berry's ''Too Much Monkey Business,'' Townshend's ''I'm A Boy'' and ''Substitute,'' and Fogerty's ''Fortunate Son.'') In that sense, the best rock writing is authentically cinematic, suggestive rather than elaborate. And Springsteen's songs, from the beginning, fit this pattern perfectly. By that measure his writing is a return to the roots of rock. By 1977, Dylan and Townshend, for instance, had begun to write more about ideas and abstractions rather than about characters and situations. The best of the singer-songwriters did the same.

Raymond Chandler once wrote that the mystery novelist, Dashiell Hammett, had used his hard-guy realism to ''give murder back to the people who commit it for reasons, not just to provide a corpse.'' Springsteen did something similar for rock, although *Greetings from Asbury Park, New Jersey* only hinted at it. Just as Hammett exposed the empty cliches of the drawing-room detective story, Springsteen's flood of images and characters were an assault upon the dry conventions of contemporary rock songwriting. Like Hammett, a former Pinkerton agent who used his experience among hoodlums and cops to add realism to his stories, Springsteen did not have to invent from scratch the reckless innocents of his songs. Because he lived among real people—rather than in the rock star jet set—such persons were his most natural material.

When Jon Landau speaks of Bruce having ''roots in a place—coastal Jersey,'' he is suggesting that Springsteen's fantasies arise from a natural environment. But since there is little room for physical description in rock songs, Springsteen's eye can't linger on the landscape: The ''Greasy Lake'' of ''Spirits in the Night'' is his equivalent of John Ford's Monument Valley, but he celebrates its inhabitants more than its natural splendor. One understands Greasy Lake as an archetype of similar places the listener has known, just as one understands the characters to be universal versions of figures in real life.

''For You,'' however, attacks stereotypes with a degree of deliberation. Springsteen has compared his songs to the films of Sergio Leone, the great director of Italian Westerns. That is to say, he is a genre artist, but operating from the *mise en scene* of the hot rod exploitation picture, with its fast cars, easy women and melodramatic tensions. Thus, when critics speak of Springsteen's ''over-reliance'' on such images, they are missing the point. (Unless one wants to dismiss genre art *per se*—but that means discarding rock and roll, too.) As Bruce himself has noted, in genre writing it isn't the situation that makes the difference—that always *seems* to be the same—but the perspective from which that scene is shown. If Springsteen's achievement counts for anything, then, it is for taking the teen milieu of cruising cars and backseat passion out of the hands of outsiders and giving it back to the people who really live it.

So it is not coincidental that ''Spirit In The Night,'' the first complete scenario based on this teenscape, took longer to write than any other song on the first album. No matter how much it is derived from experience, the best fiction is always a work of imagination. It would denigrate Springsteen's work to suggest that it is autobiographical.

''Spirit in the Night'' established the genre in which Springsteen would work. Its story, while humorous, achieves some of its emotional resonance from its connections to the teen exploitation pictures of the Fifties and Sixties. But those movies (even the best of them such as *The Girl Can't Help It*) were told from the outside, through adult eyes. Their morality and sensibility are that of filmmakers who belong to another generation; the values of the characters are presented without much sympathy or even much understanding. The point of view is precisely the opposite of rock, which has a value system of its own. (One reason that so many rock songwriters, including Bruce, were stunned by Martin Scorsese's *Mean Streets*, is that it was the first film about young adult street life that was not distanced from its protagonists.)

But those early exploitation films did help to create the American rock audience's image of itself. And in the story of a one-night getaway to a lakeside fantasy paradise, Springsteen recalls the motiveless impulse of tales like *The Wild One*—only this time, the adults have been written out of the picture. ''Spirit In The Night'' is a moment that ought to be forever; the only authority on the scene is the bond of friendship and trust that holds these people together. Not even cops come to bother Wild Billy, Crazy Janey and Hazy Davey. (Not since Chuck Berry's heyday has a rock artist developed so many ludicrously appropriate nicknames.) Unlike Bob Dylan's weirdly named denizens of the night, these kids are close to the sort of people any listener might know—they're dream, not nightmare, creatures. Their achievements are also exaggerated versions of our own. Like Berry, Springsteen creates characters with lives longer than one song. Under various guises, they have followed Springsteen through each of his albums.

The spirit of the night is the spirit of escape—that goes almost without saying. But it is also the spirit of unity, whether sexual or otherwise. When Springsteen

sings ''Spirit In The Night'' in concert, he sings the final verse amidst the crowd. The drunkeness and love-making are thus not debauched, as they would be in an exploitation story (which flaunts conventional morality to conceal its own cynicism); they are a form of ritual, which suggests the richest moments in lives that are otherwise banal. Anyone who has grown up in a small town knows that the goal is to get out, have some fun, seek The Promised Land—just as everyone knows how improbable it is that real fun, genuine escape, true promise can be found. Often, what seems from a distance to be improvement is, close up, much worse—even a trap. At Greasy Lake, Crazy Janey and her pals gain no permanent freedom; in the end, they must drive off to return to their drudgery. But what matters is the magic unity of this moment: The key word in the out-chorus (''Together we moved like spirits in the night'') is ''together.''

''Spirit In The Night'' is the heart of *Greetings From Asbury Park, New Jersey*, because it is the album's most fully realized song. But the album is framed by two numbers, ''Blinded By The Light,'' and ''It's Hard To Be A Saint In The City,'' which together create a heroic individual and begin to track his progress from the humdrum existence of the characters in ''Spirit''

toward a permanent escape.

Although the arrangements work against them, ''Blinded'' and ''Saint'' are both pure products of rock and roll. Their drive is relentless, the action non-stop. But where ''Blinded'' shows the hero as romantic inno-cent, ''Saint'' portrays that man full grown, facing a world that tempts him to abandon his single-minded pursuit of spiritual freedom. Like the protagonist of the Crystals' ''Uptown,'' the hero of ''It's Hard To Be A Saint In The City'' is nothing except when he's on his own turf:

I was the king of the alley, mama
I could talk some trash
I was the prince of the paupers
Crowned downtown at the beggars' bash
I was the pimp's main prophet,
I kept everything cool
Just a backstreet gambler with the luck to lose

This is pure brag, in the grand tradition of Bo Diddley—simply strutting one's stuff, in the confi-dence that though the world outside rock and roll can interfere, it can never win. And with this burst of self-assertion, *Greetings From Asbury Park, New Jersey* was delivered into the machinery of the record business.

The Saint in the City

From the beginning, rock stood outside the entertainment establishment, not entirely as a matter of choice. When Sam Phillips and Elvis Presley were in Memphis inventing the grandest music of the Fifties, they certainly did not view themselves as outlaws. But to the entertainment establishment—the world of big-dollar television, motion pictures and night clubs—rock was nothing more than a particularly belligerent and queerly persistent fad.

There were a variety of reasons for the showbiz attitude toward rock, but possibly the two most important were the youth and the working class background of most of the early rock and roll performers. Rock stars were resented first because they had not traveled through the normal channels. They lacked the grooming of the movie studio and night club circuit stars, and they were not only inclined to say and do outrageous things, but often didn't bother to cover them up. Jerry Lee Lewis was banned, remember, not so much for marrying his thirteen-year-old second cousin but for flaunting it. Had he lived, Buddy Holly might have faced similar problems with his marriage to a Latin-American woman.

The early rock stars also came from far less genteel circumstances than most movie or pop music stars of the day would admit to. Elvis Presley was born in a one-room house, and almost until he began recording his family lived on welfare. This was a surmountable problem, but here the lack of grooming (one might almost say, breeding) came into play again: Far from denying his working-class background, the rock star exploited it. Until the end of his life, Elvis remained in some ways a country boy. As unruly, unwashed representatives of the class that had traditionally been the audience, not the source, of American popular culture, rock stars were, from the start, entertainment establishment outlaws.

As a result, the major record companies (including RCA, despite its acquisition of Elvis Presley in 1956) virtually ignored early rock. This was a mistake of major proportions, because it gave an edge to smaller, independently distributed record companies like Atlantic in New York, Chess in Chicago, Ace of Jackson, Miss. and Specialty of Los Angeles. These companies prospered not by attempting to tailor the images of their performers, but by concentrating on developing distinctive musical styles.

But because the record companies for which they recorded, and often as not the management personnel that handled the performers, were undercapitalized, the success of the early rock stars was often fleeting. Elvis was the great exception, but when even he first played Las Vegas in 1956, he was a bust, not able to make it on supper club terms. He ended up second on the bill to comic Shecky Greene.

When it did decide that rock was something with potential for exploitation, the showbiz establishment had no idea how to sustain such careers. Often, dressing the rock star in a tuxedo and sending him to the night clubs divorced him from his natural audience—and the white adults there still found rock music too threatening for their own entertainment. The record companies developed a series of teen idols who made exploitation records, crafted with great cynicism to appeal to the teen market, but the careers of Fabian, Frankie Avalon and the rest were also not easily sustained.

Part of the problem was a lack of vision among pro-

moters. The powerful booking agents and managers who controlled the talent policies of nightclubs, casinos and resorts—where the big bucks were—had no use for the noise, and it hardly seemed likely that hip-slung jeans and ducktail haircuts were going to go over big in the Catskills or Vegas. The few entrepeneurs with sufficient expertise—Alan Freed, for instance—were ruined in the 1960 payola witch-hunt. Teen idols were rarely considered for major film roles, for similar reasons. With the rise of manufactured rock performers like Fabian and Avalon, the teen market once more became a stepping stone at the edge of a cliff, as it had almost been for Frank Sinatra. No one entertained the thought that a full-fledged, long-lived career could be built around rock or rhythm and blues.

Meanwhile, however, people were growing up with rock and roll, and not only took its values for granted but regarded the freedom and sense of exhilaration they found in the music as a kind of ideal. It's important that the rebellion of Elvis Presley and his peers (at least

as far as conventional entertainment values were concerned) was instinctive, while the outlaw posture of all later rock and roll performers was self-conscious and very deliberate. Much the same can be said of the rock audience. A teenager hearing Little Richard's "Tutti Frutti" in 1955 could respond simply to the power of the rhythm. But by the time the Beatles arrived in 1963, it had been drilled into every kid's mind that this was outlaw culture. Mature people—even "mature" teens—frowned upon it. (One of the odd effects of this was to make jazz more respectable, with the result, it sometimes seems, that every pompous young twit of the Sixties generation turned to that music—for a time.)

Having missed Elvis, the major record companies were at least somewhat prepared to cope with the advent of the Beatles, Rolling Stones and the other bands that formed the first wave of the British Invasion of 1963–1965. Consequently, the ripples these bands created quadrupled the annual dollar volume of the music industry. Still, the old-line talent packagers were

reluctant to become involved with rock. Since, this time, rock didn't go away for even a moment, other talent development mechanisms were developed to fill the gap.

Managers were developed from a pool of cronies—the legendary "fifth kid on the block"—Dutch uncles and ex-musicians. A former William Morris mailroom boy, David Geffen, became an agent, left the company with one artist, Laura Nyro, and parlayed her into a combine that eventually included Crosby, Stills, Nash and Young, the founding members of the Eagles, Jack-

son Browne and Joni Mitchell. In Macon, Georgia, R&B king Otis Redding's manager, Phil Walden, cast about locally for new talent after his star's tragic death in a 1968 plane crash—and found the Allman Bros. Band, Wet Willie, the Marshall Tucker Band and a half-dozen other Southern rock groups. They made him a millionaire well before he was thirty and eventually helped elect another Georgian, Jimmy Carter, President of the United States. In New York, Dee Anthony, ex-manager of Tony Bennett, Jerry Vale and Buddy Greco, predicted the long-term success of British rock and signed up Humble Pie, Emerson Lake and Palmer, Joe Cocker and Ten Years After for American representation. Humble Pie spun off Peter Frampton, who sold ten million albums. In England, Robert Stigwood, an Australian, joined together with Beatles manager Brian Epstein and created a hit act in the Bee Gees, a pop-oriented vocal trio, then cashed in on rock with the first power-trio, Cream. Chas Chandler, the bassist of the Animals, quit playing in order to promote the career of Jimi Hendrix. Epstein's American attorney, Nat Weiss, served as lawyer-manager for James Taylor and Bonnie Raitt. Chris Blackwell, son of a Jamaican planter, began to import reggae, the Caribbean variant of soul music, back to England, then acquired management of Steve Winwood and Traffic. Many of these men also wound up with their own record companies: Geffen with Asylum, Walden's Capricorn, Blackwell's Island and Stigwood's RSO were to become among the most important —and richest—record labels of the next decade.

Concert promotion underwent drastic changes. Before the Beatles, the biggest shows of the year were package tours put together by Dick Clark, in which a dozen acts appeared; even the headliner was fortunate if he had a half-hour onstage. And the places that the Clark Caravans and other, similar tours played were no great improvement over the high school gyms that featured groups like the Castiles—an endless round of roller rinks, decrepit teen clubs and dilapidated auditoriums.

But led by the imperious Bill Graham, with his Fillmores East and West, a new breed of rock promoter and presentation sprang up: The ballroom circuit with stops in Detroit (the Grande Ballroom), Chicago (the Kinetic Playground), Philadelphia (the Electric Factory) and Boston (the Tea Party) as well as New York, San Francisco and Los Angeles (the one major city without a long-running ballroom). Coupled with a few college gigs to fill in the gaps, a rock circuit developed that was not unlike the storied days of vaudeville—often, the converted theatres where rock groups played *were* old vaudeville stops.

But the most significant entrepreneur of Sixties rock was not a record company president like Atlantic's Ahmet Ertegun or CBS's Clive Davis, or even a sharp promoter like Graham. That title belongs to a short, balding, rotund booking agent named Frank Barsalona. Barsalona was originally an agent at GAC which was rivalled only by William Morris among the establishment booking agencies. He was one of the few younger agents in the company, and the only one who saw much potential in rock. Barsalona helped Sid Bernstein put together the Beatles tours, including their record setting engagement at Shea Stadium, but he was unable to convince anyone else that rock was here to stay. "The way the agency treated rock performers was a crime," Barsalona has said. "If you were young and had a hit record, to them you had no talent, you were just lucky and manufactured and they would treat you like that

... Rock was really the asshole, it really was." Frustrated, Barsalona decided to form his own agency, Premier Talent, and as rock performers and entrepreneurs (particularly British ones) came to understand that he was a man who understood their potential, Premier became the most influential booking agency in the business. Because he is by nature shy, Barsalona himself became a figure of almost mythic proportions. Before him, no one dared to let an act tour the country without a hit—to Barsalona, touring was the essence of hit-making. This, and his instinct for marketing rock at its hardest, were what made him so exceptional.

In the Sixties, Premier was virtually the only rock-based agency in the country. The Who, Joe Cocker and Jimi Hendrix were among the beneficiaries of its expertise; all three made as much or more mileage from live performances as they did from recordings. Premier quickly devised a simple but effective formula for large-scale rock success. It involved frequent national tours, records released at well-spaced intervals (nine months to one year between LPs—anything shorter risked over-saturating the market, anything longer risked being forgotten), and a high degree of co-ordination between the act's management, record company and the various promoters. It was a familiar process. As Barsalona told Anthony when the latter was considering switching over to rock management, "Dee, it's the same thing you used to do with Bennett, Vale and Greco, but with a different cast of characters."

That should have been all the difference in the world. But theory broke down. The second generation of rock musicians did enter show business as self-conscious rebels. And at first, this attitude armored those stars against selling out. But, when it became clear that enormous sums of money were involved, the rebel attitude became an empty shell that insulated many stars from the realities of their own compromises. By 1973, the political dreams of the Sixties were finished, and whatever allegiance was paid to rock's outlaw spirit was mostly lip service. If the freedom implicit in rock was only personal—not collective—then everyone owed it to himself to make as much money as possible before the bubble burst. So the performers were generally willing, and even eager, to accept the formula rules for success.

The first step in entering what Joni Mitchell has called the "star-making machinery" was obtaining the interest of an individual—usually a record company talent scout (A & R man) or a manager—with access to the apparatus. With recording and booking agency contracts secured, the stipulations for success were simple.

Musically, this didn't seem to involve much compromise. The focus was now on LPs, and many rock acts became successful in those years through albums alone. But the surest way to sell albums was still through radio airplay on a hit single. And radio stations that played "hits"—as opposed to the "free-form" FM stations, which by the early Seventies were on their last

legs—required certain kinds of music. Anything too raucous or abrasive, any song with "questionable" lyrics, any performer who dared to flaunt an outlandish lifestyle (and act as though he believed in it) was subject to banishment from the most important radio stations. The pressure to come up with a hit was intense; rhetoric about art was left behind, along with the political jargon.

Without an early hit, there was a natural progression in record sales. The act usually had two or three chances, sometimes a couple more, to make it to the coveted gold-record plateau (five-hundred-thousand copies sold). If, by the time of the third album, the act had not achieved sales close to that mark, it was in grave danger of being released from his contract. If he made it, then the push to platinum (one million unit sales) began. No one expected to reach that level very often.

There was a similar hierarchy of performances. Young acts began by playing clubs, for little or no money, or—with luck—opening for mid-level stars at the concert halls of the three thousand–five thousand seat variety that had replaced the ballrooms. Middle-level acts starred in such venues, or opened for top-line attractions in sports arenas and outdoor festivals with crowds of ten thousand or more. (On the way back down the ladder, some star acts found themselves opening for people who had begun by opening for them.) The idea was to get exposure, build word-of-mouth and

generate sufficient initial sales to encourage radio airplay. As with records, frequency was important. Playing the same town too often risked diminishing returns. Similarly, a brief, well-paced set was in order—forty-five minutes plus an encore was the order of the day. Two and three-hour marathon performances only risked overtime charges, damaging the profit potential.

Few acts tried to buck the formula. Bands with the communitarian ideals of the Sixties (the Grateful Dead) or strong regional bases (New York Dolls, MC5) found that without well-connected managers or agents, even miles of press clippings and strong record company support were insufficient. Of course, bands like the Dolls and MC5 played harder than most radio programmers preferred. But most groups, especially the big-name British ones, settled easily into the formula. There was no conscious design to destroy rock's early energy and idealism, but the net effect of the star-making process was to tame the music, as well as the musicians.

As a result, within the record business, the musician became not much more than an extremely well-paid laborer; having lost whatever pretensions he may have possessed as an artist, he was not quite a businessman since others were calling those shots. And the sounds became as conventional as the promotional mechanics —which from the star-making machine's perspective was ideal, since the closer the sound to some abstract standard, the easier to formalize promotional structures.

Rock stars also suffered a degree of estrangement from their original sources of inspiration, due to over-protectiveness and wealth. This was felt most severely by the Beatles era stars, who for a while literally could not walk down the street without being mobbed. By the time the hysteria quieted, such performers were permanently out-of-step with their audiences, in ways that had less to do with drug-taking and "hipness" than the natural tendency of all star-making processes to create an aristocracy. (Not to its credit, a good deal of the rock audience played along with this, settling for vicarious experience.)

Rock entrepreneurs had specific tastes. Groups that mumbled about revolution shouldn't speak up. Performers who toyed with ambiguous sexuality or openly used drugs didn't fit into the scheme—although performers who did any of these things at a certain level were admired. Thus, the commentary on decadence represented by Iggy and the Stooges was bastardized into the purely harmless entertainment of Alice Cooper, and the flashy street charisma of the Dolls was repackaged into the costumed theatrics of Aerosmith and Kiss. The development process established by promoters who were, by business standards, visionaries —whether Presley's manager, Col. Tom Parker, agent Frank Barsalona or promoter Bill Graham—had ossified into a new kind of straitjacket, just as limiting as the system it had replaced.

By 1973, it looked unlikely that anyone could afford even to attempt to break the hegemony of this new rock establishment. Rock had lost its idealism, and even the standard bearers of the past—the Who and the Rolling Stones, the individual Beatles, Bob Dylan—were sounding tired to a great many ears.

All of this is essential to understanding what happened in January, 1973, when *Greetings From Asbury Park, New Jersey* was released by Columbia Records. Without it, Springsteen's task and his impact might have been vastly different.

The label's autocratic president, Clive Davis, made it clear that Springsteen was Columbia's highest priority among new artists. This was a substantial commitment, for CBS was the largest American record company, accounting for nearly one-quarter of the nation's record sales each year. Davis ran a one-man show to a great extent, delegating authority primarily to those who could be trusted to carry out his policies to the letter. If he said that Bruce Springsteen was Columbia's best shot at a new superstar for '73, no one was about to question it. At least, not within CBS.

Normally, an artist would have been ecstatic about such strong support. But the promotional tactics that Columbia used were a mixed blessing: They offered

Springsteen an identity, but not a realistic one. In a way, Columbia's initial approach to Bruce and his music was the single most damaging event of his career; it is an obstacle he fought for years to overcome.

The dominant sound of the year was "soft rock," which was not really rock at all. It was the year of the singer-songwriter. Rock critics had identified the genre, and *Time* and *Newsweek* had certified its importance; the newsweeklies liked soft rock, feeling more comfortable with it than with the outrageous forms of other years. It was an institutional attitude shared by the record business.

Stylistically, the singer-songwriter was never adequately defined. Superficially, it meant any performer who both wrote and performed. But it certainly did not include John Lennon, or even John Fogerty, or a black man such as Sly Stone. In fact, the singer-songwriter archetype was Bob Dylan, but Dylan was so changeable that the reference was confusing. The idea seemed to be that there was a group of writer-performers who had emerged in Dylan's wake, with deeply emotional, often confessional lyrics and a light, rock-influenced (but never hard-rocking) sound. Such writers performed their own songs almost exclusively, generally in a style that owed as much to folk music and show tunes as to anything Elvis Presley or James Brown ever sang. The accompaniment was minimal—bass, drums and either guitar or piano. The mood was quiet, tasteful, almost elegant, somewhat in the spirit of Tin Pan Alley show tune composers like Hoagy Carmichael and Cole Porter. What this had to do with any kind of rock is pure guesswork.

But as a pigeonhole, the singer-songwriter tag was a masterstroke. It excused simultaneously writers who could not sing (Kris Kristofferson) and singers who could not write (Carly Simon). But in plain point of fact, the singer-songwriter was anti-rock—it offered snobs a comfortable place within popular music, and alienated a great many of the most committed listeners. It was yet another attempt to graft rock onto pop music, rather than to distinguish rock as an important pop sub-genre in its own right. The success of the singer-songwriter helped diminish the importance of rock and roll, even when the singer-songwriters were as skillful as Randy Newman or James Taylor.

The most curious aspect of the singer-songwriter boom was in fact much older: The New Dylan Syndrome. There had been one—or more—of these per year since Eric Andersen was signed by Vanguard in 1964. Phil Ochs, David Blue, Janis Ian, P.F. Sloan, John Prine and a dozen others had been saddled with the designation. In record circles it had come to be regarded as a kiss of death, since none of those performers sold many records while suffering under it. Dylan's achievements were so broad and his stature so great that no one could hope to equal him on his own terms. And it was both arrogant and idiotic for any record company to expect an unknown to do so. But the

companies needed some handle with which to distinguish one new act from another.

From a musical and historical vantage point, it was incorrect to apply either the "singer-songwriter" or the "New Dylan" labels to Bruce Springsteen. His lyrics were sufficiently intense and personal to work as singer-songwriter material, but they were clearly rooted in the rock tradition, not in the confessional, self-pitying vein of the other genre. Springsteen's music was never sedate and well-mannered in the singer-songwriter fashion; none of the performers named above could have written "Blinded By The Light." None of them could have imagined "It's Hard To Be A Saint In The City." Singer-songwriters did not boast; they complained, analyzed and philosophized. Bravado was beneath them—but it was the core of Springsteen's approach. To lump him together with them was as unwieldy as trying to make the singer-songwriters themselves fit the tradition founded by Little Richard, Chuck Berry and Elvis Presley.

The comparisons with Bob Dylan at least had more natural origins. The most obvious and superficial connection, of course, was John Hammond, who had discovered both of them. But there was also a surprising physical resemblance, enhanced by the fact that many thought Springsteen must be a Jewish name. Although Bruce is a bit taller, at five feet nine inches, his piercing

eyes, compact, powerful, but slender body and scraggly beard seemed virtually identical to Dylan's. Both men have a mass of curly hair, which under a spotlight acquires the aspect of a halo. On the back cover of *Greetings*, Springsteen looked like Dylan's tough, urban cousin. His blue work shirt might have come from the same Army-Navy store as the one Dylan wears on the cover of his *The Times They Are A-Changin'* LP. So the Columbia ads for *Greetings* featured a quote from Crawdaddy's Peter Knobler equating "Blinded By The Light" with Dylan's "Like A Rolling Stone." It was anything but apt, but it sure was an eye-catcher.

Inevitably, all great rock writing is matched against Dylan's, because Dylan's early work smashed so many boundaries and conventions, in terms of both structure and theme. As Springsteen has acknowledged, it was Bob Dylan "who made it possible for [him] to do the things [he] wanted to do." But Springsteen's similarities to Dylan weren't studied, as were those of many of the solo, acoustic guitar-playing writer-performers on the Greenwich Village scene were. In fact, although Dylan's impact on him was immediate and undeniable, Bruce's knowledge of him was centered on Dylan's 1965–66 string of hit singles, not the albums that had influenced most of the singer-songwriters. Arguably, such songs as "I Want You," "Positively Fourth Street," "Like A Rolling Stone," "Mr.

Tambourine Man" and "It Ain't Me, Babe" are the man's greatest music anyway. All of those—the first three as performed by Dylan himself, "Mr. Tambourine Man" in the Byrds' version and "It Ain't Me, Babe" as performed by the Turtles—had a sound Bruce loved, but not one that he pursued to the exclusion of all else. "Listening to one of his records was always a high point," Bruce said back in 1973—but not *the* high point. As a performer on the radio, Dylan was the equal of, not king amongst, the Stones, Manfred Mann, Mitch Ryder or The Who. None of this diminishes Dylan, but seeing his work out of context can become confusing.

In any event, Columbia's promotion (or hype) of *Greetings* put so much emphasis on the Dylan analogy that it unavoidably alienated consumers, radio people and critics. "The Dylan hype from Columbia was a turn-off," Dave Herman of WNEW-FM in New York has admitted. "I didn't even bother to listen to the album. I didn't want Columbia to think they got me." Similarly, Lester Bangs' *Rolling Stone* review of *Greetings* was so preoccupied with the New Dylan push that it missed much of Bruce's rock appeal.

Greetings showed almost immediately the symptoms of commercial failure—its initial sales could not have been much more than twenty-five-thousand copies, a bust by any standard. The Dylan hype wasn't the key factor in this—the amateurish production and wrong-headed arrangements were the truly insurmountable difficulties—but the hype was the longest-lasting problem that album created.

Soon after he was signed to Columbia, Appel also arranged a deal with the William Morris Agency for live bookings. Springsteen was already a seasoned onstage craftsman from his experience working Jersey joints, and agents Sam McKeith and Peter Golden, who made the deal, recognized him as a potential star of major proportions. It would be difficult to book him without a record, but the agency did the best it could.

When the record was released, Springsteen was sent on a comprehensive club tour: The Main Point near Philadelphia, which would become his home turf in years to come; Paul's Mall in Massachusetts, The Quiet Knight and Max's Kansas City in Chicago and New York. There weren't so many other clubs to play. A few college bookings, a couple of dates on the West Coast, and, since the album wasn't exactly a smash, that was about it. Only in Boston and Philadelphia was there much success; the strongest place for Springsteen bookings continued to be the bar scene at the Shore.

One person who caught onto Springsteen's appeal immediately was Barry Bell, a secretary at the William Morris Agency (although he was soon to become an agent himself.) Springsteen's combination of original songs, tall tales (which might make up as much as half the show) and eccentric musicality—he threw in oldies, he performed with a tuba, a violin, an accordion, you name it—was obviously unique. Slowly, a following did start to build up. Remembers Bell, "You were like the guy who went to a club before it happened. You were there and you knew it was coming." For Bell and certain others—Bruce's William Morris agent Sam McKeith, Columbia publicity chief Ron Oberman, *Crawdaddy* editor Peter Knobler, free-lance critics Paul Nelson and Karen Berg—Springsteen was already a major star on the horizon.

To spread the word, Columbia arranged for Bruce to appear as the opening act on a tour by the jazz-rock group, Chicago. It was a brief tour—only eight or ten dates. But it was a heavy token of support, for Chicago was Columbia's biggest-selling act—each of its nine albums had sold more than a million copies, and several had sold *two* million, which was then unheard of. The concert dates, including one at Madison Square Garden in New York, were certain sellouts.

But the tour was pure disaster for Bruce. It was symptomatic of Columbia's misunderstanding of the nature of Springsteen's talent and ambition. Chicago is a purely commercial proposition; its exploitation of standard jazz riffs in a pop setting qualifies as a kind of cynicism. If nothing else, Chicago is bland, and its appeal is not to people who share Bruce's intense commitment to rock and roll. This slick, professional, adult, middle-class show was the antithesis of Bruce's performance. Naturally, the audiences did not take to this hoody tough, who only delayed the appearance of what they'd paid to see and hear. (Bruce, however, remembers that the members of Chicago were unfailingly courteous, at a time when "most big bands were *not* that nice to opening acts. We got sound checks most nights. I had a lotta fun with those guys".)

In some places, Springsteen remembers, the group had things thrown at them. In Philadelphia, already a good town for Bruce, he was booed. "It was get introduced, walk on stage, blink and that's it. It's hard to show an audience what a band's about in that little time," Bruce said. "I couldn't stand it—everybody was so far away and the band couldn't hear. Maybe if they had come to see me, it would have been different. But I doubt it."

Bruce meets the press: Here, he's throttled by critic-singer Lester Bangs. Opposite, backstage with Susin Shapiro and Crawdaddy's Greg Mitchell.

Mike Appel counsels the troops.

"It left a terrible taste in Bruce's mouth as far as big buildings, as far as opening to anybody. I mean, he got booed in *Philadelphia*," Bell says, with a tone of disbelief. "The Chicago tour was a waste, and it was just sad, almost, after seeing him in the clubs, doing two hours of energy and stories and charisma. Now here he was, just another opening act on stage."

But the worst effect of the Chicago tour was the damage the New York performance at Madison Square Garden did to Springsteen's credibility with the CBS executives who saw it. Without so much as a sound check to help deal with the Garden's voluminous recesses, the group performed horribly. Even the company's biggest Springsteen fans, like Oberman, were shaken. Frustrated, Springsteen vowed he would never find himself treated as just another *anything* ever again.

For Bruce, the music always had a certain existential

purity. To play less well, or not to give as much of himself to it as he was capable of doing, was a violation of principle. After the Chicago experience, he decided that the rules of the game would change. He would never again play halls of sports arena size. No more was he to be booked as opening act to anyone, unless he could do his full, two hour show. He must have his own sound system. Above all, he must be able to perform without any time restrictions.

"That was the most important thing, I think, in Bruce's thinking," Bell says. "You can't take his show out of context. To take a part of it is to ruin it. So from then on, after the Chicago tour, it was An Evening With Bruce Springsteen. He would do the whole show, or there was a nominal opening act, like Jae Mason, the guy who later became the bouncer at the Bottom Line."

But this attitude only increased the disgruntlement

at CBS and William Morris. It made both jobs incredibly difficult; "Because you could only book him in places where he could sell tickets—which at that time, was my house and a couple other places in the Northeast," said Bell. "So he stayed out of the Midwest for a long, long time." On stops in Phoenix, Houston and eventually Los Angeles, he won sufficient fans to make returning profitable—if enough surrounding dates could be found. As Bell points out, "You can't take a date in St. Louis, even if there's an offer, go all the way out there for $500, if there's no dates around it to support it.

"Some of the other people at the agency were saying, 'He's crazy. He should get on as an opening act, go across the country.' But those are the same people who just don't understand Bruce. There's a lotta things that Bruce does that make people wonder."

Among those wondering was the staff at Columbia Records. And Mike Appel wasn't doing much to cheer people up. When an artist is obstinate the manager takes the blame, and there is no question that Mike Appel was willing to do so for Bruce. But there was more than enough blame to go around, because of Appel's bizarre and abusive style of presenting Spring-

steen's decisions. John Hammond has said that Appel is "about as offensive as any man I've ever met." Many CBS employees felt even more strongly about him, and this colored their reaction to Springsteen, which was already antagonistic because he had been unable to live up to the initial hype.

It wasn't that Appel was making particularly outrageous demands. Indeed, a good deal of the record company support he was seeking was probably just what any good manager would have requested. But Appel is a former Marine, and when he's in doubt his policy is to attack. He lacks any sense of diplomacy. Given a choice between treating someone rudely and making a conciliatory gesture, Appel never loses a chance to bully and intimidate with the language and demeanor of a drill sergeant. The result, at both Columbia and William Morris, was a good deal of animosity, a fair share of hatred and a general reluctance to cooperate or go out of the way for either Appel or his client. Only those who believed most completely in Bruce—at William Morris, agent Sam McKeith, at CBS, Ron Oberman and a few others—continued to work hard on his career.

Appel was also extremely naive. Before the first al-

bum was released, he placed a call to the NBC producer in charge of the NFL Super Bowl festivities, suggesting that instead of opening the game with ''The Star Spangled Banner,'' NBC should use Bruce Springsteen singing an original, anti-war song, ''Balboa Vs. The Beast Slayer.'' That anyone who lives in the United States could suggest such a thing is astonishing enough. But when he was immediately and understandably turned down, Appel reportedly became enraged. ''Someday I'm gonna give you a call and remind you of this,'' he told the stunned producer. ''Then I'm gonna make another call and you'll be out of a job.'' (So the story goes. Appel admits making the call and the suggestion but denies the threat: ''All I said was, instead of doing something creative, he was gonna do the same old hack thing.'')

''Remember,'' Appel told a new CBS employee, ''Bruce Springsteen isn't a rock act. He's a religion.'' This attitude no one denies. Even Hammond, who clearly finds the man despicable, acknowledged at the time, ''Mike is utterly selfless in his devotion to Bruce.'' Appel has taken the statement about religion further. ''I always thought of myself as John the Baptist, heralding Bruce's coming to the world,'' he says. Since he was operating with little capital and a family to support—he would eventually mortgage his home to keep the organization going—there seems little doubt that such comments were made partly to sustain Appel's own conviction. As Bell says, ''I don't think Mike Appel did anything without checking it with Bruce first. I think that was how, to some extent, Mike got into trouble with Bruce. They started having different opinions on things—a lotta things, like where Bruce should go, what he should get paid and all the rest." Left to himself, Appel would never have made the decision to buck the system. But there is no denying that he could have—should have—conducted himself more discreetly and less emotionally.

All of these problems were exacerbated in May, 1973, when Clive Davis was mysteriously fired (actually, it seems, in a corporate *putsch*). With the dismal sales record and a poor performance at the CBS Records Convention in San Francisco in July, Springsteen was in big trouble with CBS. And although the live show was coming along, it, too, had problems, mostly stemming from the erratic rhythm section.

The convention appearance was especially damaging to whatever credibility Bruce had left within Columbia Records. "Bruce came on with a chip on his shoulder," Hammond says, "and played way too long. People came to me and said, 'He really can't be that bad, can he, John?'" Many at the record label were prepared to write him off as a particularly embarrassing mistake.

But Bruce remembers differently. "I followed Edgar Winter with his smoke bombs, and the salesmen loved that. You can't compete with that. So Danny and I did 'Sandy,' which I had just written, just accordion and acoustic guitar. Then the band came out to play 'Saint in the City,' 'Thundercrack' and maybe another one. All these ladies in gowns in the front rows had their fingers in their ears, but I thought we played good, and so did [promo man] Mike Pillote, Ron Oberman and [concert producer] Chip Monck. At least, that's what they told me. What can I say?"

As for the rest of the world, it seemed to have forgotten more than it ever wanted to know about Bruce. Disc jockey Dave Herman summarized the attitude: "He was just another media hype that failed. He was already a dead artist who bombed on his first album."

Undaunted, the young corpse prepared to record his second LP.

Wild and Innocent

The Wild, The Innocent And The E Street Shuffle was recorded in the summer and fall of 1973 and released that November. At Columbia Records, it was a less-than-ideal moment to be considered a Clive Davis protege, especially if your first album hadn't sold enough copies to justify a heavy promotional budget. *E Street* was released with the absolute minimum of fanfare. The CBS field people who had pushed hard for sales and airplay on *Greetings* now had several projects of much higher priority—not an uncommon circumstance for an artist whose first album has been a widely publicized flop, although it was perhaps taken to extreme lengths by the CBS national promotion man who encouraged a Houston station to cease playing Bruce's record and begin programming Boz Scaggs and Billy Joel instead.

Springsteen did have one small, but vocal, part of the rock establishment on his side: the critics. CBS publicity director Ron Oberman made *The Wild, The Innocent And The E Street Shuffle* his highest personal priority. Oberman was a believer who had attended enough shows to know what Bruce could do onstage. In fact, Oberman was one of very few CBS executives who had seen Springsteen frequently enough to know that the Chicago tour and the convention show were just flukes. In addition, he recognized Springsteen's appeal among the press: Bruce's instinct about what made a great record was completely in line with most rock critics' thinking.

In terms of influence, rock critics have never been as significant in their field as reviewers of drama, film or "serious" music, partly because the audience for rock is often barely literate. Poor reviews will close a Broadway play; good ones in the right places will sometimes make a novel a bestseller. But even the top rock critics have exerted little public influence—though their impact on the music industry itself has not always been inconsequential. Oberman didn't need to manipulate the press in this instance—he was too canny to try. Besides, he understood that, from the point of view of critical taste, Bruce's music didn't require hype. Now that the

"New Dylan" bullshit had settled down, *The Wild, The Innocent And The E Street Shuffle* was certain to be widely praised. Oberman's publicity job consisted of assuring critics who hadn't seen Bruce that he was everything the others were beginning to say, and encouraging those who had been converted to listen, and to write.

There had been some enthusiasm among critics even for the first album, and the early shows had earned astonishingly good reviews. "Our enthusiasm was sustained because of the press," says Bell. "All you had to do was read the newspaper and you would think that *Greetings* was the Number One album, instead of number one thousand. Every time we booked him anywhere, we got nothing but rave reviews."

This enthusiasm was beginning to trickle down to the promoters, as well. "I *never* have had a phone call when somebody said, 'Boy, Bruce stunk!' or 'What's this guy about?'" Bell said in early 1979. "Which always happens at least once or twice with everybody— including the Rolling Stones. Somebody will call up and say they didn't play good this night. But people were saying, '*This* guy's got potential.' There was always something good coming back."

If Springsteen were still only last year's failed hype to the disc jockeys and the record stores, he was, in the eyes of many writers, a young artist with potential for greatness. Most critics have a historical perspective, and one of the startling things about even Springsteen's

With Clive Davis.

On the street in Long Branch, N.J.

early shows was their dramatic sweep of rock history, the way they incorporated songs, styles and fragments from every era. Besides, Springsteen wrote with incisive intelligence of the street life that so many critics idolized (though very few of them had lived any part of the tough guy image). And his reference points were similar to the kind of half-forgotten, away-from-the-trend nuances critics cherished: early Elvis, Dylan's great Sixties rock, the soul of Motown and Stax (as transmitted through Van Morrison, it seemed) and the pop production extravaganzas of Phil Spector and Roy Orbison.

It wasn't surprising then, that Ken Emerson, writing in *Rolling Stone*, called *E Street* one of the year's best albums, or that Ed Ward, in *Creem*, dubbed it "great." Ward added that he hadn't been "so mystified and entertained by an album since *Astral Weeks*," Van Morrison's most spellbinding record. And, he said, although Springsteen's unfettered spew of lyrical imagery would seem to contradict it, "one person I know who's met him reports that he doesn't use drugs, by the way." At a moment when many rock critics were becoming hostile to the decadent lives of rock stars, that was especially significant.

For Bruce himself, *The Wild, The Innocent And The E Street Shuffle* was a breakthrough. "On the second album, I started slowly to find out who I am," he said,

"and where I wanted to be. It was like coming out of the shadow of various influences and trying to be yourself."

What he found was a sensibility totally shaped by rock and pop culture Americana. The result was not quite pastiche, for Springsteen took the best bits and shaped them into a distinct vision; like many another genre artist, he saw the stock situations from such a personal perspective that they seemed unique. In some senses, *The Wild, The Innocent And The E Street Shuffle* might have been made by a different person than the one who did *Greetings From Asbury Park, New Jersey*. Although the key stylistic elements remained the same, and they were allowed free play, there was no talk about "folk music," this time. The result is a record that is more confident, mature and disciplined—and when the discipline fades, as it sometimes does, one is still left with more than simple sloppiness.

"The new album was a little more what I wanted to do," Springsteen continues. "There was more of the band in there and the songs were written more in the way I wanted to write." And it was at this time that the advantages of New Jersey's isolation from the rock mainstream began to show up. Because Bruce had not been pressured into joining a scene or following a trend, he had never confused the idealism inherent in early rock and roll—the notion that it could set you free—with the mass-marketed bohemianism of the Sixties. So he understood from the start that it was important to retain control of as many aspects of his career as possible. Elvis Presley was the root of his inspiration— Elvis the King, the man who had it all and threw it all away. Springsteen's ambition was just as limitless.

At times, "all" seems the most important word in Bruce's vocabulary. It is the explanation for the sweat-drenched three-hour shows, for the painstaking way he records, and for the distance he keeps from rock's cocaine-and-limousine set. Springsteen wants to be the Complete Rock Star: great singer, greater writer, great producer, great arranger, great guitarist, great live performer. Surround himself with the best band, best stage crew, best lighting. To do it *all*, his own way. "My parents used to tell me that they wanted me to have something more than they did," he said on stage one night. "What they didn't understand was that I wanted *everything*."

Perhaps it is naive, but Bruce's faith in rock and roll and what it can do—not just for him, but for anybody—is complete. Rock and roll is the great spiritual alternative of the age; Bruce understands this as well as anyone, and he articulates it better than any spokesman rock has had since Peter Townshend's heyday.

"Sometimes people ask, who are your favorites?"

Bruce told *Creem*'s Robert Duncan in 1978. "My favorites change. Sometimes it's Elvis, sometimes it's Buddy Holly. Different personalities. For me, the *idea* of rock and roll is sort of my favorite. The feeling. Rock and roll came to my house where there seemed to be no way out. It just seemed like a dead-end street, nothing I liked to do, nothing I wanted to do, except roll over and go to sleep or something. And it came into my house—snuck in, ya know, and opened up a whole world of possibilities. Rock and roll. The Beatles opened doors. Ideally, if any stuff I do could ever do that for somebody, that's the best. Can't do anything better than that. Rock and roll motivates. It's the big, gigantic motivator, at least it was for me. There's a whole lot of things involved, but that's what I think you gotta remain true to. That idea, that *feeling*. That's the real spirit of the music."

But at the end of 1973, in pursuit of fame and fortune, the rock machine had forgotten that feeling. When the idealism of the Sixties crashed, more than just political and artistic pretension perished. So did the notion of rock and roll as something bigger than entertainment—the idea that rock was a cause and a salvation, the idea that it offered something greater than fun. That it offered, in Pete Townshend's word, *triumph*.

When rock joined in the typical pop pursuit of big bucks, when the musician ceased to be an outlaw and began to cooperate with the show business establish-

ment, the *idea* of rock was corrupted. It may be true, as British critic Charlie Gillett has said, that any term which can encompass both Elvis Presley and the Velvet Underground is musically meaningless. But it is not *emotionally* meaningless—at least, not until rock becomes a synonym for any pop music, no matter what its inspirational potential. That is the tragedy of the Seventies: Rock became whatever people marketed as rock, rather than something special.

In such a medium, to return to the historical roots and impart new life to them seems more worthwhile than to experiment with such things as "artrock." And in any event, the stars who had made technical breakthroughs in the early Seventies—Pete Townshend himself, Stevie Wonder, Sly Stone—were beginning to run into dead ends, or out of gas. Acting almost as if their experiments had never existed, Springsteen investigated many of the nooks and crannies they and their peers had ignored.

Thus, the methodology by which Springsteen came to his music is perhaps less interesting than the tenacity with which he held to his ideals. Bruce was never caught up with what was fashionable in terms of technique, and because he was a remarkably prolific songwriter, he could discover ruts and dead ends more quickly than those who worked more slowly. He also had a memory for every honest moment ever put on wax, it sometimes seemed, whether it was Gene Pitney's "Love My Life Away" or Harold Dorman's "Mountain of Love." At a time when the demarcation between black and white popular music was severely drawn, Bruce slipped easily into grooves based on soul rhythm patterns—thus the frequent comparisons to Van Morrison, who was at that time almost the only other white performer who consistently used soul music elements in rock. Bruce built a style as deeply imaginative as the Beatles or Bob Dylan had done, because he was one of the few performers who understood that rock did not begin and end with superstars, but with a hundred—or a thousand—half-forgotten records whose stars had flickered for only an instant. *The Wild, The Innocent And The E Street Shuffle* found an audience without resorting to the usual music business routine because those who had once been committed to rock couldn't forget it. And because those who were too young to have known it before couldn't believe it.

The album is certainly flawed, sometimes in fundamental ways. The sound is muddy, and although this time the band arrangements are integral to the sound, the drumming is still erratic, one of the most serious problems from which rock can suffer. The piano parts were recorded on a creaky instrument: the action of the foot pedals can actually be heard during soft passages. The lyrics are still too wordy, but at least they're focused on a single theme per song.

The Wild, The Innocent And The E Street Shuffle is a transitional record, serving for Bruce much the same purpose that albums like *Revolver* and *Bringing It All Back Home* did for the Beatles and Bob Dylan. In essence, the album consolidates Bruce's perspective on the best elements of rock's first twenty years, while making the first step toward a genuinely personal style.

In a way, the album's two sides seem like separate records. The first, "E Street," side is something of a holdover from *Greetings*, full of energetic songs whose potential has not always been fully exploited. But Side Two contains Springsteen's first fully realized thematic concepts—a three-song suite of tales about wild and innocent kids on the loose.

The themes of Side One deal with escape. "Wild Billy's Circus Story," a mood sketch of an evening at the circus and a young boy's seduction by carnival life, is too mannered in its pursuit of the calliope—it is almost a parody. Similarly, although "The E Street Shuffle," which opens the record, contains wonderful street-life imagery—"teenage tramps in skintight pants do the E Street dance"—with powerful, soul music horns, the recording lacks the crispness and punch to move it along. This is even more problematical on "Kitty's Back," a classic bar band shouter that is obviously meant as a performance piece, but whose best qualities are swallowed up in the mix. Springsteen's prowess as a guitarist should have been immediately apparent after this song, but because of the fuzzy recording, the playing here reveals itself only with extremely concentrated listening.

In the end, Side One's most fully realized production is "Asbury Park Fourth Of July (Sandy)," a nearly perfect ballad, the story of the boardwalk kids and their hot rod/pinball environment. The arrangement is built around acoustic guitar and accordion which are haunt-

ing in their simplicity. Springsteen's raspy vocals quaver in a way that is reminiscent at times of the Band's Richard Manuel. That's appropriate. The Band sings about an America most of us have felt, but never seen. Springsteen sings about a version of the nation most of us have seen without feeling.

The story of "Sandy" is a B-movie plot about kids on the loose, running from dream date to low-key rumble. The singer's girlfriend (a boardwalk waitress) has left him, and he's looking for new romance and a way out of this ritualized existence. The street is full of "switch-blade lovers," "boys . . . with their shirts open," and "greasers in their high heels." A mysterious fortune teller, Madame Marie, is busted by the cops for "knowing more than they do." As the music rises and falls, the singer pleads with Sandy to follow him:

For me this boardwalk life's through
You oughta quit this scene, too
Sandy, the aurora is rising behind us
The pier lights; our carnival life forever
Oh love me tonight and I promise I'll love you
    forever
Oh I mean it Sandy girl

Here, the boardwalk becomes something more enticing and more ominous than the one pictured on the post-card cover of *Greetings*: a symbol of hope, and an omen of wasted possibilities. In the second verse, the singer wistfully remembers making love to his boss's daughter. (Onstage, Springsteen caps the verse with a simple interjection of delight and pure triumph. "Ain't got no boss, no more," he exults.)

The Wild, The Innocent And The E Street Shuffle's first side is characterized by a remarkable exuberance. Even the slower songs like "Wild Billy" and "Sandy" have a quality of release, a delight in the simple joy of existence. But Side Two is much darker—while it is never defeatist, it is certainly much more raw. All along, Springsteen has had a tale to tell, an epic of life as lived not so much by car crazy kids or the urban underworld, but on the rough edge, under the thumb of a system that beats back hope for sport. On the first LP, the celebration of the subway rider in "It's Hard To Be A Saint In The City," the shootout in the Bronx that's the peak moment of "Lost In The Flood," and here, Kitty's failed attempt to find a big city romance in "Kitty's Back" are all of a piece. The names change but the characters do not. And all of them point toward the narrative second side of *The Wild, The Innocent And The E Street Shuffle*.

It's a story rich with lust and humor, of victory snatched from the clutches of defeat, of victories lost at the last moment, of life lived for thrills and lives that

are barely lived at all. What's most remarkable is that Springsteen's view of this nightworld is, in the end, affectionate. He finds beauty in its empty echoes, in its milieu of dirty sheets and barren cupboards, trashy gutters and broken-down cars. As with any outsider, his belief in the City is stronger than a native could ever afford.

"Rosalita" is Side Two's rocker, sandwiched between the two ballads "Incident On Fifty-Seventh Street" and "New York City Serenade" the way the weekend is crammed between Friday and Monday. It might have been recorded at a demolition site. And the story is a marvel. Rosalita is locked in her room. Her parents disapprove of her boyfriend—the singer—because he is a rock and roller. The lyric is mostly a plea for her to break past their inane regulations; the singer stands beneath her balcony, shouting like a madman for Rosie to free herself. But she's confused. So he coaxes her, while the wild guitars bump into the horns and finally slam the punch line home:

> But now you're sad, your mama's mad
> And your papa says he knows that I don't have any
>   money
> Well, tell him this is his last chance
> To get his daughter in a fine romance
> Because the record company, Rosie,
> Just gave me a big advance

It's a giddy spoof of a conclusion—for once, the characters really have found a way to beat the trap of their lives. If anybody had doubts that Bruce Springsteen would someday write a classic rock song, "Rosalita" dispelled them. The music is equal to the lyric, literally archetypal rock and roll. For five years, it has been the final number of his show; it may be his final song

forever.

"Incident On Fifty-Seventh Street" and "New York City Serenade" begin more quietly, and never gain the raucous heights of "Rosalita." But they lack nothing for energy—long, winding, slower tempo songs they may be, but they both end on emotional peaks. Most writers take years to write songs that meld classical virtues with a unique perspective, but Springsteen did it when he was twenty-three, on his second album. "When I write something and I *know* it's good," Springsteen says, "I get a little spark. It's like a little light that goes off inside me that says, 'Bing! You've just fulfilled your life's purpose.' "

"New York City Serenade" is about exactly such moments of self-discovery. Bruce croons it with all the faith of the truly wild and innocent, describing a fool's paradise and the rules by which one lives within it: "It's midnight in Manhattan / This is no time to get cute. It's a mad dog's promenade. So walk tall . . . or, baby, don't walk at all." In the end, the city and the song merge in a single metaphor:

> Hey vibes man, hey jazz man, play me your
>   serenade
> Any deeper blue and you're playin' in your
>   grave

There's great delicacy in this song, with its acoustic guitar and light piano, rumbling bass and crying strings. But in the guitar, there's an edge like a knife, and Bruce's voice aches with desire. At the very end of the song's ten minutes, the music glides and soars with a singsong celebration of a junkman, whose singing, singing, singing becomes a triumph of life itself. For in this place, beauty is everywhere balanced by something sinister.

Here is Springsteen the great seducer. It's as though he were whispering secrets and promises in our ear, drawing us just close enough to make us want to hear more. You can imagine Johnny Shines hearing Robert Johnson's blues and finding in them something like this that encouraged him to follow the great country bluesman. The beat is not rock and roll—it is just a rolling heartbeat. But it is something very like Springsteen's own statement of the blues: What it is that matters, how one might gain it, and lose it, and the price paid for the attempt. For if this is not a version of the blues, then it is very like a Pied Piper's tune; one has about as much hope of resisting.

Springsteen does not know the City well. These songs have less sense of place and physical detail than, say, the New York Dolls' demimonde epics. What he does know is the sort of person for whom the place has killer depths, for whom this town chokes off all that's young and beautiful, whom the town uses its own beauty to destroy. It's the same place that the Drifters found, uptown, "On Broadway." That story was too long for one song, or three. It would swoop over to the next album, and the next. A simple tale, it's a long way from "Sandy's" Little Eden—a world away, or a lifetime.

In "Incident On Fifty-Seventh Street," Johnny's a flashy dresser, hanging out with hard girls and pimps. Puerto Rican Jane picks him up, but Johnny's torn between his love and his partners in crime. Temptation is the central fact of his existence—temptation and looming failure, demons that only grow larger until he challenges them.

With "Incident On Fifty-Seventh Street," all the funny street names suddenly come to life, leaping from the earlier songs to swagger down boulevards and creep down narrow alleys. The names have changed again, but we recognize the same figures. In the end, these characters bring the teen exploitation era up-to-date, only this version is truer than ever before. Geographically, Bruce Springsteen is as far from Latin New York as he is from Leonard Bernstein. Spiritually, he has always been there, down with the losers and the hopeless, the not-quick-enough and the dead, where the margin of life is music.

It's the music that makes the difference. In other hands, Spanish Johnny and Puerto Rican Jane's love affair could easily have become maudlin. But Springsteen, marshalling his band like an army, makes the lovers triumphant. Danny Federici's organ is as open and warm as a fresh bullet wound, and Springsteen's own guitar surges at the end like anti-aircraft fire. When Johnny says "Good night, Janey," it is not a mournful farewell, but a promise on which he means to deliver; the difference is precisely the intensity of the performance.

The story itself is as old as Romeo and Juliet, but it is told with the passion of someone who must, sometimes in the dark of night, wish that he had lived it—or fear that he still might. This is rock not just on the edge, but over it. The best way—finally the only way—to tell it is to let the boy do it himself.

Incident On Fifty-Seventh Street
By Bruce Springsteen

Spanish Johnny drove in from the underworld last
   night
With bruised arms and broken rhythm and a beat-up
   old Buick
But dressed just like dynamite
He tried sellin' his heart to the hard girls over on Easy
   Street
But they sighed, "Johnny, it falls apart so easy and you
   know, hearts these days are cheap."
And the pimps swung their axes and said, "Johnny,
   you're a cheater."
Oh the pimps swung their axes and said, "Johnny,
   you're a liar."
And from out of the shadows came a young girl's voice
Sayin' "Johnny, don't cry."
Puerto Rican Jane, oh, won't you tell me, what's your
   name?
I want to drive you down to the other side of town
Where paradise ain't so crowded and there'll be action
   goin' down on Shanty Lane tonight

All the golden-heeled fairies in a real bitch-fight
Pull .38s
And kiss the girls good night

Good night, it's all right, Jane
Now let them black boys in to light the soul flame
We may find it out on the street tonight, baby
Or we may walk until the daylight, maybe

Well, like a cool Romeo he made his moves
Oh, she looked so fine
Like a late Juliet, she knew he'd never be true
But then she didn't really mind
Upstairs the band was playin'
The singer was singin' something about going home
She whispered, ''Spanish Johnny, you can leave me
    tonight
But just don't leave me alone''
And Johnny cried,
''Puerto Rican Jane! Word is down the cops have found
    the vein.''
Them barefoot boys, they left their homes for the
    woods
Them little barefoot street boys they said their homes
    ain't no good
They left the corners

Threw away all of their switchblade knives
And kissed each other good-bye

Johnny was sittin' on the fire escape
Watchin' the kids playin' down the street
He called down, ''Hey little heroes, summer's long
But I guess it ain't very sweet around here any more.''
Janey sleeps in sheets damp with sweat
Johnny sits up alone and watches her dream on,
    dream on
And the sister prays for lost souls
Then breaks down in the chapel after everyone's gone
Jane moves over to share her pillow
But opens her eyes to see Johnny up and putting his
    clothes on
She says, ''Those romantic young boys
All they ever wanna do is fight''
Those romantic young boys
They're callin' through the window:
''Hey Spanish Johnny, wanna make a little easy money
    tonight?''

And Johnny whispered
''Good night, it's all right, Jane
I'll meet you tomorrow night on Lover's Lane
We may find it out on the street tonight, baby

Or we may walk until the daylight, maybe

Aw, good night, it's all right, Jane
I'm gonna meet you tomorrow night on Lover's Lane
Now we can find it out on the street tonight, baby
Or we may have to walk until the morning light,
   maybe."

There are a few precious moments in rock when you can hear a musician overcoming both his own limits and the restrictions of the form. At those times, the music flows into something so awesome that its force is undeniable. Van Morrison's *Astral Weeks,* Eric Clapton's "Layla," Dylan's "Like A Rolling Stone," Phil Spector's "Da Doo Ron Ron," Roy Orbison's "Running Scared," perhaps Neil Young on "Helpless" and *Tonight's The Night,* certainly the entire first Jimi Hendrix Experience LP and the Who's "My Generation" and "Substitute" are moments such as that. For Springsteen, the watershed came on his second album. If he has already written greater music, explored the possibilities of his ideas more completely, made better recordings, none of it can ever sound quite this *fresh.* Neither he, nor we, will ever again be quite so astonished by the dimensions of his talent.

7

FREEZE OUT

"You don't see no music on the records unless you watch the grooves. And that ain't much. That's pretty boring."—Bruce Springsteen

It may have been clear to rock critics that *The Wild, The Innocent And The E Street Shuffle* was a major piece of rock artistry. But to almost everyone else the album looked like a certified commercial flop. The reasons were more complex than Columbia's lack of promotion, although, as was later demonstrated, the album could have done better if the most elementary promotional efforts had been expended. (For instance, there was not a single trade paper advertisement for *The Wild, The Innocent And The E Street Shuffle*, although record companies routinely take at least one ad for every new release.)

Electronics aside, the differences between AM and FM radio in America are principally matters of taste. Both sorts of stations have a tendency to seek music that conforms to the bland standards promoted by the rock machine (although that is putting the cart before the horse, since those standards were developed as a response to radio's role as the principle promotional vehicle for American popular music), but rock on AM radio must conform to very different standards than rock on FM—and this difference was much greater in 1974 than it is today.

The most obvious restriction on AM radio concerns time. Such stations are extremely reluctant to play any song more than three minutes thirty seconds long. Go over four minutes, and you risk kissing the AM Top Forty stations goodbye—not a light matter, since AM is by far the larger marketplace, with audiences measured in potential millions of listeners and with similar benefits in potential sales. Of the seven songs on *The Wild, The Innocent, And The E Street Shuffle* not one was less than four and one half minutes long. (At the time, Springsteen claimed that he simply couldn't say or play what he wanted in a briefer format.)

There are also ways to mix the sound of a record to make it sound brighter and more immediately exciting on AM radio, which has very low fidelity and is most often picked up on tinny automobile and table radio speakers. Because *The Wild, The Innocent And The E Street Shuffle* sounded muddy even on expensive stereo equipment, the AM radio market was written off—for all intents and purposes, since no singles were released from it—the moment *E Street* was released. This made it drastically unlikely that the album would achieve sales beyond the quarter-million level.

FM radio is another story. Theoretically, FM—the so-called Album-Oriented Radio of the Seventies (AOR for short)—is much freer than AM, playing hits that are too long or too loud for the broad-based listenership of their brethren. But in 1974 very few stations on even the FM band were willing to take a chance on adventurous sounds. FM programmers liked to blast AM radio for its stale conventions and its preference for bland performers like Tony Orlando and Elton John. But FM itself was (and is) in something of a rut. What started in the late Sixties as an exciting movement toward radical broadcasting had become merely another trail in the hunt for large listenership; FM rock radio also looked for a least common denominator, although admittedly its ideal sound was a bit more adventuresome.

Only a few loyal disc jockeys, usually at FM stations that allowed the deejays to pick a proportion of their own music, bothered with Springsteen's second album. In New York, WNEW virtually ignored it, at least at the onset, despite the fact that "New York City Serenade" —for one—was a natural for its hometown listeners. KILT in Houston, WBCN in Boston and, above all, Ed Sciaky at WMMR in Philadelphia and, later, Kid Leo at WMMS in Cleveland did play Springsteen, partly because they liked the music, partly because the Springsteen cult was growing to substantial proportions—through live shows—in those cities.

This situation is not altogether unusual. There are thousands upon thousands of albums released yearly in the United States, and several hundred others released in the English language abroad. The majority remain unheard on any radio station at all. But the quality of Bruce's songs is so self-evident that it is mystifying that so few FM stations picked up on them. For Mike Appel, who had all of his own and (soon-to-be-departed) Jim Cretecos' savings tied up in Springsteen, the lack of airplay was more than disconcerting. It was infuriating.

Appel began to badger Columbia for more support; again, something many a manager might do, but given Appel's penchant for verbal abuse, it proved self destructive. The company was unresponsive. Appel hardly cared how he appeared to the record company. His dedication to Springsteen, in whom he had both believed and invested, was complete. But to call his approach to promotion merely counter-productive is to understate the case considerably.

Appel is said to have sent a letter containing torn-up $10 bills (according to another version, photocopied twenties) to stations that he considered the worst

offenders; the implications that he thought the programmers took payola could not be more clear. He also phoned and berated them. At Christmas, he sent bags of coal, rather than the usual presents, to everyone he felt was hurting Springsteen's career by not playing the record. (Appel denies that he sent the shredded or photocopied bills. But he admits the rest, contending that the coal was meant as a gag.)

The radio programmers went berserk, but what was worse, it hurt Springsteen with the record company. Columbia, like any other label, cannot afford to offend radio stations; unintentional slights require immediate fence-mending. From the company's point of view, there's always another album to promote, which requires the programmer's continuing cooperation. The coal outraged CBS executives. Appel had left a lot of programmer feathers to smooth—more, many executives felt, than either he or his act were worth. Word came down from near the top: *The Wild, The Innocent And The E Street Shuffle* was a dead issue. What little promotion there was dried up. Rumors began to hit the street that CBS was even thinking of releasing Springsteen from his contract.

Undoubtedly, Springsteen would have been signed by another record company if CBS had dropped him. That was one thing that kept CBS from doing so. But a new label would have meant starting from scratch, and whatever the problems, it was hard to find another label—particularly another New York–based label—that was as effective in selling records as Columbia.

Springsteen found himself blocked at every turn. Radio was not interested. The record company had virtually given up hope. Touring in the usual fashion seemed to violate his artistic conception. Like a one-horse shay, the record machine stopped working all at once.

The point isn't that the machine was attempting to prevent Bruce Springsteen from becoming a success. But confronted with a performer who did not meet specifications, the machinery was simply unable to process him. Unless one believes that rock is purely product, never art, and that therefore the performer is obliged to tailor his work to the standards of the marketplace, the failure was not basically Springsteen's. It was, rather, an indication that the promotional process developed by the rock establishment in the Sixties and early Seventies had lost a great deal of its effectiveness.

Springsteen and Appel fell back on their confidence in themselves. Bruce soon began to think about making another record—although the suggestion from CBS that he try recording with session musicians fell on deaf ears. Springsteen would rather fail than compromise the essence of his sound. As for the live show, they simply slogged it out in the half dozen markets—Philadelphia, New York, Boston, Washington, Phoenix, Houston—where he had caught on. It was mostly club dates and small halls, making just enough money to

keep going. The key was Philadelphia, where *E Street* had sold more than half its total copies in the early going.

Of course, this approach contradicted standard music business logic, according to which an artist who made himself available too often in a given market would soon become "overexposed." Why this was supposed to be true of concert attractions and not of records—which are ideally played on radio as often as possible—is mysterious. In any case, it proved untrue: Some of the major success stories of the Seventies (Bob Seger, Ted Nugent, Styx) developed precisely by exploiting this sort of regional popularity.

The judgment was irrelevant in the case of Bruce Springsteen anyway, because anyone who went to see his show more than once did not see the same thing. As agent Bell remembers, "I would go there and I would be surprised every night. Where, with somebody else, after seeing the act two nights in a row, you'd say, 'Okay, let's go home.' But here, you know, I wanted to be there the next night, to see what the new surprise was gonna be, what the new innovation was gonna be, what the new material was gonna be, where would he jump this time, what would he do crazy next time."

In his early dates, Springsteen offered a mix of his own material tied together with a few stories that served as introductions along with the occasional oldie. Although his tales were always more witty than the usual slam-bang introductions, and while the oldies were inevitably performed with zeal, the most unusual fixtures of the early appearances were Danny Federici's accordion and Garry Tallent's tuba. But as Springsteen became more experienced and more confident, he wove the introductory stories into the fabric of the music itself: The material changed endlessly, with old hits recast completely and new material being worked out before the audiences' eyes. And always, the intensity was remarkable; Springsteen was not happy unless he left the stage completely drained. As Bell says, "He would do things that people just weren't used to. They weren't used to commitments like that onstage. His whole concept—he always had the public in mind in his shows. The long sound checks, even in the clubs—everything. There was a reason for his being there. His show was always . . . perfect.

"It was weird. It was spontaneous, yet it was not spontaneous. The spontaneity was so evident, yet you would think that the guy rehearsed for six years before he went on stage. He would always know how to put new material in the show. In the beginning, the pacing of the show wasn't great, but as he performed more and more it got better.

"I think that what most people were just shocked at, when they saw him, was his energy. Everybody else that you would normally see—Chicago, Blood Sweat and Tears—was just *tired* on stage. Everybody was getting used to the forty-five minute set. Bruce was out there for two hours. That was the one complaint we used to

get about Bruce: that he was on too long. According to the promoters. You couldn't tell the kids that—the kids would have liked him to play another three hours."

The live show really took off after drummer Ernest "Boom" Carter replaced Vini Lopez. Springsteen agonized over sacking Lopez, with whom he had played since Steel Mill. But the move was necessary. Carter was a last-minute addition when a gig turned up before auditions for a new drummer were completed—he was Sancious' friend, and readily available. Boom's arrival stabilized the rhythm section, letting the natural drive of the songs come through. People began to talk about Springsteen's E Street Band as one of the most powerful club acts in rock. Now Bruce could say truthfully, "I play for two and a half hours every show. I put myself on the line."

The length of his shows was made mandatory by Springsteen's sense of obligation to his audience. "If I leave the stage feeling, well, if I'd played just one more song, maybe somebody out there would have been won over, if I feel I could have given more, it's hard for me to sleep that night," he has said. As a result, despite his fragile looks, Springsteen has the physical condition of an athlete. His biceps ripple, and his agility is notorious; it is not uncommon for him to begin or end a song by leaping headlong from a piano or a speaker column, or to pursue Clarence Clemons around the

74

stage at a furious pace through a one-minute instrumental bridge in ''Rosalita''. After each show, Springsteen virtually collapses into his dressing room, soaked with sweat. Yet good or bad, his dedication extends into the heart of the night; he leaves the concert hall hours after the show is concluded, but if any fans are still waiting outside, he always has time for a few words, an autograph, a joke or two.

The classic rock songs that Springsteen began to drop into his show were more carefully chosen and performed than the oldies used by most singer-songwriters. Whereas someone like Elton John made obvious choices, picking up on ever-present Beatles songs like ''I Want To Hold Your Hand'' and ''Lucy In The Sky With Diamonds,'' Springsteen picked his older material in a way that integrated it into his own music. Bruce never used more than two or three such songs per show, but when he did Fats Domino's ''Let The Four Winds Blow,'' Chuck Berry's ''Little Queenie,'' or Elvis Presley's ''Wear Your Ring Around Your Neck,'' he made them his own, without violating the stylistic basis of the original. The archetypal examples of this are Springsteen's version of ''Quarter To Three,'' the half-forgotten Gary ''U.S.'' Bonds hit that became his standard encore, and the Crystals' great Phil Spector production, ''Then She Kissed Me.'' But his version of Bob Dylan's ''I Want You,'' slowed down and intensified, lifted that song from a mixture of lust

and disgust to a tune of pure aching passion, without sacrificing Dylan's ironic intent.

This was an astute move, because it gave Springsteen access to the entire span of rock and roll at a moment when rock was especially historically self-conscious. If he was more than two steps from the blues, Springsteen was barely one removed from the Sixties hard rock of the Beatles and the Rolling Stones. Playing for audiences that were not always certain which were his originals and which the ''oldies,'' Bruce simply took everything and stamped it with his own identity. Fans old enough to remember the originals were still jarred by a jolt of reminiscence.

For his part, Springsteen never considered any part of his repertoire ''oldies'' in the sense of Sha Na Na's bogus nostalgia. ''They're just songs that I've always liked. Whenever a song's got that life, that ability to move you and is still very relevant to today, to what's happening, that's important.

''We don't play no oldies. They may be older songs, but they're not nostalgic, really. I was never into that whole nostalgic thing, because it's stupid. But these songs are different. It's obvious by the reaction they get. It's great today, it's great right now, and if somebody plays it and people hear it, they'll still love it tomorrow.'' In an industry whose sense of history often overwhelmed its sense of tradition, that statement was nearly revolutionary: It drew the line between mechanical masturbation and the genuine ability to perceive and create links between past and present in popular culture.

Springsteen never played other people's songs with reverence, because that would have sapped the life from them. His own material was also not fixed into any single shape or style. On the LP, for example, "The E Street Shuffle" is an approximation of Stax Records' version of soul music, with a jaunty brass section and raspy vocal. Live, it sometimes became a slow ballad or a straight-forward rocker. Partly, this was compensation for the E Street Band's lack of a brass section. But it was also a measure of Bruce's relentless searching, his willingness to rethink his material constantly, exploring all of its possibilities. "For You," to take another example, might be performed solo, just Bruce at the piano, on one night, and in a full band version the next, done as a fast-paced rocker or as a slow ballad as the mood struck him. There were a dozen different ways to sing his songs, and Springsteen felt no need to confine himself to the version that was recorded. And this applied not only to whole songs but to details within numbers, as well (although once a song's *lyrics* were recorded they rarely differed onstage.) But rhythm, tempo, instrumentation and phrasing all shifted nightly—that was a major element of the "surprise" that Bell talks about.

But Springsteen's biggest concert risk was playing unrecorded material; most recording artists had long since ceased performing anything but recorded material for only that material could have a calculated effect. Springsteen used new songs, to let him see whether they fit into the performance and to determine audience reaction: In fact, songs like "Thundercrack" that never made it into any of the albums were audience favorites in Philadelphia. And one could hear Springsteen shifting the good ideas and images from one song to the next: The lines "French cream won't soften those boots, baby/ French kisses will not break your heart" originally appeared in a song called "Contessa," but were later incorporated in slightly altered form into "She's The One" from *Born to Run*. The original live performances of "She's The One," in turn, contributed the phrases "hated the truth that ran us down" and "hated you when you went away" to "Backstreets". "Thunder Road" itself had two different verses that changed the narrative line drastically, although certainly the emotional thrust of the song never varied.

Springsteen's show was so far away from the standard rock presentation that it's difficult to compare the two. The live shows of recording artists feature their own material, done in versions as close as possible to the album they're trying to sell; the artists perform songs associated with other performers exceedingly sparingly, for fear of being thought uncreative; new songs aren't performed because they haven't been established as product yet. In contrast to the others, with their

standardized forty-five-minute sets, Springsteen's concerts were epic, not just in length, but in their scope of material. Yet throughout, they kept the audience on the edge of its seats, with the feeling that anything might happen next.

Oddly, these innovations made Springsteen seem even more the repository of rock and roll tradition: His energy and creativity linked the comparatively primitive experiments of Presley, Little Richard and Chuck Berry to the relative sophistication of the Beatles, Bob Dylan and the Rolling Stones. Yet this is precisely what made his performances so utterly up-to-date, for Springsteen grafted the enthusiasm and recklessness of the Fifties rockers onto the self-aware innovations of the Sixties.

In addition, Bruce seemed always on the verge of unlocking the last secret cupboard of rock and roll, so that the music would finally stand naked, its essence revealed. Rock history is made up of moments—hit singles that have no follow-up, careers that end in airplane crashes just as they are about to blossom. Because there is not yet an orthodox and complete version of that history, one can never be sure that something hasn't been overlooked. Suppose *the* great rock single had flickered over the airwaves just once, on the night you had passed out in the backseat? Probably not, but still ... For Bruce, rock and roll has always had this sense of possibility. He brought it back to a great many of his listeners as well.

Ultimately, it was his showmanship—the physical aspect of his presentation—that nailed the point home. Bruce uses his body to dramatize not just the content of his songs, but every moment of his stage life. Faris Bouhafa, who then ran Max's Kansas City, remembers that "Bruce has always done the street rap on stage, and he always had an incredible sense of drama. The first shows were very spontaneous. After a while, every movement looked spontaneous, but he'd been doing it so long, it had to be calculated. He opened the shows acoustically then, and the band was different, but he always captured the audience."

This ability to make the rehearsed appear spontaneous and the spontaneous seem well-crafted is in its way as great a gift as Springsteen's musical instinct. As a result, Springsteen's stories were rarely the random, shaggy dog variety like the one about Ducky Slattery. More often, they are like the introductions to "The E Street Shuffle" and "It's My Life" recounted above. All of them have a point to make about the music—or, rather, the music has a point to make about the stories. "The E Street Shuffle" narrative plays across the notion that blacks are dangerous and innately hip, two ideas central to the broad appeal of Clarence Clemons—a man who probably does know who put the bomp, although he isn't telling.

Eventually, in the introduction to an old Manfred Mann hit, "Pretty Flamingo," Bruce found a way to deal with the one subject that, up to that point, his writing had sometimes shied away from: sex.

"I lived on this street," the story sometimes began. "It was South Street. Highway Nine passed right by my house. But it was real close to town and every day about five o'clock, there was this one girl, she used to work downtown, I guess, and she used to walk past my house, every day. And we'd sit out on the porch and we'd find out what time it is—it's four-thirty, man. And at quarter to five we'd hustle out there and we'd sit down. And I'd say, 'Today, you're gonna go up, Steven, and say, "Hi, my name is Steve. What's your name?" '

'Umm humm.'

"See, we'd plan all this stuff out, how we were gonna do this. 'Cause she was one of those girls that you sit there like a fool and you're afraid to go up and say hello to, you know. And we'd try to get everybody, everybody on the street, to go up and try to find out what her *name* was. And the only cat that'd go near her was this one crazy guy. And we'd say, 'Now go on up, go on up to her. You're crazy, see, she won't...' "

The laughter drowns him out.

"No, really, if you're crazy, see, you can get away with lots of stuff. People always afraid of somebody who acts nuts. This guy was a little guy; he was littler than me. I used to hang out with him on weekends. Like, he'd go into pool halls and go up to the table where all the heaviest cats are playin'. You know they got a lot of money on the game. And he'd take the eight ball and throw it across the table, you know, knock it into all the balls. But they never used to beat him up, 'cause they thought he was nuts.

"So I was hangin' out with him, but even he wouldn't go up and say nothin' to her. So this went on for like a few ... years, I guess. And then, like I moved away. But we never found out what her name was; we used to always call her somethin', we used to have this name—should I tell 'em?

"*All the guys on my block called her Flamingo...*" By the time he finishes the verse, the audience is wild, half in love with its image of the girl, riveted to the song. The guitar line is elegant and the singing impassioned. For a few moments, you're just lost in the magic of a moment, and then Springsteen snaps you out of it. "Gonna find that girl!" he bellows and then:

"Clarence, what can I do? I think I'll hire some private detective. I don't know. I looked in the phone book. I'm gonna hire somebody famous. They found Patty Hearst; it took 'em awhile. Somebody famous—Charlie Chan—somebody with a gun. And when I get 'er, I know what I'm gonna tell her now. I know what I'm gonna tell 'er. I'm gonna tell her, I'm in a *band.*"

"E Street," "It's My Life," and "Pretty Flamingo" are narrative set pieces, but on occasion, Bruce used other songs to the same effect. "Spirit In The Night" can become a full-fledged, detailed narrative, and when Bruce enters the audience to sing the final verse, as he began to do in 1975 and continues doing even in large halls, it is a major thrill. "Kitty's Back" became a

tale of terror one night, when Bruce claimed that she had sent a blood-stained knife backstage. Then he ducked into the audience during the middle of the song, while Clarence Clemons solemnly declaimed: "Ladies and gentlemen, Bruce Springsteen will not be appearing here tonight." Then Bruce raced back to the mike, as if there was a hellhound on his trail, to hit the "Here she comes" chant and explode with "Kitty's back in town!"

At the end of "Incident On Fifty-Seventh Street," Springsteen would describe Spanish Johnny leaving Puerto Rican Jane:

"He pulled on his pants. He pulled on his shirt. He pulled on his *tube socks*. And he went out into the car.

[Bluffs turning the ignition several times; the car won't start. Finally he smiles as the engine catches. He begins to sing.] Maybe we can slip away . . . maybe we can steal away." Over and over he repeats those lines, whispering them, seducing everyone. "Just for a minute, just for a second." When the music ends, even a packed room feels drained.

It wasn't just the length of the shows, then, that made them the talk of rock. They built from quiet opening numbers ("New York City Serenade," later "Thunder Road") to the wildest rocking conclusion, "Rosalita," and then into a series of encores: "Quarter To Three," "For You," "Wear My Ring Around Your Neck," "Sandy." If it went on long enough, Bruce

would call for the Isley Brothers' "Twist And Shout" and finish standing atop the piano.

And this sense of complete exhilaration came along at the perfect moment. Since rock had begun to be taken seriously, an arrogance of musicianship had grown up among the biggest and most popular performers. Aside from a few old timers—the Who, the Stones—showmanship was disdained, particularly by the heavyweight English and Californian groups. The Grateful Dead, Yes, the Eagles, Emerson Lake and Palmer, Led Zeppelin, Crosby, Stills, Nash and Young, regardless of their musical diversity, shared a common refusal to project as entertainers.

A cult of showmanship did appear in the Seventies, partly as a reaction to the standoffish attitude of big-time rock bands. But Elton John and Alice Cooper—later, Kiss as well—put rock in the backseat, playing music that was purely exploitative and derivative. Mick Jagger, Rod Stewart and Roger Daltrey all continued to put on flamboyant shows that complemented their music but they had begun to seem like aging throwbacks. There was not a single American performer

who had been able to combine showmanship and creative music. In fact, the very best American rock bands, Creedence Clearwater Revival and the Band, were the most immobile of all. The heyday of Jimi Hendrix and Joe Cocker was barely a memory.

Springsteen, able to see himself as both a fan and a player, was as fed up as some parts of the audience were becoming. "They're just people who wanna crawl back in the womb," he said of such performers, "people who have built their own reality and are afraid of reality itself." It was part of his compact with his fans that he would never isolate himself in that way.

Springsteen felt that his relationship with his audience implied an obligation: "When you're up on that stage, you can't think about you and them. You got to look out there and see yourself as a kid and see how you're reacting to what you're doing. When you lose the kid in you, you can't deal with performing anymore. If you look at things too objectively, you lose that spirit that the audience has come looking for.

"It's just being honest with the audience and yourself," he continues. "You can't conform to the formula of always giving the audience what it wants, or

you're killing yourself and you're killing the audience. Because they don't really want it either. Just because they respond to something doesn't mean they want it. I think it has come to the point where they respond automatically to things they think they should respond to. You've got to give them more than that. Someone has to take the initiative and say, 'Let's step out of the mold. Let's try *this*.' ''

Bruce Springsteen's combination of showmanship and musicianship, his recklessness, and his dogged commitment to the pursuit of perfection, harked back to the Presley-led Fifties and to the Sixties when Jagger was really sashaying and the Beatles could spin the world with a nod of their heads. Audiences responded immediately because they had missed this combination, or else had never known it. In Springsteen, the Seventies had acquired their first *complete* star, one who did not have to compartmentalize his talents. As for the rest of them jokers, there's a line in ''Rosalita'' that says it all: ''Someday we'll look back on this and it will all seem funny.''

Now all that remained was for the rock industry to take notice.

Thundercrack

On a chilly Thursday evening in early April, 1974, Bruce Springsteen was in the midst of a three-night benefit at Charley's, a small bar near Harvard Square in Cambridge, Massachusetts. The club could not have held more than three hundred people, and it had rarely been so packed. Outside, lines stretched around the corner, despite the weather. Springsteen had been playing in Boston a good deal recently, and word-of-mouth was making him a local cult hero there, as it was all over the Eastern Seaboard.

Springsteen's choice of Charley's for his Boston engagement is indicative of his loyalties. He had originally been slated to play Joe's Place, an even smaller dive that specialized in Chicago blues, because Joe Spadafora (who owned Joe's Place) had booked Springsteen in his scuffling days and they had become friendly. Then, the weekend before, Joe's Place burned to the ground. Springsteen called Mike Appel to tell him he was going to play a benefit for Spadafora, and discovered that William Morris had booked him into the larger, more prestigious Performance Center in the heart of Harvard Square for the same nights.

This precipitated a crisis of sorts. The growth of his Boston following would clearly make the April date Springsteen's final club appearance in the area; next time, the sheer demand for tickets would make it necessary to move to a concert hall. Bruce felt he owed Spadafora his final club date.

That upset the booking agency. Once more, Springsteen was refusing to take the course most advantageous to his career (not to mention reducing their commission). For a time, both the Performance Center and Charley's were advertising the appearance. Eventually, Bruce won—he would play for Spadafora, or not at all.

By Thursday's late show, sweat was pouring off the walls at Charley's, mingling with the stench of spilled beer and stale cigarette smoke. The crowd was a socially mixed group—a rarity in Cambridge, where audiences tend to be exclusively collegiate or rough-house townie —and the blend helped make the sense of anticipation for each set as high as at a concert by the Stones or Led Zeppelin, while the listeners were as attentive as at

shows by Jackson Browne or Bonnie Raitt.

Reports from the early shows, and repeated listenings to *The Wild, The Innocent And The E Street Shuffle,* drew the attention of Jon Landau. Landau, at twenty six, was probably the most influential rock critic in the country. From his Concord home, he ran the record review section of *Rolling Stone,* the nation's most prestigious rock consumer publication. Tall and bespectacled, a former guitarist himself, Landau was one of the few critics who took the time and trouble to learn the business side of rock, which further increased his stature in the record industry. Landau had also produced records—the MC5's second album, *Back In The USA,* plus two by Livingston Taylor, the brother of James— before being forced to return to journalism because of a chronic intestinal disease. In the Boston-Cambridge area, Landau's clout was even greater, because of his regular column in *The Real Paper,* one of the city's two *Village Voice*-style weeklies. Landau knew how to wield his influence: He had been instrumental in getting the J. Geils Band signed to Atlantic Records, and his review of Maria Muldaur's ''Midnight At The Oasis'' had been a key factor in convincing Warner Bros. Records to back the song, which eventually became a major hit.

On the Sunday before Springsteen's appearance at Charley's, Landau wrote an anticipatory *Real Paper* column that called *The Wild, The Innocent And The E Street Shuffle* ''the most under-rated album so far this

Jon Landau tries on Bruce's cap backstage at Widener College, 1974.

year, an impassioned and inspired street fantasy that's as much fun as it is deep.''

Landau was ordinarily cautious in his judgements. Because of his position in Boston, and at *Rolling Stone,* such a strong statement would have had some impact on the record company in any event. But unlike other critics, who had celebrated Springsteen's successes without being able to pinpoint the fundamental flaws in his recordings, Landau also spotted the problems. Drummer Lopez, he said, was ''the album's consistent weak spot.'' In additon, he noted, ''The album is not as well-produced as it ought to have been .... The recording is still a mite thin or trebly-sounding, especially when the band moves into the breaks. With Springsteen's voice so rough in the first place, the album occasionally becomes unnecessarily shrill. But these are minor blemishes on a very major work.

''Next time around,'' he concluded prophetically, ''he ought to work a little harder on matching the production to the material, round out a few rough edges and then just throw some more hot ones on the vinyl. The subways he sings so much about keep rolling all night long; and the way this boy rocks, it's just a matter of time before he starts picking up passengers.''

Still, at this time, Landau knew virtually nothing about Springsteen. He hadn't listened to the first album, although, after receiving a phone call from Clive Davis, he made certain it was reviewed. And though he had heard from Oberman, *Rolling Stone* reviewer Ken Emerson and others about Bruce's live show, Landau had yet to see it himself.

So it must have been fate that Landau walked up to Charley's that night at just the moment Springsteen had come outside to read the copy of the *Real Paper* column posted in the window. Springsteen was wearing only a light jacket, and to warm himself he was bouncing up and down on his toes as he read. Somehow, the fans standing in line didn't recognize him, but Landau did. Walking over, Jon asked Springsteen if he liked the piece. ''It's good,'' Bruce replied. ''I've read better, you know.'' Then Landau introduced himself. Laughing, they entered the bar.

Inside, Bruce introduced Landau to Mike Appel, who immediately asked, ''So you don't like the album's production, huh?'' Landau spent the few remaining minutes before the show amplifying and explaining his remarks for Appel, and listening to Bruce and Mike's story of their problems at CBS. Bruce himself said little; he spent most of the time listening to the exchange between the other two.

Despite the rave, Landau's friends were surprised by his appearance at Charley's. He had quit going to concerts, except for performances by real favorites or old friends, yet here was the man who joshingly (but deliberately) styled himself King of Rock and Roll at a concert by a virtual unknown.

That evening's show confirmed Landau's impressions from the album, and raised his hopes. Springsteen opened with ''New York City Serenade,'' accompanied only by David Sancious, who added snatches of Mozart

to the song's lush introduction. This could have made for a confusing beginning, but instead it announced that this was one rocker who was bound by no one's preconceptions.

Visually, the band was a hodge-podge. After Bruce, dressed as usual in leather jacket, plain T-shirt, jeans and boots, the focus of attention was Clarence Clemons, whose size dwarfed both his tenor sax and the relatively diminutive Springsteen. Garry Tallent had long hair, and a beard halfway down his chest. Sancious and Boom Carter wore their hair closely cropped, and they dressed neatly, almost as if they were preppies themselves. Danny Federici's long blond locks curled down past his shoulders as he swayed at his organ. The music they made was all of a piece—hard, tight, driving. What really impressed Landau, though, was Springsteen's projection of a complete artistic persona. The singing was classically rock and roll, unabashedly passionate and powerful, and Bruce expanded upon it with a series of short introductions, witty stories that served to frame the songs. He also acted out the songs with grand gestures full of the innocence and toughness of the lyrics.

By the time the group came out for their second encore, a raucous version of Fats Domino's "Let The Four Winds Blow," the place was in pandemonium and,

surprising even himself, Landau—seated only inches from the stage—led the applause. He left raving, not only to his Boston colleagues but to his fellow editors at *Rolling Stone,* where he made certain that *The Wild, The Innocent And The E Street Shuffle* was named one of the seven best albums of 1973.

A month later, on May 9, Springsteen played Cambridge again. Once more, this ran counter to music-business orthodoxy: Playing the same towns too frequently was "saturating" the market, becoming *too* available. Still, Springsteen was making it work for him. At the Harvard Square Theatre, he was only the opening act; Bonnie Raitt, the headliner, had agreed to allow him to play his full two-hour show. It was something Raitt may have regretted: Springsteen concluded to a thunderous ovation, and a good portion of the crowd walked out after his set, despite the fact that Cambridge is Raitt's home turf.

It was the night before his twenty-seventh birthday, and Landau drove home in a daze. It was hard for him to believe that he was feeling this way, but, by early morning, he had himself so worked up that he sat down and wrote an exceptionally long and intense *Real Paper* column about the experience.

"It's four in the morning and raining," began the *Loose Ends* column that appeared in the May 22, 1974,

The E Street Band in 1973 (left to right): Garry Tallent, David Sancious, Vini Lopez, Bruce, Danny Federici, Clarence Clemons.

Real Paper. "I'm twenty-seven today, feeling old, listening to my records and remembering that things were different a decade ago." The piece went on to chronicle the richness of Landau's personal history in rock and soul music: the Righteous Brothers, the Four Tops, the Rolling Stones, each initial encounter special and emotionally devastating. Landau told, too, of his disenchantment as the fan became a musician, critic, and producer.

"But tonight," he concluded, "there is someone I can write of the way I used to write, without reservations of any kind. Last Thursday at Harvard Square Theatre, I saw my rock and roll past flash before my eyes. And I saw something else: *I saw rock and roll future and its name is Bruce Springsteen.* And on a night when I needed to feel young, he made me feel like I was hearing music for the first time."

The piece went on for another column and a half. But that one paragraph, besides containing the most frequently quoted line in the history of rock criticism, sealed Jon Landau's future and, in a way, Bruce Springsteen's. The stage was set. In a few weeks, the "rock and roll future" tag would rocket literally around the world.

9

The Future Delayed

Columbia Records seized "I saw rock and roll future and its name is Bruce Springsteen" and used it as the headline of a full-page ad featuring the last half of Landau's column. The line quickly became one of the most misquoted in rock. Landau's original is almost Dickensian, with its spoofing allusion to the spiritual resurrection of Scrooge, but the other versions made it seem as though Landau were attempting to write advertising copy. Still, if Springsteen's future at Columbia had seemed a bit hazy before, the column went a long way toward clearing it up.

It would be ingenuous to suggest that Landau had not anticipated the effect of his words. There is a certain kind of very partisan criticism that, when written by a highly regarded critic, can raise the level of rhetoric about an artist's work. (Pauline Kael's review of Robert Altman's *Nashville* is an even more celebrated example.) When such reviews appear, they force other critics into a reactive position. Since such an esteemed colleague has called the work a masterpiece, those are the grounds on which it must be judged, rather than the usual terms of good/bad/indifferent/interesting. Chances are, many lesser critics will follow the lead of the big-time pundit, but even the critic's relative equals must match the stakes laid on the table. Moreover, Landau was not writing about a single work—he was making a claim for the artist *himself*. For the rest of his career, Bruce Springsteen will be judged not on whether he is good, but on whether he is great. The question is no longer whether his style is unique and expressive, but whether it really represents the future direction of rock; not whether his songs are special, but whether they are classics. And because the record business—and in many ways, rock criticism itself—is so short-sighted, Springsteen was immediately faced with the notion that he was the first wave of a trend. Landau had wiped out the middle ground, and although he certainly didn't calculate every effect his article might have, in a general way he understood very well what the column might accomplish. What was more surprising was that so many fans and critics jumped over to his side.

In the next few months, such prestigious critics as Robert Christgau of *The Village Voice* and *Newsday*, John Rockwell of The New York *Times* and Robert Hilburn of The Los Angeles *Times* also wrote enthusiastically of Springsteen. (Hilburn, in fact, had been raving about Springsteen for quite a while.) More importantly, Landau's line struck a responsive chord with Bruce's swelling audience: He had put his finger on just what made people care so passionately about Bruce's music, and about rock in general. If some who saw only the ad were skeptical, those who saw both the ad and Springsteen felt confirmed in their judgments.

CBS reactivated Springsteen's albums, offering a discount to stores that bought them in quantity. Sales (particularly of the second album) picked up fast. By August, *The Wild, The Innocent And The E Street*

Shuffle was approaching one-hundred-thousand sold, a highly respectable figure, particularly considering the company's initial disinterest. (More than half of these initial sales were in Philadelphia, where a pair of WMMR-FM disc jockeys, David Dye and Ed Sciaky, were rabid Springsteen followers. Sciaky, in fact, sometimes taped his radio show in order to travel to distant Springsteen appearances.)

Springsteen was of two minds about Landau's quote and the resultant advertisement. He told friends that he resented the ad, because it capitalized on ''a very personal thing.'' But he also appreciated Jon's enthusiasm. ''It came at a time when a lot of people—including the record company—were wondering whether I really had it,'' he says. ''It gave me a lot of hope. Landau's quote helped me reaffirm a belief in myself. The band and I were making $50 a week. It helped me go on. I realized I was gettin' through to somebody.''

For his part, Jon Landau felt he had found something in the Harvard Square Theatre that he had always been seeking in rock and roll: ''When I had my band, my dream was to write a show that would tell the whole history of rock and roll—sort of like Eric Burdon's 'Story Of Bo Diddley.' And one night, long after Barry and the Remains [an early Boston band with which Landau was close] had broken up, I saw Barry Tashian actually do it.

''He was playing with this terrible band in some bar in Boston. They began to do Chuck Berry's 'Let It Rock', which is one of my favorites in the first place. Barry got so deep into it, he just waved off the other guys, one by one, until he was all alone, playing guitar and making up the words. He was telling this incredible story about Elvis, Berry and the rest of it. And that's what I saw in Springsteen: an ability to tell the whole damn story.''

Some saw the column as Landau's bid to become Springsteen's record producer. But, the transparent honesty of the piece aside, Landau's Chrone's Disease (an intestinal disorder aggravated by stress), made it physically impossible for him to do any producing. That was the reason he had stopped in the first place. However, the column did bring Springsteen and Landau together as friends. Shortly after the article appeared, Springsteen phoned Landau to thank him, and they became embroiled in a lengthy discussion. CBS still felt that Bruce had serious production problems that were preventing him from being successful. What, Springsteen wanted to know, did a producer do, anyway? Landau explained the range of functions a producer might perform: Some are merely engineers, simply responsible for the proper recording of ideas an artist has already worked out thoroughly. Others help arrange songs, or, for artists who do not write, assist in

choosing material. At the most extreme, the producer imposes his ideas on the recording to the point where it becomes more his record than the artist's. Springsteen was fascinated; he knew almost nothing about standard record business procedure. (As he once put it, "I never knew anyone who made a record or was involved in the record business. If they'd told me that part of the deal was mopping the floor, I suppose I'd have mopped the floor.") From there, the conversation meandered into more personal matters, winding up with both men promising to stay in touch. They did.

Meanwhile, the pressure was mounting for Bruce to make a record as good as his live show. At the Harvard Square Theatre date, he had played "Born To Run" for the first time live. Shortly afterward, he recorded a four-and-one-half-minute version of "Born To Run," clearly hit-single material but the song was too long in that rendition. Editing it proved almost impossible; Springsteen was stymied. June and July passed with no resolution.

Springsteen had recorded some other material after his second album, including "The Fever," a fine Ray Charles-style R&B number. Bruce decided that he hated it, but not before an enthusiastic Appel had run off a few copies and sent them to disc jockeys who had been supportive. When Bruce arrived in Austin, Texas, and Phoenix, Arizona, for shows that summer, he was barraged with dozens of requests for the song, which had become an underground hit. This displeased CBS, who had hit material, but no product to sell.

"Born To Run" was likewise distributed to a few disc jockeys, with even stronger results. Appel was apparently confident that Springsteen would soon

make an album—there was almost enough material for one—so he gave tapes to Sciaky, Kid Leo in Cleveland and a few others. Everybody who heard the tape wanted to buy it, but again, there was no hope of that. It became an even bigger underground hit than "The Fever," Leo playing it every Friday at 5:55 PM on WMMS-FM in Cleveland to "officially launch the weekend."

Columbia was again annoyed; Springsteen's perfectionism stood in the way of obvious sales. "Born To Run" might be too long, but then again, it might be that rare number that becomes a smash despite its length. And according to a hoary record business shibboleth, advance airplay such as this is disastrous to sales. Only certain radio stations had the tape, for one thing, which meant that their competitors would feel slighted and might refuse to play the official release. Perhaps radio stations who had the early tape wouldn't play the record as often when it came out, because their listeners were already too familiar with it. Besides, records are bought on impulse; if a kid goes into a store and asks for a song, it had better be there, because the chance he'll come back—even once—is slim. Yet CBS was stymied. Springsteen was not yet satisfied with "Born To Run," and as far as he was concerned, the song would be perfect before it was released, or it would not be released at all.

A similar perfectionism stalled the recording of the rest of the third album. If things didn't go right during the first couple of sessions in a week, the dates fell apart. And things were not going right. Bruce couldn't put his finger on it, but he felt stalemated in the studio. For one thing, 914 Studios, where the first two LPs had been made, was in Rockland County, New York, more than sixty miles from the Jersey Shore where the band members lived. By the time they arrived at the studio, everyone was already tired. Also, 914's tape equipment tended to malfunction and its piano was frequently out of tune.

So Bruce would cancel out, play whatever live dates he could get, or just stay at home, writing and arranging material that often never got performed onstage, much less on record. This was nothing new. Those who had known Bruce longest accepted it as his way. Back in the Steel Mill era, Danny Federici remembers, "Bruce was writing about a song per day. It was crazy. It got so I didn't want to go to rehearsal, because every time there'd be this mess of new songs to learn. And they were all gone so soon. Bruce just goes, 'That's yesterday,' and throws 'em away."

Springsteen's attitude in the recording studio itself was similar. Just as his arrangements were becoming increasingly complex, necessitating trying a variety of approaches to each song before laying it down, he wanted to experiment with the recording process. That was one reason for using 914 Studios, where the rates were much lower than in a Manhattan studio. Many of his most unusual effects were created by taking outrageous

chances: "Born To Run" itself features strings, more than one dozen guitar tracks, sax, drums, glockenspiel, bass, multiple keyboards and a variety of voices. Because he worked by trial and error, the young wizard proceeded even more slowly.

What sustained the band was its live shows. The band was still being booked by agent Sam McKeith, whose confidence in Springsteen's talent kept enthusiasm alive at William Morris. But McKeith was on vacation that August and so it was Barry Bell who booked Bruce as an opener at an Anne Murray show at the Schaefer Music Festival in Central Park on August 3rd. "Shep Gordon and Johnny Podell managed and booked Anne Murray. [Gordon and Podell were also involved with Alice Cooper.] And [promoter] Ron Delsener wanted to put this package together of Anne Murray, Bruce and an opening act, Brewer and Shipley," says Bell. "So I told Ron, 'That's fine with us. If that's the only date you've got, that's *fine*. We advise you that it would be a good idea if Bruce closes the show.' Ron agreed. However, Shep Gordon did not agree. Shep Gordon wanted Anne Murray to close; he said it was an important New York date for her. Johnny Podell wanted her to close. He said, 'Who's Bruce Springsteen? He has a cult following in New York. "Snowbird" is a big hit. Murray should close.'

"I said, 'Hey, I don't care. I'm just trying to do this for your sake. You're not gonna want to follow Bruce Springsteen in New York City.' But evidently they wanted to follow him in New York City. And they did.

"So Bruce goes out there. There was a buzz in the amplifier, I remember, for which Mike Appel got yelled at after the show. But Bruce goes out there and really

kicks ass. It was one of his better shows that I had seen up to that point. Now, he's on for about an hour and twenty minutes. Mike Appel is walking around with his safari hat on; he doesn't even want to talk to Gordon or Podell.

"So they come over to me, like I'm their best friend. 'C'mon, get this guy off the stage.' I said, 'Hey *no*. *You* wanted to follow him. That's just the way it is. You had the choice. We advised you that this was gonna happen. We wanted to close the show. You wouldn't let us. He's got another ten or fifteen minutes to go. He's gonna do it.'

"So then he goes into 'Rosalita' and completely killed the audience. It was about ninety-nine per cent Springsteen fans, it seemed. There were about five thousand people there and they went wild.

"Now these people are screaming, 'Get him the fuck outta there!' I said, 'No. He gets his encore. He does his one encore,' I forget what it was. The crowd went wild. Anne Murray went on, and was booed off the stage. 'We want Bruce,' the whole thing. She has never come back to New York since then."

Unfortunately, the Central Park gig was one of the last shows that David Sancious and Boom Carter played with Bruce. Sancious had been offered a recording contract with Epic, Columbia's sister label, and he decided to take it. Carter left with him, as part of a band called Tone, which has since made several electric jazz records.

Springsteen respected Sancious's ability enough to appreciate David's need to make his own sound. ("Davey could get off on playing anything," Bruce remembers. "When we first played together, in the ten-piece band, he was a real wild man. He had that rock 'n' roll thing in him—it always seemed like he might be the next Jimi Hendrix. He had the potential to be that.") But the absence of a second keyboard player and a drummer made things difficult. For someone else, it might have simplified the recording issue. The obvious move was to hire studio professionals for those instruments. But Springsteen wanted none of that. "I don't hire studio musicians. I don't want guys with big houses playing for me. I just put an ad in the paper and people come out and play. You take a kid off the street and he'll play his heart out for you. If someone's primarily interested in how much money he's going to make, I don't want him playing for me."

At a 1974 rehearsal with pianist David Sancious.

Anyway, Springsteen needed replacements who would fit into the live act permanently. And, since Sancious, Tallent, Clemons and Federici worked with Bruce to form one of rock's most distinctive sounds, it would not be easy to find substitutes.

In one way, Springsteen had very little to offer. "I ain't makin' that much money. I've got some great musicians in my band, and I'm payin' 'em terrible money," he said around this time. "I pay myself the same, but it's terrible for me, too. I mean, we're barely makin' a livin' scrapin' by." But there was no lack of candidates for the new post. Springsteen and Appel placed an ad in *The Village Voice:*

Drummer and keyboard player wanted for Bruce Springsteen and the E Street Band. Must sing.

Calls flooded Appel's office. With characteristic serendipity, after auditioning about thirty other performers, Springsteen found a pair of musicians who not only matched Carter and Sancious, but who brought whole new dimensions to the band.

The drummer, saturnine "Mighty" Max Weinberg, was another Jersey boy, who had come to New York to study with Bernard "Pretty" Purdie, the great soul drummer. Max had played in rock bands since he was thirteen, and later in pit bands with Broadway shows like *The Magic Show* and *Godspell.* But rock and roll was closest to Weinberg's heart; he played with something of the power of Keith Moon, though with a good deal more restraint. And the pit band experience made him a grand onstage foil for Bruce—Weinberg keyed the rhythm to Springsteen's physical and vocal movements, no matter how unpredictable. Max added drama to the band, and enhanced its rhythmic power. He was a real find.

Pianist Roy Bittan was, if anything, even more of a discovery; he quickly became known as technically the best player in the group. He so impressed Bruce that the diminutive, balding keyboard wiz (who looks a bit like film director Martin Scorsese) was dubbed "The Professor." He ate up all the Sancious parts and reached for more. Having grown up in Far Rockaway, near Coney Island, Bittan was the only non-New Jersey kid in the band. Roy was also the only member who had recorded with anyone but Bruce. And, in addition to an array of rock bands, he'd toured with *Jesus Christ, Superstar;* he'd served as musical director of a Broadway flop, and he'd even played with the Pittsburgh Symphony.

The addition of Weinberg and Bittan was crucial to Springsteen's sound, because they professionalized it without losing its essential spirit. Tallent was steady as a rock, while Clemons and Federici were highly stylized players—neither Clarence nor Danny could be described as master technicians, but they had heart. Max and Roy were pros with the sense not to let what was "correct" get in the way of what felt right. They let Bruce range as far as his imagination.

The band at this time also had a sort of floating sev-

At the Asbury Park Casino, in 1974.

Backstage with an ecstatic Bob Seger, a big Springsteen admirer whose "Night Moves" was inspired by "Born to Run."

enth member—the willowy blonde violinist Suki Lahav, wife of engineer Louis Lahav, who worked on the first two LP's and the early stages of *Born To Run*. Onstage, Suki's ghostly pale figure was a fine contrast to Bruce's darkness and toughness, and, musically, the addition of a violin was a luxury that quickly became a necessity in songs like "Incident On Fifty-Seventh Street," "New York City Serenade," Dylan's "I Want You" and a new song called "Jungleland."

Now all that was left was for Bittan and Weinberg to learn the material, and for Bruce to adapt it to their style. Then the record could be completed. But November, 1974—the first anniversary of the release of *The Wild, The Innocent And The E Street Shuffle*—came and went with no progress. Sales of the second album had passed one-hundred-fifty thousand, but a new record was needed to spread Bruce's name beyond the East Coast. Things still weren't right in the studio; no one seemed to understand why not.

Outwardly, Bruce was as phlegmatic as ever, al-though he, too, must have been disheartened by the lack of progress. "When it's ready, it'll be there. I can't be pressured," he said. "I decided a long time ago, I know who I am and where I come from. And I know what it is to be caught up in the pressure. You start thinking that you're something else. You start becoming a product of the entertainment business. I try to keep my perspective on the thing. It's even for the good of the record company that I do that, because I'll give 'em my best and it'll work out for the best in the end."

However, Bruce wasn't nearly so decisive in the studio, agonizing for hours and sometimes days over details some thought irrelevant. He was essentially marking time. CBS was unimpressed by his rationale—like any corporation, it cared more about his biggest selling than his best work. Yet, although he hadn't seemed very important when the year began, Columbia Records entered 1975 with Bruce Springsteen once more near the top of its priorities. All he had to do was get a record out.

10
Prisoner of Rock and Roll

"The record company was confused. The kids in the audience were going nuts, but the record wasn't selling. It got obvious that we needed a rock and roll album."—Bruce Springsteen, September, 1975

What Springsteen needed more than anything, some thought, was a relatively objective third party to assist him and Mike Appel in the studio. (Perhaps this was a function Jim Cretecos had performed on the first two records, which at least were completed in short order.) Because Springsteen thought of a "producer" as someone who would separate him from control of his own music, he was hostile to the idea. But CBS never quite gave up on it. As a record company spokesman put it early in 1975: "It's true that his recordings have been rather poor. But I have yet to meet anyone who knows more about what he's after than Springsteen does. He's really fascinated by the studio, and he has a great ear. The problem is that he's not interested in documenting what he's learned. He does not cater to marketing."

In June, 1974, Jon Landau entered the hospital for an operation that would cure his stomach trouble; he spent four weeks flat on his back in a hospital bed, and could barely get around for another month or two. When Bruce and Mike saw him at Springsteen's October 29 show at the Boston Music Hall, Landau had lost so much weight they hardly recognized him. Bruce again let Jon know how much he appreciated the *Real Paper* column, and reiterated his difficulties with CBS about record production.

They didn't see one another again until late November. By then, Landau was fully recovered from the operation and in the midst of a divorce. As a result, Jon was moving to New York, where he and Bruce spent an afternoon going through records and evaluating their production, talking generally, and ending up at the movies, where they ran into Jim Cretecos. A couple of weeks later, Bruce phoned Jon, and they met again. This time, Bruce played him a demo of "Jungleland" and asked what Landau thought of the production. Jon suggested they compare it to the second album. When they did, it was clear that little, if any, progress had been made.

For Landau, this was a time of decision. He was sufficiently recovered to think about record production again, but he was leaning toward working in a record company for a while to get some more experience. Producing Springsteen was at the back of his mind, perhaps, but Landau considered that possibility only with caution. Besides, he still had some obligations to *Rolling Stone,* which had kept him on salary during his convalesence.

There were other considerations, too. Landau's last rock band production, of the MC5, had been controversial; a later attempt at producing his friends, the J. Geils Band, had not worked out. While the more folk-oriented Livingston Taylor productions had both sold better and sounded more professional, Springsteen would mean taking a third shot at rock and roll. If the record was bad, Landau's reputation would suffer—though after the *Real Paper* column, that was true no matter who produced. As Landau moved back to the

city where he'd grown up, his mind seemed settled. He would work in the record business and he would someday produce more records, but at the moment, Bruce Springsteen was too hot to handle.

Still, Jon and Bruce formed a natural friendship. If Bruce found himself stranded in Manhattan, after the last bus back to New Jersey, he would call Landau and stay at his Eighty-Fourth Street apartment, where they would stay up all night, talking about a hundred things, but most of all about the difficulty of getting a record out. During this period, Landau heard demo versions of "Backstreets," "Born to Run" and "Jungleland." Later, Paul Nelson, writing in *The Village Voice*, caught the essence of their relationship: "If Landau was somewhat in awe of the kind of instinctual genius who could resolve esthetic problems by compounding them, Bruce had no less respect for someone who invariably got to ten by counting out nine individual numbers, one at a time. It was the ideal artistic marriage of creative madness and controlling method."

In February, Springsteen invited Landau to visit one of the sessions at 914 Studios. It was a frustrating night. Playing the same song over and over again is part of the studio process, but Bruce didn't seem to be making any progress. Drawing Jon aside, Springsteen asked him what he thought. Landau suggested that the essential problem was in the rhythm section, which fit with Springsteen's own thinking.

A month or so later, Springsteen and Appel invited Landau to stop by a late-night mixing session at the CBS Studios on Fifty-Second Street. By the time Landau arrived at two A.M. there was no hope left of accomplishing much that night. The aim had been to put together a version of "Born To Run" suitable for single release, but the chemistry just wasn't right. After the session broke up, Bruce asked Jon if he could stay at the Eighty-Fourth Street apartment. They stopped off for a bite to eat, and it was then that Bruce first suggested that he would like Landau to work on the album. Despite his qualms, Jon was interested. A meeting with Appel to work out the business details was arranged. But Jon and Mike couldn't come to terms.

A few weeks later, Bruce invited Landau to come down to New Jersey for a band rehearsal. Landau agreed, spending the night on a ratty old couch which, Springsteen told him the next day, had been rescued from a neighbor's trash. It was indicative of the group's $100-a-week living conditions.

When they arrived at the rehearsal hall, Landau was surprised to find that Springsteen expected him to participate as more than a friend. Bruce expected Jon to give suggestions, and even some orders. The song was "Thunder Road," and the problem was a sax break in the middle of the song that disrupted the flow of the tune. Jon suggested moving the solo to the end, which worked beautifully. He also tinkered a bit with the rest of the arrangement, cutting the rendition from more than seven minutes to about four. Both Bruce and the

group were impressed; the next day, at Springsteen's insistence, Landau was hired as the album's co-producer with Bruce and Mike.

Mike Appel must have been perplexed that Bruce had chosen this upstart rock critic to assist them—after all, Landau's other rock records had been flops—but he went along. Not that anyone has much choice when Springsteen sets his mind to something. Still, the album was not yet set, primarily because the songs were not yet written. Also, 914 Studios was technically not as good for the kind of record Springsteen wanted to make as some Manhattan facilities. After only one session with Landau at the Westchester studio, the project was moved to the Record Plant, near Times Square, a studio favored by hard rockers like Aerosmith and John Len-

non. They also signed on a young engineer named Jimmy Iovine, from Red Hook, Brooklyn, whose previous work had been done principally with Lennon, on the Harry Nilsson *Pussycats* album and with Lennon and Phil Spector, on John's *Rock and Roll* oldies set.

Publicly, Springsteen was still confident. "I just don't work on a schedule," he would say. "If I'm gonna do this, it's gonna be fun." But the strain did begin to show; Paul Williams recounted one instance in his 1975 *Gallery* piece on Springsteen.

"At a recent concert, he mentioned between songs that his former piano player, David Sancious, would have an album coming out soon. A voice from the audience shouted: 'What about you?' Bruce paused for just a moment. 'Me? I'm not putting out records any more. I'm just . . .' He paused again, aware that his joke could turn into a putdown. 'No, y'know, pretty soon. . . . I don't know, it sorta tells me. It's like . . .' And the band began the next song."

"The album became a monster," Springsteen remembered later. "It wanted everything. It just ate up everyone's life."

Of the songs Springsteen had written—"Born To Run," "She's The One," "Thunder Road" and "Jungleland"—none were short enough to qualify as hit singles. Both "Born To Run" and "Thunder Road" were immediately memorable, but neither was less than four minutes long. "Jungleland" was a ten minute narrative, and it was impossible to shorten it. "She's The One" could have been adapted but Bruce wasn't even sure he wanted to include the song on the album. If one of those songs had been a possible single, it could have been released immediately to slake the appetites of fans and the record machinery. But Springsteen just didn't feel that he had a single to give them.

Various attempts were made to edit "Born To Run," which had not been recorded terribly well—the tempo falls apart near the end—but which had the inexpressible quality of magic that is the hallmark of great rock. The record company had a staff engineer make a few passes at an edit; Springsteen literally laughed at the results. "Born To Run" is a pure creation of the studio, an incredible hodge-podge of effects. If any part is eliminated, the rest of the song becomes a jumble.

The addition of Landau to the production team was the first encouraging sign in weeks. Bruce would finish a few live dates booked for April, then do nothing but work on the record. Certainly, there was no reason it couldn't be finished in a month or two. The album would surely be out by July.

It was going to be an educational summer.

Landau's greatest contributions to the project were, first, a firm commitment to the concept of a hard rock LP, and second, professionalizing the recording process. The symbol of the latter was the Record Plant. There were no long delays for mechanical failure here, and Iovine, trained by Record Plant boss Roy Cicala and further educated by Lennon and Spector, knew exactly how to get the block sound—without needless instrumental separation—they needed. Iovine's engineering and the more up-to-date standards of the studio contributed to the closest approximation yet of Bruce's live sound on vinyl.

Landau also encouraged Springsteen to go for a focused rock sound, which would focus attention on just those elements the first two albums had underplayed. The original idea, spawned by the track of "Born to Run," was to do a group of guitar based songs. But for some reason, Springsteen wasn't comfortable playing guitar in the studio, or with experimenting with the instrument as he had done in Steel Mill. He found the requirement of playing the same figure identically on each take too restrictive. In the end, the mass of guitars on *Born To Run* made the album *seem* guitar dominated, although in fact the most important instrument is Roy Bittan's piano. As Bruce puts it: "We decided to make a guitar album, but then I wrote all the songs on piano."

In any event, people expected a rock album. But the decision to do one also gave the record a cohesive organizing principle. And someone had finally made decisions in an organization riddled with an inability to decide anything. "The indecision came from fear," Landau later said. "If you do one thing, that means you can't do another. Bruce wants it all; he always wants it all."

By his own admission, Springsteen was simply trapped in the forest of his own ambition. "It was the weirdest thing I have ever seen. We did attempt to work on it earlier. We did "Born To Run" a year ago. And over that period, we did attempt to start the record many times. But we'd always get bogged down. Things broke. Sessions didn't work.

"The main factor that changed things around, I guess, was Jon Landau. He was an interested party. He said, 'Listen, man you gotta make an album.' Like he said, I wasn't doing right by myself putting the album off as long as I did. He sorta impressed on me this fact. Whenever we talked, he'd have something important to tell me. It became obvious that I needed somebody with an outside perspective.

"But it wasn't like he came in and said, 'Don't do it your way; do it my way.' When Jon came in, he just said, 'Do it your way. But *do it*!' " The problem was that Bruce wasn't certain what his way was.

There was another psychological advantage to stalling. The third album was make-it-or-break-it time; the world was waiting. The longer Springsteen could delay, the longer he could put off his day of reckoning. As he said at the time, "Here comes the third album, and I guess everybody's excited about it. My time has come, but I'm not going to count on it. I don't count on nothing. I stopped doing that a long time ago. Anything that happens now is icing on the cake."

There was no problem recording basic tracks for the songs already written—"Jungleland," "She's The

One'' and "Thunder Road" were swiftly laid out. It was decided that "Born To Run" was not to be tampered with, since fiddling with the song only confused it. The remaining difficulties were twofold: finishing the writing and adding overdubs that would flesh out the songs. The vocals weren't difficult to get down—that was mostly a matter of concentration. But the other songs only trickled from Bruce's pen. And it took the band some time to learn them, which could only be done after Springsteen was sure he knew what arrangement he wanted to use, which often took days.

Prodded by Landau, Springsteen agonized over the arrangements. It was mostly a choice of what to leave out. Unlike Phil Spector, Springsteen could not use all the instruments of his dreams in his songs. Sometimes, there were minor battles, but everyone worked with the knowledge that, in Landau's words, "Bruce works instinctively. He is incredibly intense and concentrates deeply. Underneath his shyness is the strongest will I've ever encountered. If there's something he doesn't want to do, he won't." And he took his time making up his mind, too. The work was intensive, from three P.M. to six A.M., and often longer, every day. Pressure couldn't speed things up; only constant, gentle prodding spurred Springsteen on. At anything else, he balked.

Almost any other artist would have tried to rush. Bruce would not. As he brought in new songs, he would sit and rework the lyrics with assiduous attention to detail, sometimes calling on Landau's editorial experience. The wordiness of the previous record was

curbed; every image was streamlined, and as a result, each one packed more punch.

But whatever advice he may have taken from his co-producers, as Landau says, "Bruce made every important artistic decision on the LP. The biggest thing I learned from him was the ability to concentrate on the big picture. 'Hey, wait a minute,' he'd say, 'the release date is just one day. The record is forever.' "

Occasionally, they all must have felt condemned to a lifetime in the Record Plant, endlessly waiting to complete just a little bit more. Unlike most delayed sessions, the production problems with *Born To Run* weren't a matter of trying to get things musically correct or of searching for the right song. The task was lengthy and arduous because Springsteen had unleashed his drive for perfection; every note and nuance had to be perfect, exactly what he intended, with no possibilities overlooked.

Occasionally, all that kept voices down and fists unclenched were long walks around the seedy block in the middle of the night. By August, neither Bruce nor Landau nor Appel had any vestige of a tan; their skins were ivory white, like rock and roll ghosts. Outsiders didn't notice that. Around the Record Plant, the word from the start was that an extraordinary album was being created. Everybody who dropped by the studio inquired about its progress or tried (usually with no luck) to hear some of it.

Robert Duncan published Bruce's ghoulish version of the experience in *Creem* Magazine that winter:

"Let me tell ya, I had this *horrible* pressure in the studio, and for the whole last part of the record, I was livin' in this certain inn in New York over on the West Side. And the room there had this crooked mirror . . . and every night when I'd come home, that mirror was *crooked* again. Every time. That crooked mirror . . . it just couldn't stay straight.

"So I'm in there with this crooked mirror, and after about a week, the room started to look like Nagasaki . . ." He pauses suspended in a gesture that indicates the room, and begins again. "Junk all over the place. So every day I'd go in the studio and that was *that*—every day was *supposed* to be the last, it stretched out for weeks—and then I'd come home and there'd be this crooked mirror.

"One night," he says, getting serious once more, "toward the end of the record, I was sittin' there at the piano tryin' to get down the last cut, 'She's The One,' and Landau's in the booth, and we've been at it for hours and hours. I just lean my head down on the piano. It just won't come. And everybody's tryin' to tell me how to do it—they were all there to help me and they were really tryin'—and Landau's sayin' this and that and freakin' out . . . and, all of a sudden, everybody looks around and Landau has just disappeared, just walked off into the night—night, it was like *six* A.M.—couldn't take it.

"He was smart to go home and get some sleep. The whole thing was like that. And when I got home around ten in the morning, to the room with the crooked mirror, my girlfriend, she says to me—she says it every night when I come home—'Is it finished?'

"And I say, 'No.' I could've cried. I almost cried. Well, maybe I did cry a little." (Springsteen himself became so exhausted that he dozed off during the mix of "Thunder Road," with the result that the sax part which he intended to use only on the final chorus was left in the entire song.)

When the horn parts for "Tenth Avenue Freezeout" had to be added, Bruce realized that he wanted some saxes and trumpets to accompany Clarence Clemons' sax. But nobody seemed able to articulate what was needed. Bruce and Roy Bittan wrote some charts that sounded like Chicago, which was far from what they had in mind. "There was no direction. Everybody was waiting for Bruce. The date's falling apart and all these expensive guys [the Brecker Brothers] are out there," Landau remembers. "Then I notice this guy, Miami Steve, standing around."

Landau had met Van Zandt in Asbury Park the previous winter, when Steve was playing guitar in the Asbury Jukes with Southside Johnny Lyon—a group that featured precisely the Stax soul music that the "Tenth Avenue" horn part was supposed to evoke. Springsteen pointed to Van Zandt, and Steve moved to the door separating the control room from the musicians. "OK, Steve, this is the big time," said Landau.

Van Zandt looked about nervously. Like many another natural-born rock and roller, he does not cut a commanding figure—sort of a cross between the anarchic Keith Moon and the irrepressible Keith Richard. But when he entered the studio and confronted the superstar sessionmen, he became cocky. Putting his straw hat firmly on his head, he marched up to the Brecker Brothers and said to the most experienced studio horn players in Manhattan, "OK, boys, put those charts away." In the control room, eyes were popping. Everyone knew Steve, but no one knew whether he could pull this off. That is, not until he *sang* each horn player his part, with the lines, the timing and the inflection all perfect. The sessionmen obediently played their parts, and the horns were recorded. When they'd finished, Springsteen turned to Mike Appel. "OK," he said. "It's time to put the boy on the payroll. I've been meaning to tell you—he's the new guitar player." From that night, Miami Steve has been a fixture in the E Street Band.

Bruce made precisely one commercial concession. "Every letter I got about the second album—and I got a bunch—asked why the lyrics weren't printed on the sleeve. I'll be glad to give 'em that," he said.

Fittingly, the recording itself went right down to the wire. As Springsteen finished the final vocals, he, Landau and Iovine mixed them in another room, supervised band rehearsals for the forthcoming tour in a third room, and made certain that the lyrics were accurately transcribed. In fact, Bruce did a few shows during the mastering period, afterwards flying or driving back to Manhattan to work on the album. Finally, just before a gig at the Carter Baron Theatre in Washington, D.C., that would take Bruce out of town for the best part of a week, every detail was complete. Sort of.

Mixing is a major part of record-making that involves placing all the sonic elements in their proper relationship, since too much of this guitar or that backing vocal and the record doesn't sound as good. But even the best mix can be spoiled by an inferior master. Mastering involves translating the tape mix accurately to the metal parts from which the records are actually pressed. It is precision work that only a few people do well. Bruce rejected almost a dozen *Born To Run* masters. "Once, down in Virginia," he remembered, "Jimmy sent down a master and I had to go to a local hi-fi store and ask the guy to let me play it. It was defective and the guy musta thought we were nuts." Another master was so bad that Bruce flung it out of his hotel room window and into a river.

Iovine now acknowledges that Bruce was right about the first few masters, but, he claims, Springsteen was "nuts" about the last one. In Washington, where Bruce got the master, the only available record player was an $89.95 cheapie portable, and that's what he and the band heard it on. Low fidelity was the word, and Bruce decided he hated the whole damn thing. He was going to scrap half of it, he told Appel, and substitute live recordings from upcoming dates at the Bottom Line in New York.

Landau got the word in San Francisco, where he had gone on vacation. Landau is usually reserved, but this time he lost his cool. No one knows exactly what he said, but he has reported the gist of what he told Bruce on the phone that night. "Look," he told him, "*you're not supposed to like it.* You think Chuck Berry sits around listening to 'Maybellene'? And when he does hear it, don't you think that he wishes a few things could be changed? Now c'mon, it's time to put the record out." It was an argument Springsteen could understand, and he accepted it. So it was over. The "monster" was tamed at last. Springsteen could now answer the question, "Where's the album?" with, "It'll be out in two weeks."

Bruce onstage with Southside Johnny, at the Asbury Jukes' Memorial Day, 1976 celebration of the release of their first album, broadcast live in New York and Cleveland from the Stone Pony bar in Asbury.

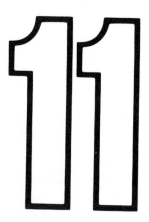

Thunder Road

Born To Run was an instant classic. Anyone who loves rock and roll must respond to its catalogue of styles, the rough and tough music, the lyrics that sum up the brightest hopes—and some of the darkest aspects—of the rock and roll dream. The album may have been a monster in the making, but it was also, as Greil Marcus has said, "like a '57 Chevy running on melted-down Crystals records. And it shuts down every claim that has been made for him."

Born To Run makes no stylistic breakthroughs, as the fundamental Elvis Presley and Beatles recordings had done. But it does represent the culmination of twenty years of rock and roll, and when it was released in October, 1975, it was the strongest possible testimony to the continued vitality of that tradition. Springsteen had synthesized his music largely from secondary sources. Rather than delving directly into blues or gospel or even early rock, he went for what he recalled of the forgotten, sometimes-junky hit singles he and his friends had loved when they were kids.

There is something about a one-shot hitmaker, like Little Eva, or an under-rated one, like Roy Orbison, that is more fascinating than the big league musicians who have been prominent for years. Springsteen's record recalled, and in a sense redeemed, this important part of rock and roll. Part of the appeal of these brief successes is what they tell the fans about themselves, people who love the music as a secret world not easily discovered, and whose place in the music is confirmed through a memory that is more than nostalgic.

Another part of the magic of one-shot hits lies in what they tell about the transience of success and fail-

ure. Rock and roll, in this sense, typifies the American dream: The star on the wane, like the one-shot hit, reminds us that everyone has a shot at the top. And *Born To Run* takes us out there among those whose shot has arched off into the distance, beyond the possibility of recovery. It is a record that explores the horizon and examines people whose horizons are closing in. "My early albums were about being some place and what it was like there," says Bruce. "*Born To Run* is about being nowhere at all."

But Nowhere is not Anywhere. *Born To Run* is as locked into an America of screen doors, fast cars and casual violence as the Beatles' "Penny Lane" is locked into the English everyday. To miss the point is to miss the reason why Bruce Springsteen is such a powerful influence on his fans. As the American Incarnate, he has become the first American hard rock hero since . . . well, I'll argue, since Elvis himself.

With one exception, the figures who unified the Sixties rock scene were British. And that exception, Bob Dylan, lacked a commitment to rock as music; his rock period was, in fact, brief—lasting only from *Bringing It All Back Home* (1965) through *Blonde On Blonde* (1966) and *The Basement Tapes* (recorded 1967, released 1977). Before and after, Dylan played music that could be identified as rock only through its association with a similar audience.

In fact, none of the American groups of the Sixties had the sort of commitment to rock and roll as a form that the Who, the Rolling Stones and (at their best) the Beatles brought to it. The Beach Boys diddled with dreary, if complex, pop forms after 1966. The folk rock bands—the Lovin' Spoonful, the Byrds, the Buffalo Springfield—were too concerned with their own cool. So were the acid rock bands of the San Francisco sound; their LSD experimentalism may have been chic, but that sort of music never had any connection with rhythm and blues or the Elvis Presley/Buddy Holly rockabilly school. It was, instead, a melange of effects pilfered from West Coast jazz, from the cool school, from campus folk music, from country and western —from almost anything but rock and soul themselves.

In any event, none of these groups had a figure of sufficient charisma to challenge British rockers like Keith Richard, Keith Moon, John Lennon or Pete Townshend. Only three American stars of the Sixties had the commitment and personal magnetism to challenge the English rock hegemony. Of them, the Berkeley-bred John Fogerty was dishonored in his own backyard, as a result of which he denied his natural instinct in vain attempts to make Creedence Clearwater Revival conform to the artificial aesthetic of the "album rock" groups across San Francisco Bay. Nevertheless, Fogerty's great series of CCR hits is the closest thing to rockabilly since the Fifties.

Sly Stone was an inspirational figure in his own right, but he rarely turned his considerable imagination to rock itself, preferring instead to demolish the conventions of soul music and afterward to march to his own distinctive beat. (In the Seventies, Sly's rhythm inventions would be codified and repackaged as disco music—a form which has more merit than the white rock audience is willing to grant it, but which has yet to move beyond Sly's original concepts.)

After Presley's decline in Hollywood, the closest we came to an American rock hero was Jimi Hendrix. Not only was Hendrix black, which presented problems of perception (rock racism did not *start* with the anti-disco movement) but he had to escape to England to live out his fantasy that a black man could do what Dylan and Presley had done. Hendrix was great at everything he set his hand to, but even today his immeasurable influence is underacknowledged. And in the Sixties the rock audience in America was already too far gone on its pretentious path to see Jimi for what he was: The One.

Everybody else was either a hippie or an entertainer. Left without an American rock star, the underclass rebels who formed rock and roll's natural constituency drifted away from music, toward motorcycles and petty crime. The few who stuck with the music listened more often to black music than to white sounds, which left an enormous vacuum. Bruce Springsteen was the first American rock performer in nearly a decade—since Jimi's death—to attempt to fill that space. And his emergence would create, in surprising ways, a flood of followers and would reopen issues many had thought closed. If the meaning of "punk" has changed drastically since 1975, *Born To Run* must be counted as the record that set the stage for its re-emergence at all. It was a record that took the music from the hands of

craftsmen and profiteers and gave it back to the sort of people who loved it because they lived it.

But *Born To Run* is much more than a resurrection of the punk esthetic. It is also the story of where such people had been since the rocker became an *artiste:* truly Nowhere. *Born To Run* is a record for everyone who grew up during the heyday of Woodstock and peace and love and couldn't embrace such foppish trappings. Everyone in America with a chip on his shoulder can accept these stories. In fact, the little stories add up to one big story, one that simply follows a boy and his girlfriend through a long, tragicomic day, a bit like *American Graffiti* without the saccharine. In some ways, though, it is more like *Mean Streets:* There is a sense that every life we encounter has a half-realized potential not just for violence but for catastrophe.

This time, Springsteen's concept was deliberate. At one point, it was jokingly suggested that the albums's opening song, "Thunder Road," might begin with a clock radio clicking on and blaring Orbison's "Only the Lonely." In fact, Bruce wrote the song in a morning mood, adding a reference to the Orbison song in the fifth line.

The record moves through a series of encounters, some of which are flashbacks—"Tenth Avenue Freeze-out," "Night," "She's The One"—but all of which are harrowingly current in their emotions. "Backstreets" ends Side One evoking the heat of the afternoon; "Born To Run" begins the second side with the early evening mist. By the time "Jungleland" is over, we have reached dawn of the next day. Much has happened, here in Nowhere, but nothing is finished. There is the feeling that these characters may be condemned to repeat such days forever.

"Thunder Road" is a statement of purpose; in its way, it encapsulates the whole story of the album. It celebrates the virtues of day-to-day living and loving, while articulating the hero's deepest fears:

So you're scared and you're thinkin'
That maybe we ain't that young anymore
Show a little faith! There's magic in the night
You ain't a beauty but hey, you're all right
And that's all right with me

This is not a story of salvation or heroism (searching for such imponderables is declared a "waste"), yet there's always a chance if the girl (here Mary, though she has other names) will only believe as deeply as the singer: "Roll down your window and let the wind blow back your hair/The night's bustin' open/These two lanes will take us anywhere."

Cars and guitars are not a panacea, of course—but they may be a way of escaping these cruel streets, of leaving the poverty and desperation of the empty lives around them. The singer has both car and guitar, and he's splitting; it's up to Mary (and to every listener) to take a chance with him, or to risk being trapped. To call this temptation isn't fair—anyone half-alive has to take the chance; this romantic ambition is too seductive to

ignore. Plus, we know these characters—from time to time, we may have been them—and we have to find out what's coming next. The past is a gang of departed lovers:

> They haunt this dusty beach road
> In the skeleton frames of burned-out Chevrolets
> They scream your name at night in the street
> Your graduation gown lies in rags at their feet
> And in the lonely cool before dawn,
> You hear their engines roaring on
> But when you get to the porch, they're gone
> On the wind—so, Mary, climb in
> It's a town fulla losers
> And I'm pullin' outta here to win!

It is such a brave boast that the fact that they're going to drive in circles doesn't really matter—at the moment. Later, it might be the only thing that counts.

"Backstreets" and "Born To Run" are alternate consequences of running away. (Perhaps "running away" is a bit extreme; as Pete Townshend has said, rock will not let you run away from your problems—but it will let you dance all over them.) Neither of the songs' locations is geographically far removed from the other, but psychically the distance is extreme. Taken separately, they are impressive. Taken together, these two numbers alone would be enough to make Springsteen's reputation as one of the great rock writers, singers and musicians.

Musically, the songs are opposites. Both are bursting with ideas, riffs, images, throwaway lines that burn into the memory. But "Born To Run" is driven, possessed (the man with the hellhound on his trail once again), propelled by the mighty roar of God-knows-how-many Fender guitars slamming into the same riff, racing to a climax on a deadend street. "Backstreets," on the other hand, owes more to the stately, fugue-like music of the electric Dylan. It is led along by organ and piano interplay, the guitar understated and used to punctuate the phrases mathematically (as Dylan described Robbie Robertson's playing). Both songs are reaching for an orchestral effect, and largely achieve it, though there's nothing remotely European about either. Springsteen sings "Born To Run" flat-out, as though his life depends on getting through a tight corner at maximum speed. He sings "Backstreets" with true grief, so mournful that he seems ready to swallow the whole world for solace.

In "Born To Run," Wendy and the singer are racing down a cruising strip right out of real life, the endless highway, lined on either side by drive-in restaurants, movie theatres and amusement arcades, that seems to run through every town with more than a handful of teenagers. Springsteen has temporarily slipped away from Jersey—there are a minimum of references to the Shore, nothing so explicit as in "Sandy," which is really the same story at a more conservative speed. This place may be Nowhere, but it is now a Universal Nowhere.

There's something furious about the song's celebration of life; there's a sense of what price a man must pay to attain such peak experiences in this world. Even here Springsteen hasn't completely escaped the world of small town New Jersey—in fact, he doesn't seem to want to. Perhaps it's symbolic that Springsteen the man still chooses to reside there. As Jay Gatsby discovered (and as Magic Rat will learn in a few moments) there is no way out:

> In the day we sweat it out on the streets of a
>   runaway American dream
> At night we ride through mansions of glory in
>   suicide machines . . .
> Baby this town rips the bones from your back
> It's a death trap, a suicide rap
> We gotta get out while we're young
> 'Cause tramps like us, baby, we were born to run

"Born To Run" is a snapshot of this endlessly circled paradise, girls primping their hair, boys trying on hard faces. It is impossible to hear it without some apprehension—what might happen is anyone's guess: The place can explode at any second. In its way, "Born To Run," as lively a piece of music as anyone has ever made, is a song about death; consider the title's allusion to the old punk tattoo, "Born To Lose." It is a message of hope, but also a message of doom. Like the ghost-lovers of "Thunder Road," the heroes of "Born To Run" are condemned to roam the strip forever, seeking what cannot be found.

In "Backstreets," Springsteen's roving punk loses everything to love. In the midst of all this fantasy, the song serves as a blast of icy reality—a paranoid's reality, maybe, but real enough. "Backstreets" is a song in which innocence is not so much lost as discarded. But it is also a song about how even rebels try to hold onto their illusions. Its opening lines are ominous:

> One soft, infested summer
> Me and Terry became friends
> Tryin' in vain to breathe the fire
> We was born in

Those words come as close to poetry as any lyrics in rock but they have much more to offer than verbal felicity. "Backstreets" establishes a situation in which a man and a woman are not just lovers, but best friends; in which the lover's loss is not mourned because she is an idealized angel, but because it robs the singer of a special companion who shares what seemingly cannot be shared. In a medium that has been noted for its unyielding dominance by males, and for its callous attitude toward women, "Backstreets" is a landmark. Terry is neither Bob Dylan's goddess/angel "Isis," nor the "Stupid Girl" of Mick Jagger's and Neil Young's fantasies. If she seems a dream, that's only because she is an equal—something people rarely are in life.

But Terry leaves the singer, and he is crushed, bellowing his hurt and disbelief throughout the song. Without her, he may have to grow up—in the worst sense of that term—exchanging his dreams and hopes for "maturity," or whatever it is that society calls a life without prospects.

It would be a mistake to consider Springsteen the protagonist of these songs. The emotions are real, but the actions aren't his. The characters are idealized and universalized, and their function is to symbolize and develop the themes of the songs. In a sense, Springsteen is all of the men and most of the women on this album; but in that same sense, so is any listener.

This is never more clear than in "Jungleland," the mini-opera that ends *Born To Run*. Springsteen is no more Magic Rat in this song than director Martin Scorsese is one of the crazy aspiring hoods in *Mean Streets*. But, like Scorsese's, Springsteen's remove is not the detachment of the exploiter; rather, he keeps his distance in order to maintain artistic perspective. And his ability to create dramatic situations and arresting characters is unparalleled in contemporary popular music. The links

between his characters are by now patent—Magic Rat *is* Spanish Johnny, and Bruce has suggested that "Jungleland" might be what happened to Johnny after he left Puerto Rican Jane's bed and went out into the night at the conclusion of "Incident On Fifty-Seventh Street."

In the two most menacing songs on the album, Springsteen's characters find their fate. The stranger of the two—and the shorter—is "Meeting Across The River," a terse, moody vignette that parallels the small-town hustlers of "Born To Run" to the big city hoods of the second album. "Meeting Across The River" is unlike anything Springsteen had previously done—brief, spare, non-rock: The arrangement features Bruce's voice set against piano and trumpets, only. Originally, the song was called "The Heist," and it depicts two small-time guys getting ready for the big score, preparing to meet the kind of guys who "don't dance." Although "Meeting" is striking on its own terms, on the album it serves primarily as an introduc-

tion to ''Jungleland'' shifting the mood of the record from exuberance to exhaustion.

''Jungleland'' opens with a sweet violin passage that gives way to a tinkling piano. As Magic Rat pulls into town and picks up his girl, there's no sense that anything but another romantic interlude is taking place. But that mood is suddenly shattered as the Rat and the girl move across a twisted landscape, pursued for unknown reasons by Maximum Lawmen. Although their crime is unstated, the fact that, this time, the escapees are pursued for real casts a new light on the hope that was held out in the early songs. In the second verse, the guitars explode and the drums crash in:

From the churches to the jails
Tonight all is silence in the world
As we take our stand
Down . . . in . . . Jungleland.
From this point, the song takes on a furious pace and

tone. Even the rock and roll bands, which represent the route out of the town full of losers, are transformed into street-fighting gangs. An Exxon sign looms on the horizon like Moby Dick. The faces have hardened: The characters have become a battalion rather than a bunch of hot-rod innocents. This moment is Springsteen's way of saying, ''You can be my partner in crime.''

The scene moves to a wild dance party, then changes again, via a smoky sax solo, to a funky bedroom where lovers wrestle but love can't win. Outside the window, Rat, the potential hero, is smashed to the pavement. Uncaring, the girl inside reaches for the light. As it goes out, Springsteen sings, ''Outside the street's on fire / In a real death waltz,'' and the music smashes in for the kill, threatening, lethal, expressive of all the destructive potential of these mean streets.

And the poets down here
Don't write nothin' at all

They just stand back and let it all be
And in the quick of the night
They reach for their moment
And try to make an honest stand
But they wind up wounded,
Not even dead
Tonight in Jungleland

Springsteen's voice takes over, soaring above strings and sax, flat-out wailing. Anyone who ever says he isn't a great vocalist—this isn't exactly singing—is going to have to reckon with this moment, when Bruce simply lets the pure anger, frustration, pain and glory of rock and roll ooze out of him.

Magic Rat isn't dead, though. There's hope. It is not clear how much more Rat (or we) could stand—but the idea remains that we have seen only the beginning of his story, even now.

Next time, the world will wait to hear it.

12

"Hype"

In Philadelphia, Washington, D.C., and Boston, *Born To Run* advance sold more than any other album in history. In D.C., orders tripled those for Elton John's current record. *Born To Run* made *Record World's* Top Ten its first week out (something only Led Zeppelin and Elton John had done previously), selling well even in a few areas where Springsteen had not often performed. The demand was so heavy, in fact, that FM airplay was saturated with Springsteen for more than two weeks, with nearly every station in the country reporting that they had programmed it.

In Philly, the Top-Forty AM station, WFIL, was so impressed by phone requests and retail sales that it began playing "Born To Run" without waiting for Columbia officially to release a single. For its part, the record company wasted no time in naming "Born To Run" as the single from the album, and, despite its four-and-one-half-minute length, the song began a steady march up the charts. The album lingered in the national Top Ten.

Springsteen began his first national tour ever, playing forty dates from coast to coast. Reaction to the shows everywhere was incredible; the Bottom Line dates had especially helped to spread the word, because CBS had specially flown in a number of non-New York press and radio figures. And where Springsteen played, he sold records. *Born To Run* quickly went gold, and it was clear that the album would reach the platinum level in a matter of a few months.

Born To Run also received an extraordinary display of press attention. *Rolling Stone* ran a feature, a long record review and a review of the live show. John Rockwell, pop critic for The New York *Times,* wrote a lengthy piece on the Bottom Line gig. Nearly every daily, college newspaper and lifestyle weekly in the country devoted some space to the Springsteen album, tour, phenomenon.

Moreover, nearly every album review was an outburst of praise, and, if anything, the live reviews were even more glowing. The demand for interview time became so great that Mike Appel granted access only to those publications that agreed to feature Springsteen on their

front cover. An exception was made for *Playboy,* but Appel counseled the sex magazine that if it was serious about changing its image, putting rock's "next big sex symbol" on the cover would be only to its advantage.

It's important to understand, though, that the press could not have made Springsteen's record a hit. In the end, reviews have little to do with record sales, except that they encourage people to check out the show. It was the live appearances, in conjunction with radio play, that accounted for the tremendous sales of *Born To Run.*

Still, the press had played a very important role for

Springsteen, nurturing his talent when everyone else seemed to have given up. And even more importantly, it provided a more sympathetic (if not necessarily more accurate) image for Bruce than the one that the record company was able to give him. After all, it is Springsteen's identity that assures him, not of hits, but of a career. "Born To Run" might have established him in any case, or it might have simply become a lost one-shot for the next inspired outsider to draw upon. But Springsteen created a remarkably strong image on stage, and it was the press—more than, and long before, radio—that exposed that image to the rock

audience. Bruce's mug, staring out from all those review illustrations, was easily the most distinctive that rock had produced in years; Springsteen with one hit became more identifiable than faceless groups like Chicago, the Doobie Brothers and the Guess Who, who had had whole strings of Top Ten songs.

The press explosion was in fact a groundswell. Nonetheless, the massive press coverage Springsteen received, and its overwhelmingly favorable tone, led those who knew little or nothing about rock (which includes most of the straight media, and even a great many on the staff of such "rock journals" as *Rolling Stone*) to conclude that it was all a gigantic hype. *Rolling Stone,* although it had an inside story, did not put Springsteen on its cover in 1975, because of its San Francisco bias and over-sensitivity to Jon Landau's involvement. Instead, it ran a twenty-five hundred word profile by John Rockwell.

Admittedly, CBS spent a great deal of money promoting *Born To Run:* Initial expenditures probably totalled around $250,00 for advertising, concert tickets and related expenses. But CBS spent more time merely trying to keep pace with the press demand for interviews and concert seats than it did trying to engineer favorable comments. Indeed, since the departure of Ron Oberman to the West Coast marketing department, the New York publicity staff—with the notable exception of Glen Brunman, who was responsible only for liaison with "out-of-town" papers—had not been exceptionally enthusiastic in its support of Springsteen. Brunman became known as the key man in getting access to Bruce, but he was hardly well enough known among most writers to have pulled off the supposed publicity coup single-handed. Glen wound up with two grocery boxes full of *Born To Run* clippings, but it was all he could do to gather them in and make certain that those who were supposed to see the show did.

As Brunman points out, the regional reviews—outside the East Coast media centers—were at least as important to Springsteen's 1975 success as were the big city reviews. In fact, the sheer quantity of clippings was a factor in *Newsweek*'s final decison to run their "Making Of A Rock Star" cover story. But Brunman acknowledges that he talked Bruce up from a "Go-see-for-yourself," angle, which is a long way from a hard sell. "Everything I said was designed to push people to see him," says Brunman. "But only because I knew he could back it up. Which he did."

The fact is that the press was pre-sold on Springsteen. Jon Landau's influence had something to do with this, as did that of several other prestigious New York writers, including John Rockwell, Paul Nelson, Robert Christgau, and myself, whom Christgau has dubbed the Rock Critic Establishment. And, as Christgau has recognized, Springsteen was made to order for that Establishment, who believed, in Christgau's words, that "the early 60's were a rich if somewhat silly period that nurtured both the soul style . . . and a wealth of not-so-ephemeral pop rock and roll, consummated in the enlightened hedonism of the Beach Boys and the great production machines of Motown and Phil Spector. This is Springsteen's era—he may talk Berry and Presley, but his encore is Gary "U.S." Bonds. I sometimes wonder whether half of Springsteen's [critical] fans aren't delighted by his music because they weren't lucky enough to have been glued to their radios in 1963; clearly, the other half are delighted to experience the most unequivocal pleasure of their adolescence all over again . . . The stock explanation of why successful media professionals identify so intensely with an idealized youth rebel like Springsteen is that they want to preserve their own youth, but this is stupid. Say rather that they want to preserve their rebellion."

The most significant articles about Springsteen were written by just such professional fans. Robert Hilburn in The Los Angeles *Times,* Peter Knobler at *Crawdaddy,* Paul Nelson in the *Voice* itself—not to mention Landau—wrote pieces closer to critical essays than objective reportage. In terms of the media brouhaha to follow, this was not terribly significant. As Christgau pointed out, "The first tenet of newsroom cynicism . . . is that hard news 'digging' is a more blessed endeavor than feature writing, of which reviewing is the lowliest example." It was not the reviews in the rock papers, or even the daily paper critiques, that landed Springsteen on the covers of *Time* and *Newsweek* simultaneously.

Rockwell's piece in the daily *Times* on the phenomenon of *Born To Run* piqued the interest of Henry Edwards, rock critic without portfolio (or interest, or much expertise) for the Sunday *Times* Arts & Leisure section. He wrote a piece called, "If There Hadn't Been A Bruce Springsteen, Then the Critics Would Have Made Him Up," which ran in the *Times* on October 5. Written with all the felicity of phrasing embodied in its title, the piece's highlight was an attack on Springsteen for repeating the phrase "hiding on the backstreets" twenty-five times (which count, incidentally, is incorrect).

Edwards' central points were that Springsteen appealed to rock critics purely out of nostalgia and that the critics alone had made him a phenomenon. Nevertheless, the two contradictory articles in The New York *Times* were just the sort of controversy needed to generate interest among the other Establishment press organs. *Newsweek* senior editor Lynn Young had been

contemplating doing a piece on the "making of a rock star," and she decided that the Springsteen "hype" was worth a cover story.

It is clear that *Newsweek* approached the story with the premise that no rock star could make it big on merit alone. Newsweeklies—not to mention the majority of American publications—are run by the sort of people who can't understand why rock continued to exist after the "scandal" of payola was exposed in 1960. The magazine had already done a brief Springsteen piece in its September 8 issue, which concluded on this ironic note:

> Still the star's manager, Mike Appel, was reluctant to spring Springsteen into the full spotlight, banning interviews 'except for a cover story.'

There was also a note of sour grapes: When *Time*'s Joan Downs had done a Springsteen piece the year before, he had talked with her.

Young determined that the magazine would do an "inside story on how the music industry creates a star." Unfortunately, she had chosen the one star that the music industry had *not* created—the one performer of the past five years who had not allowed himself to be packaged. But *Newsweek*'s real intent was to discredit Springsteen, and hopefully the rock business, for which the publication does not conceal its disdain. Maureen Orth, a glamour sniper recently returned from a European vacation, was assigned to research and write the story. Orth had occasionally written about rock performers before, although her style is about as compatible with rock as cannibalism is with missionary work.

One way or another, Jay Cocks of *Time* got wind of *Newsweek*'s plans and convinced his editors that they should not be scooped. Cocks was the magazine's film critic, but he was also a rock fan (in 1978, he would become *Time*'s rock critic). He had the support of staffers Downs, James Willwerth (who had co-authored Clive Davis's book, *Clive: Inside The Music Business)* and researcher Jean Vallely. *Time*, too, decided to do the Springsteen story as a cover: Willwerth interviewed the principals, Vallely talked with some others, and Cocks did the writing.

Columbia's public relations people could hardly believe what seemed to be their good fortune. It was all they could do to keep the two ferociously competitive reporting teams separate. (According to some versions of this story, it was also all Columbia could do to get Bruce to agree to interviews for either piece.)

Time and *Newsweek* used almost identical material to write diametric stories. Orth's thesis was that Springsteen was the creation of CBS—although she never got around to explaining just how CBS had done the job, despite the "Making Of A Rock Star" cover headline. According to *Newsweek*, Springsteen was an unlettered dummy, and Landau and Appel were shadowy, sub-criminal figures manipulating gullible press people who in turn twisted a captious public around their typing

fingers.

In *Time,* Cocks championed Springsteen, while acknowledging that the press reception might have gone a trifle overboard. His piece, which, like Orth's, appeared in the issue dated October 27, 1975, accepted the "hype" as a natural consequence of exposure to Bruce's talent. The resulting furor over the simultaneous covers was not dignified with comment by Walter Cronkite on the CBS Evening News—but Cronkite seemed to be the only pundit in the country who didn't claim that the two newsweeklies were only expanding the "hype."

In its next issue, *Newsweek* felt compelled to run an "explanation" of the double-cover barrage, assuring its readers that there had been no collusion between the two magazines. To its credit, *Time* refrained from bitching about the situation in print. But some time later, editor-in-chief Henry Gruenwald was allegedly heard at a party to say that he considered the Springsteen cover the greatest embarassment of his career.

The rest of the print media had a field day with the double-cover sweep. Snide remarks and intimations of idiocy were the rule of the day, reflecting the national news media's antagonism toward rock and roll, or toward any other expression of non-Milquetoast culture. In truth, the *Time* and *Newsweek* stories reflected the bankruptcy of American cultural coverage more than anything else. Lacking any grasp of artistic phenomena not certified by Europeans and/or academics, such publications almost invariably play follow the leader, the leaders in this case being John Rockwell of the *Times* and Jay Cocks at *Time*, who are

the only critics at any of the Establishment bastions who have any feeling for what is going on at street-level.

The pity was that somewhere in the midst of this the music was forgotten. *Born To Run* might never have been reviewed with much real insight anyway, because Landau's quote had been blown out of proportion. But with the *Time* and *Newsweek* autohype, the fact that this record was one of the finest and most startling of the decade was lost in the ensuing controversy. Springsteen's success, and the album itself, had raised many questions about the state of rock and roll, but with the exception of Christgau's *Voice* piece and one by Langdon Winner in *The Real Paper,* almost nothing written about the man or his album touched on those issues. The editors of *Time* and *Newsweek* may have felt that they were just running a story on another popular entertainer, like the bland Elton John or the elegant, empty vocalizer and political groupie Linda Ronstadt. But Bruce Springsteen was something else: An authentic American street kid, who wasn't particularly interested in the insular concerns of media management, and whose music was so unpalatable to

the pop tastes of non-rockers that it inevitably spawned a backlash.

The real irony was the amount of space the press spent pondering its own actions. The obvious parallel is the Evel Knievel story. After Knievel's abortive Snake River Canyon jump, nearly every editor that had sent along a reporter to cover the story then assigned long articles questioning whether such events were in fact newsworthy, or simply exploitative—"hype" again. It is a pathetic commentary on American journalism that such issues are not considered in advance. But, in the Springsteen case, none of the commentators (except rock critic Christgau) were able to see past their own biases clearly enough to resolve such issues.

Of course, the stories and recriminations took their toll on Springsteen himself. Three years later, during his summer 1978 tour, he could look back with some humor on those days. "It's later been written that it was all hype," he said. "And that's silly. 'Cause it wasn't. There wasn't a lotta hype. There were a lotta good stories and positive things written about the band, but there was no bullshit involved.

"Like the *Time* and *Newsweek* thing, which for a long time I had funny feelings about. Now I look back and think that it was good, because we got the record out to maybe more people than might have otherwise heard it. And that was the important thing for me . . . My pop said the best thing about it. 'Why not you on the cover of *Time*?' he says. 'Better you than another picture of the president.' ''

But in October 1975, the hype charges were not a matter for joking. It was almost as if the spectre of the promotional debacle on the first album had returned to haunt Springsteen. Certainly, everything written about him for the next few years—maybe forever—would be colored by this incident. Bruce retreated, tried to readjust to both notoriety and success. For a few weeks, it was hard for him to believe that he was the same person.

For Springsteen's early fans and most ardent supporters, it was difficult to believe that, despite the fact that he had become a star of major importance, rock had not immediately turned back toward its earlier values. But Springsteen's success was not the sort that

121

Miami Steve, with some of his many hats.

creates a watershed, as Elvis Presley and the Beatles had done; the rock audience was by now too fragmented for any single figure to unite it. Presley and the Beatles were able to catch their fans (and their detractors) unawares, but these days both the rock crowd and the media were too self-conscious for anything like that.

But *Born To Run* did set the stage for fundamental challenges to big-time rock and roll. Springsteen clearly was the key influence on struggling Midwestern rocker Bob Seger and his ''Night Moves,'' which was the best hit single since ''Born To Run.'' It is also hard to believe that an impassioned British rebel like Graham Parker would have gotten much of a hearing without *Born To Run* and its emphasis on root values. Springsteen set people thinking about fundamental issues again, so that when a new generation of punk rockers did emerge in the next two years—beginning with Patti Smith and the Ramones and winding up with a bagful of English anti-stars such as the Sex Pistols and the Clash—the established interests had to reckon with it.

As for Bruce himself, he soon recovered from the flap. By the time the tour hit L.A., he could laugh about it a little. When the cheers died down at his second show at the Roxy, he was exuberant. ''There ain't nobody here from *Billboard* tonight!'' he exulted, glad to feel at home with ordinary fans. And by the final show of the *Born To Run* tour, in Philadelphia on New Year's Eve, he seemed fully in command again, even changing the key verse of ''Rosalita'' to:

Tell your daddy I ain't no freak

'Cause I got my picture on the cover of *Time* and
    Newsweek!

In 1976, there would be rare cause for such joy.

Killers in the Sun

The *Born To Run* tour was a triumph not just for Bruce Springsteen, but also for the E Street Band, to which people were beginning to pay special attention. Playing across the country, solidly booked for two months at three-thousand-seat theaters and concert halls improved everything—the sound was fine, and Mark Brickman's lights were beginning to reach for unparalleled effects, working on tighter cues than anyone else in rock, bathing the songs in sheets of color that perfectly complemented the music. Most important, the band was growing together musically, knitting into a genuinely individual sound. Springsteen himself had that much more flexibility, able now simply to sing on some songs where previously he had also had to play guitar, able also to accentuate his moves through Max Weinberg's precision percussion, with Clemons and Van Zandt standing by to lend dramatic support. The net effect was of a group of professionals who played for much more than money.

The key factor in this transformation was Miami Steve Van Zandt, not because he led the band, but because he balanced its diverse tendencies. The professionalism would have come eventually in any case; although Weinberg and Bittan had originally signed on for salaries of only $75 weekly, their seasoning in studios and pit bands guaranteed a new technical polish. Federici, Clemons and Tallent, on the other hand, were notable for a close-knit feeling, stylized but not studied. It was these two diverse approaches that Miami Steve was able to blend. As a charter member of the Asbury Park Upstage crowd—while still in high school—he was part of the casualness and intimacy of the older members. But after his period on the road with Dion, the Dovells and other oldies acts, Van Zandt also understood the rules of the game for hired guns. Van Zandt was capable of saying that "If I had it my way, we'd do the records in mono," but he also recognized the value of professional technique.

Van Zandt's presence was also personally important for Springsteen. Federici, Clemons and Tallent had played with Bruce for years—Danny had been with him even longer than Steve—but, except for Clarence, they were as reclusive as Bruce himself. Like him, other Asbury Park players believed that, "What you dig is the respect for doing what you do, not the attention," in Bruce's words. "Attention without respect is jive. Plus, I was always the kind of guy who liked to walk around and slip back into the shadows."

But Van Zandt is as voluble as Springsteen is taciturn. Steve makes friends quickly and easily, regaling them with quick wisecracks, self-deprecating shaggy dog stories and the rocker's perspective that necessitates dancing on every grave, including (especially) your own. Steve found it simple to take people at their word, socially, and hope for the best. He did not hang back, although while Bruce could forgive almost anything in a friend—once you're in, you're in—Steve believed that friendship was proved by adhering to certain rules of behavior, and those who broke them could get themselves lost. It is no coincidence that Van Zandt's favorite is Sixties soul music, loose and convivial, while Springsteen's tastes lean toward the more insular white rock and roll of the Sixties.

But when the chips were down, there was no doubt that the two stood together. Both were driven by a sense of rock and roll as the Way Out of the Trap, into which almost everyone with whom they'd grown up had fallen. And Van Zandt was intensely loyal to Springsteen, seeing in Bruce the one-of-a-kind friend and band leader most musicians must dream about. "Bruce is the best possible boss," he has said. "He's hip enough to let everybody do other things, to express themselves in other ways. All that does is make your gig better. When you go back to playing in the band, it's like coming home to foundation and security."

As an emotional liaison between Bruce and the band, Steve's role was crucial. Although things were terrific onstage, behind the scenes, as far as the group was concerned, the joint was a mess. Springsteen cared nothing about money or business, but the band watched such things closely, and what they saw made them wary. Equipment that should have been purchased was rented. Laurel Canyon didn't always make Clarence Clemon's child support payments on time, once forcing Clarence to spend a night in jail until Appel showed up to bail him out. Steve's guitar was stolen from a rehearsal studio, forcing him to play an important Boston gig with an unfamiliar instrument; he was so depressed that Springsteen played off him for the whole show, just to try and cheer his friend up.

Mike Appel managed Bruce Springsteen, but not the E Street Band. It was a situation Appel wanted to change; he offered contracts to all the members, and Danny Federici and Clarence Clemons actually signed them. When the rest of the band convinced them that they had made a foolish move, Springsteen asked Appel to tear the documents up. To his credit, Appel did so. But the band was left with the impression that Danny and Clarence, the band's great innocents, had been tricked.

As far as Springsteen was concerned, such problems were of little consequence. But the band never hid its dislike of Appel, nor its distrust of him. Neither did the road crew, which is the backbone of any rock touring organization. When Appel showed up at the E Street Christmas party that year, the celebration was in full swing. Within minutes after his arrival, the room was empty. Bruce viewed such incidents with chagrin. He well understood that Appel was abrasive and rude; during the *Born To Run* sessions, he had asked Mike to stay away from the studio for a month because of the counter-productive tensions he created. (It was Jon Landau, ironically, who engineered Mike's return.) Yet Bruce also saw the other side of the man. "I can't help it—I like the guy," he told friends.

It was hard not to think that "like" was stretching it. Like Pike Bishop in Sam Peckinpah's *The Wild Bunch*, Bruce believes that "When you side with a man, you stay with him. And if you don't do that, you're like some animal." Mike Appel was the first music business person to believe in Springsteen's talent—or anyway, the first one who had any notion of what to do with his skill—which made up for a great deal. Certainly, any intelligent person must have seen that Appel created a problem for every one that he solved. Yet Springsteen's loyalty ran deep; it was predicated on trust. Once you're in, you're in.

Born To Run was a success on every level—with the fans, with the press, in radio airplay, and among other musicians. "After the Bottom Line," remembers Barry Bell, "Bruce went from a Northeastern cult figure to a nationwide figure—by playing ten shows. When I look back on that I can't understand how he did it. He would start at eight o'clock at night and end up at five o'clock in the morning. It was like he was punching a clock, he did so many hours—he'd be like a wet rag when it was all over."

From Bell's point of view, the hype issue was also an advantage. "Look," he says, "if a guy writes in Beaumont, Ill., that Bruce Springsteen is all hype and he can't be as good as he is, then the people are gonna come out and judge for themselves. I can remember that in Seattle or Portland, one of those, he sold out a two-thousand-seater going in for the first time, just based on all the word going around. And after the show, the kids were screaming for more while they were tearing the set down. I always knew that once Bruce got his audience there, they'd never lose him."

Yet even Bell is willing to admit that "it was not a tremendously successful tour as far as business. We did what we wanted to do as far as exposure in certain markets. It was a process of building him up."

In Los Angeles, the show drew all sorts of scenemakers: Carole King, Jackie De Shannon, Joni Mitchell, Nils Lofgren, Jackson Browne, Tom Waits and actors Robert De Niro and Jack Nicholson. The latter, in fact, another boy from the Jersey Coast, led the cheering from atop his table. That same week, Spring-steen encountered his penultimate idol, Phil Spector. (He would never meet the ultimate idol, Elvis, although as we shall see, he tried.) Spector was typically cool. "I'm hip to what the kid is doing. I'm mildly interested," said the man to whom *Born To Run* paid homage.

Spector invited Bruce to visit a session he was producing for Dion. It was a more relaxed encounter, although describing anything about Spector as relaxed risks overstatement. Iovine, who had worked with Spector on Lennon's records, was in town, and Miami Steve knew Dion well from the oldies circuit. The session lasted five hours, peppered with wisecracks from the maestro: "OK, fellas. Bruce Spring*street* is here. He's on the cover of *Time* and he's born to run. So let's show him how to make a record." But during the evening, the former boy genius drew the new one aside. "If I were with you, your records would be clearer and better," said the man who had produced *Let It Be,* the muddiest of all Beatles LPs, "and you'd sell five times as many." Bruce reportedly thought the offer attractive, though others were amused: Spector, too, has a reputation for taking a long time to finish records.

Spector was reserved about Springsteen, but only up to a point. When one of the producer's friends suggested that the meeting was like introducing the great Sixties pitcher Sandy Koufax to the new Dodger star Don Sutton, Spector corrected him, "No, it's more

the first time, it's a thrill," said Bruce. "But after that, it's just a stupid car." The items that got messed up, on the other hand, were just those that mattered most —ones involving Bruce's ideas of integrity and independence.

In Washington, D.C., for instance, Appel and William Morris booked Springsteen into a ten-thousand-seat hall. No one had bothered to consult Bruce, and cancellations, explanations, apologies, rebookings and recriminations ensued—with predictable fallout in the press.

Then disaster set in on a brief European jaunt in November featuring two dates in London and one-nighters in Amsterdam and Stockholm. The mini-tour was booked by William Morris, but its promotion was largely in the hands of CBS International, which didn't quite get the picture. London was chosen for the most excessive hype, partly because of a series of enthusiastic articles written over the past year by Mick Watts and other American correspondents for *Melody Maker*, the largest of the English pop weeklies. The city was plastered with stickers bearing the "I saw rock and roll future and its name is Bruce Springsteen" quote; Hammersmith Odeon, the theatre where the shows were held, was festooned with "At Last London Is Ready For

like Babe Ruth and Hank Aaron." Home-run kings.

Musically, the show was constantly growing. Playing in Detroit for the first time, the group worked up a medley of Mitch Ryder hits, a perfect opportunity for Weinberg—by now, known as Mighty Max—to shine. The so-called "Detroit Medley," worked so well that it remained as a semi-permanent encore. In Oakland, Calif., the crowd was so wild by the end of the set that the balcony nearly collapsed.

Somehow, though, Springsteen was uneasy with success. It was true that he'd come all the way, from virtual rags to potential riches. Life should have been a dream come true. But it wasn't. Things just weren't going right, though knowing Bruce's penchant for perfectionism this might only have meant that they were not going perfectly. And the things that went right were a bit too smooth to be trusted. "You ride in a limousine

Bruce Springsteen!'' posters and flyers (which, before the show, Bruce went around tearing off the walls and ripping to shreds). The tour went by in a daze—the All-American eating habits of the band were confounded by European cuisine, the brevity of the tour left little time to recover from jet lag, and on the final night, in his London hotel, Clarence Clemons was denied permission to bring his—black—friends up to his room. (Clarence, never at a loss, changed into his most outrageous clothing and returning to the lobby glowered at the white businessmen, arriving with their hookers, challenging all who entered as to whether all of *their* party was registered.)

When the band returned to the States, Springsteen withdrew, hardly seeing anyone—not the band, not Appel, not Landau. He spent most of his time with his girlfriend, an odd circumstance for a man who had often stated, ''I can't have any women. I gotta give everything to my music. And I'm not ready to write married music yet.'' At that moment, Springsteen felt the need for a truly private life. He had felt the pressure earlier, asking Jack Nicholson in Los Angeles how the movie star had dealt with fame. But Nicholson's reply—that he had waited a long, long time for stardom and so welcomed it with little reservation—was no help.

Springsteen's sombre mood affected the show. Bruce changed from the black leather jacket, jeans and T-shirts he had previously worn to a pair of baggy pants and a long-billed cap that made him look more like one of Ducky Slattery's gas-pump jockeys than the hard-edged punk of the past. The effect was comic but soothing, removing some of the bluster from the shows.

Mike Appel was determined that the fourth Bruce Springsteen album should be recorded live, preferably as a double or triple set. To this end, he recorded a few shows at the end of the year, using the Record Plant's mobile unit with Jimmy Iovine at the controls. (The live broadcasts from the Bottom Line in New York and the Roxy in Los Angeles were among those put on tape, as were the shows at C.W. Post College on Long Island, at the Tower Theatre in Philadelphia, and at Ryerson Theatre in Toronto.) Bruce, however, was convinced that the live album—for which fans had been clamoring since *The Wild, The Innocent And The E Street Shuffle*—was still premature. His attitude wasn't simply obstinate, although one factor was certainly his suspicion that making records by just going out and playing was too easy. He felt that the band's onstage excitement wasn't ready to be captured yet; when he heard the shows on tape, Bruce thought that the playing lacked consistency, particularly in terms of tempo. Also, he was confident that his fourth album should be a set of completely new songs.

Once more, Springsteen was flying in the face of the rock formula. It is instructive to compare his career with that of Peter Frampton, the young English rocker whose solo career (after leaving Humble Pie) had started about the same time as Springsteen's. Frampton released three studio albums with increasing success (although none went gold) and followed with a live set that was the blockbuster of 1976. *Frampton Comes Alive* sold between five and ten million copies (depending on whose figures one believes), an absolutely unheard-of sum that kicked off the record industry's multi-platinum binge of the late Seventies.

Frampton was managed by Dee Anthony and booked by Frank Barsalona's Premier Talent Agency, and he had followed their rock packaging ideas to the letter, touring as many as two hundred nights a year, more for exposure than for profit, interspersed with albums released at clockwork intervals. As it happened, *Comes Alive* wasn't a bad record, given Frampton's limited talents. But the volume of sales it generated disoriented Frampton, and his follow-up record, *I'm In You*, was burdened with syrupy pop arrangements that overlooked his most distinctive ability (as a guitarist) in favor of teen-idol singing. Although the singer has remained a formidable concert attraction, *I'm In You* sold less than half as many copies as the live set, and Frampton did not release another LP until May, 1979. His career seems as damaged as that of any teen idol before him, particularly given his catastrophic ''acting'' debut with the Bee Gees in Robert Stigwood's horrid

film version of *Sgt. Pepper's Lonely Hearts Club Band.*

Peter Frampton is perhaps the classic example of the limitations of rock's starmaking machinery. While he is insured of wealth for the rest of his life, it is doubtful whether Frampton will ever be a creative—or even commercial—force in rock music again. His credibility is simply exhausted, for although he had worked hard to gain it, his gigantic victory was premature. The formula could turn drastically counter-productive. Only his instinctive mistrust of the easy ways had saved Springsteen.

In the end, the only product of Appel's 1975 live recordings was a tape of the holiday chestnut "Santa Claus Is Coming To Town," based on Phil Spector's arrangement for the Crystals, which was sent out to a few radio stations during the Christmas season. The song has been given considerable airplay every year since then, some of it on major Top-Forty stations such as WRKO-AM in Boston, but "Santa Claus" has never been officially released to the public.

Perhaps the final measure of the toll that fame was taking on Springsteen was that the ordinarily prolific songwriter performed no new material on the *Born To Run* tour. His set instead consisted of the complete new album, minus only "Meeting Across The River," plus highlights from the first two LP's and a few older songs; toward the end of the year, "Santa Claus" and "It's My Life," complete with the story about his adolesence, were added. But Bruce wrote no new songs, or at least none that he was ready to sing in public.

The *Born To Run* tour ended with four sold-out shows at the three-thousand-seat Tower Theatre in Philadelphia. Ticket requests numbered ninety-thousand; it was clear that Springsteen would either have to play someplace larger next time or simply work full-time in Philly, if he wanted to reach all of his fans in the area.

When the last set was over, long after midnight on New Year's Eve, no one was terribly surprised when Bruce expressed more relief than exhilaration. Now he could relax, grow into his new situation.

His life would never be so simple again.

East of Eden

Lee said uneasily, "I told you when you asked me that it was all in yourself. I told you you could control it if you wanted to .... He couldn't help it, Cal. That's his nature. It was the only way he knew. He didn't have a choice. But you have. Don't you hear me? You have a choice."

John Steinbeck, *East of Eden*

The early days of 1976 were filled with promise. Jon Landau flew to Los Angeles to begin recording a new Jackson Browne album, *The Pretender*. Pianist Roy Bittan was in Philadelphia, working with David Bowie on *Station To Station*, an album for which Bowie recorded a few Springsteen songs (they never appeared). Miami Steve got back to Asbury Park and decided that his old band—retitled Southside Johnny and the Asbury Jukes—was ready to record. With Van Zandt producing and Jimmy Iovine engineering, the Jukes cut a debut album called *I Don't Want To Go Home* for the CBS Epic label; its highlights were the title track, written by Steve, and Bruce's "The Fever." Pure mainline soul in the old style, with guest appearances by Lee ("Ya Ya") Dorsey and ex-Ronette Ronnie Spector, *I Don't Want To Go Home* sold acceptably for a debut record—more than one hundred thousand—and the Jukes began a national tour.

Toward the end of 1975, Barry Bell and Mike Appel began discussions about creating a new booking agency with Bell running the business and Appel providing the office space—a small enterprise with only Bruce and a couple of others as clients. Barry was eager to leave William Morris, and there was a feeling among the E Streeters that the big agency wasn't right for them.

If anyone was unhappy, it was Mike Appel. He had, perhaps, supposed that success would make Bruce see the light about large concert halls and other methods of maximizing profits. But it soon became clear that, left to himself, Springsteen had no intention of making such concessions to stardom. Appel had big ideas—he wanted to set up a cross-country tour in a circus tent, establish the booking agency, release a live album as quickly as possible to cash in on the *Born To Run*

success. At the very least, Appel felt, he needed additional protection as Springsteen's manager. While Bruce was still contracted to Laurel Canyon for two more albums (and to CBS for seven), the management contract had only one year to run.

The *Born to Run* tour hadn't been profitable; it had not lost much money, but playing in small theatres, traveling with more than twenty people in the crew, keeping the band on salary year-round, the debts had increased. The obvious solution was to play some big gigs and cash in—Larry Magid offered Bruce $500,000 for playing the one-hundred-thousand-seat JFK Stadium in Philadelphia on the Bicentennial Independence Day. But Springsteen rejected anything so gross and obvious—which had Appel worried.

Mike arranged for CBS to advance Laurel Canyon $500,000 against future Springsteen earnings. The company was happy to do so, the success of *Born to Run* (nine-hundred-thousand units sold and counting) having proved that if Springsteen were not *the* future, at least he had one.

What happened next is unclear. According to Appel's attorney, Leonard Marks (as reported in *Rolling Stone*), "When things started looking up, Appel offered to renegotiate the contracts with Springsteen —including giving him half the stock of all Laurel Canyon companies. Springsteen said he didn't want to deal with a written contract but wanted to work it out with Appel on a day-to-day basis with a verbal agreement based on trust. Appel had an audit done by Mason and Company and then sent Springsteen a letter saying that 'the books are open' and inviting another outside audit by Springsteen."

That is certainly accurate. But it seems that Appel's tactics while renegotiating proved rather heavy handed. He told Springsteen of the half-million-dollar CBS advance, saying that half of it could be his—if Bruce agreed to re-sign with Laurel Canyon Management for an extended period of time. Otherwise, Appel assured him, he would have to hold Springsteen to the letter of their agreement—and Appel made it clear, for the first time, how disadvantageous were the contracts Springsteen had originally signed. For instance, Bruce was entitled to a three and one-half per cent (about ten cents) record royalty (based on wholesale price), while Laurel Canyon's agreement with CBS gave Appel's company at least forty cents per LP. The manager/producer kept the difference. Similarly, the management contract did not specify the standard fifteen-twenty per cent commission to Laurel Canyon/Appel; in high-earnings situations, it provided for a *fifty per cent* commission. Springsteen did not control his own song publishing rights either; Laurel Canyon held them, and could grant or refuse right to use the material to whomever it chose, whatever Springsteen's wishes.

Springsteen found this shocking, since he had never bothered to read the contracts when he signed them. "It was my own fault," he would later say. "I knew what a lawyer was." If he didn't, he was soon to find out. Still, in January and February 1976, Springsteen wasn't taking Appel's assertions too seriously; mostly, they were about money, and cash had never been at the top of Bruce's priorities. He retained his confidence that matters could be worked out.

On the other hand, he had to be sure. Heading to California to visit his parents, Springsteen stopped off to visit Landau in Los Angeles. He had the contracts with him, and asked Jon to read them. Asked what he thought, Landau replied that Springsteen clearly needed the advice of an attorney. A few weeks later, when both men were back in New York, they visited the offices of Mike Mayer, of Mayer Nussbaum and Katz, a respected music business law firm that represented—in addition to Landau himself—Atlantic Records, Phil Walden of Capricorn Records, the Otis Redding estate and Rod Stewart.

Mayer immediately saw the unfairness of the contracts, and the conflicts inherent in Appel representing Bruce's over-all career on one hand and acting as his record production company on the other. Bruce retained Mayer, Nussbaum and Katz to represent him in renegotiating the deals. He also had accountant Stephen Tenenbaum audit his dealings with Appel, from early 1972 through Feburary 1976. Springsteen regarded these maneuvers as overdue but simply matters of form—he was preparing to work out some sort of agreement with Appel, not for a lawsuit. Despite Appel's admissions about the nature of the contracts, there were still bonds between them.

Meanwhile, Appel continued to plan a booking agency with Barry Bell. "We were all ready for the next tour," Bell recalls. "But a lotta things started to happen. It began slowly. I was at Bruce's house and Mike still hadn't made an arrangement with me yet, so he

Miami Steve after first hearing the single he produced for Ronnie Spector (sitting on case in rear), backstage in Cleveland, 1976. "Say Goodbye to Hollywood," released on Epic, also featured the E Street Band although not that funny looking fellow to the right of Ronnie.

and Cheauteau Merrill, his assistant, had started to book a small tour out of Mike's office. Bruce says to me, 'What do you think about Cheauteau booking my tour? I said, 'You're asking the wrong guy, 'cause I want to do it.'

"Mike was telling me that what was holding the deal up was that Bruce wasn't sure he wanted to do it. I said, 'You can't just hire anybody to do the booking. We're [agents are] professionals. You want the best record company, don't you? You want the best of everything else. You should also have the best agent.'

"Bruce said, 'Oh I didn't realize that was it; I thought it was something else.' By the time the conversation ended, what it came down to was him saying, 'Look, Mike Appel's my manager, he's my producer; I don't want him to be my agent, too.' So I assured him that every dollar he paid to an agent was going to go to me. All Mike was doing was giving me an office and a telephone; if I signed any other acts, I'd give him some of what I got in order to pay the expenses. But Bruce was my thing. I told him, 'You will not sign any contract with Mike Appel as far as an agency.' He said, 'Fine, let's do it.' And we went off to the Carole King show at the Palladium, had a great time; Bruce jammed with Carole. It was a great night in my life."

The next day, Bell called Appel to tell him that everything was resolved. Appel said they should have lunch, and over the meal explained that Bruce's deal was running out and that Springsteen was reluctant to sign a new one. "I don't know why I should have to give him a new deal," Appel said. "I've already got him on paper." Bell could see that the sides were being drawn, which worried him, especially because the rumors that he was starting his own agency were starting to filter through the music business grapevine. If the gossip ever got back to the bosses at the Agency, Bell knew, he wouldn't be able to quit—he would be summarily dismissed for his contemplation of competition.

"Now what happens is they really start to spread apart," Bell says. "Then they get back together. And Bruce calls me up one night, I think it was in February. He says, 'O.K., quit your job tomorrow and let's roll.' That was exactly what I wanted to hear. I said, 'Wow, you worked it out.' Bruce says, 'Yeah, Mike agreed to my deal.'

"The next day, I go into the office with a big grin on my face, ready to say, 'See ya.' But a sixth sense says I should call Mike Appel and congratulate him on making the deal. And Mike didn't pick up my call. Now I'm starting to sweat bullets.

"Around five-thirty I finally reached him—I'd spent the day in the office without quitting. I said, 'Mike what's going on?' And in the most hyper, nervous voice I have ever heard on the telephone, he says, 'The whole thing's off, the deal's off, I changed my mind, I talked to my father and it was not a good deal; I can't do it!' "

So they went to the mats.

Appel started out with crucial leverage: the half-million dollars from CBS. Except for whatever publishing royalties trickled in, that was all the income he had, since he represented no other clients. But it was

Clarence, Bruce and Miami Steve at the Bottom Line in August, 1975.

enough.

Springsteen, on the other hand, was jammed for cash. He needed money to mount the tour that Appel had booked for him, and since CBS had courteously paid off Mike, the record company wasn't the place to get it. William Morris agreed to lend him the money, provided he would re-sign with the agency for another year. This Bruce agreed to do, and Bell and Sam McKeith, his co-agents at the time, arranged for the cash to be advanced.

The tour was meant to cover secondary markets, but it had not been properly structured. William Morris did its best to straighten the gigs out, but Springsteen was still left with a long jaunt through the South, the area of the country where he had the least appeal. The tour featured, for instance, five dates in Tennessee, where Bruce had never before appeared, and where he eventually would not draw terribly well.

Still, Bruce kept his spirits up. After his show in Memphis on April 29, mid-way through the tour, he and Miami Steve, along with publicist Glen Brunman, got into a taxi to look for a bite to eat. "We told the cab driver, take us someplace quiet," Bruce later recalled. "He said, 'Are you guys celebrities?' 'Yeah.' So he said he'd take us out along the highway, by Elvis' house. I said, 'You *gotta* take me to Elvis' house.' He says, 'Okay. Do you mind if I call the dispatcher and tell him where we're going?' So he calls the guy, says, 'We got some celebrities here. We got . . .' and he shoves the mike in my face, so I say, 'Bruce Springsteen.' They didn't know who I was, but they were *pretendin'* to, y'know? He told the dispatcher we were going to Elvis' house; he was crackin' up because the dispatcher thought we were gonna drink coffee with Elvis.

"When we got to the gate, I looked through. It was three A.M., but all the lights in the house were on. I said, 'I gotta go see if he's home.' So I climbed over and started up the driveway; it's a long walk 'cause the house is set way back. And I was almost at the front door, just getting ready to knock, when I see this guy looking at me from the trees. He says, 'Hey, come here a minute.' I said, 'Is Elvis here?' He said, no, he was in Lake Tahoe or something.

"Well, now I'm pullin' out all the cheap shots I can think—you know, I was on *Time*, I play guitar, Elvis is my hero, all the things I never say to anybody. Because I figure I've gotta get a message through. But he just said, 'Yeah, sure. Why don't you let me walk you down to the gate. You gotta get out of here.' He thought I was just another crazy fan—which I was."

Springsteen was also writing songs again—notably a new rocker, "Frankie"—in preparation for his fourth album, which he and Jon Landau hoped to begin recording as soon as this tour was completed, in late May or early June—provided that Jon could finish the Jackson Browne LP, which was also dragging on.

Mike Appel, meanwhile, was making plans of his own. He requested in several places that concert receipts be held in escrow so that he could be sure of obtaining his management commissions; in the few places where the courts granted his plea, however, Appel found that the money had been paid in advance—there was no box office money to attach. This was crucial for the coming struggle, for Springsteen's only hope of generating income was through live performances.

On May 14th, Laurel Canyon sent Springsteen a check for $67,368.78 "which represent[ed] the balance of all monies due [him] from the inception of our relationship through March 31, 1976." But it is interesting to note that this was the first accounting Springsteen had ever received from Laurel Canyon, although the relationship began in March, 1972, more than four years previously; under the contract, he was owed accountings every three months. The audit also disclosed some interesting facts: although Laurel Canyon's Springsteen-derived income over the four year period totalled between one and two million dollars, Springsteen's total income for the period was less than $100,000 through March 31, 1976. Only one tax payment, from 1975, was recorded. Although some of this was explained by the fact that most money was turned over to the organization for salaries and expenses, accountant Tenenbaum's report said that Appel's records showed that Laurel Canyon had "conducted Springsteen's business in a slipshod, wasteful and neglectful manner; that he failed to maintain adequate and complete books and records relating to Springsteen's activities; and that enormous amounts of expenses and disbursements are charged to Springsteen which are in large measure unsubstantiated . . . My audit reveals a classic case of the unconscionable exploitation of an unsophisticated and unrepresented performer by his manager for the manager's primary economic benefit."

Certainly, Mike Appel hadn't gotten rich off Bruce Springsteen, but just as certainly, Springsteen was entitled to more than ten per cent of money he had generated. Bruce clearly had a right to expect that his management organization would make sure that his taxes were paid; not to do so is the kind of fiscal irresponsibility that has so often resulted in catastrophe for entertainment and sports figures (the fighter Joe Louis is only the most obvious example).

Meanwhile, it was clear that the Jackson Browne sessions were not going to be completed by June 1. That was no real problem, since, despite Springsteen's many ideas for new songs he'd actually completed only a few. But on July 2, Appel sent Springsteen a letter stating in no uncertain terms that he would not allow Jon Landau to produce the fourth LP, citing paragraph 2(b) of their contract as his authority. Three weeks later, on July 27, 1976, Springsteen filed suit in Federal Court in Manhattan, alleging fraud (in that Appel had represented himself as a knowledgeable and experienced businessman), undue influence and breach of trust. In the legal parlance, Appel had allegedly breached his "fiduciary"

trust as manager—which trust obliged him to act first and honorably in the best interests of his client.

According to Springsteen's lawsuit, the Laurel Canyon management was a massive conflict of interest, in that Appel's managerial responsibility was suspended in any of Springsteen's dealings with Laurel Canyon companies and in that it attempted to deny Springsteen the right to any advisers other than Mike Appel. In dealing with any of Appel's companies, in other words, Springsteen stood naked.

The CBS contract boondoggle, in which the number of albums Laurel Canyon contracted for was twice as many as Bruce was obliged to give the production company, was also revealed in the suit. Springsteen said that far from being advised of his rights in these matters, he had seen only one page of the CBS agreement—the one which he signed, appropriately enough, on the hood of a car in a dark New Jersey parking lot.

Two days later, on July 29th, Appel filed suit in New York State Supreme Court, asking the court to bar Bruce and Landau from entering a recording studio together. In an affidavit, Appel claimed that only Laurel Canyon had the right to appoint a producer, and, he said, he preferred the "winning combination" of himself and Springsteen, conveniently ignoring the fact that only one track, "Born to Run," had been produced by that pair without assistance of a third party.

Springsteen's legal team had apparently underestimated the persuasiveness of Appel's argument. Judge Arnold Fein, who has a reputation for taking the phrase "unique and exclusive services" in a contract very seriously, saw only that Appel's rights were being infringed, and granted the injunction, effectively barring Bruce and Jon Landau from recording together. Appel had gained the upper hand, dividing the opposition.

First, Springsteen was not barred from recording; he was only barred from recording with *Jon Landau*. (Appel would later attempt to appoint as producer Brooks Arthur, owner of 914 Studios and producer of previous hits by Janis Ian—a move that Bruce would greet derisively in a later affidavit.)

Second, CBS was involved in the lawsuit, against its corporate instinct. Indeed, company attorney Walter Dean would later characterize CBS as "an innocent third

party," which was hardly the case. The truth was that CBS could hardly afford to have the case go to trial, for if it were determined that Appel's contracts were invalid, the CBS deal might be voided along with them. And, as a free agent, Springsteen would clearly be worth millions. The company was pushed into a position of false neutrality very much to Appel's advantage. Third, Landau was effectively isolated by Appel's strategy and by Fein's strongly worded opinion, which said that Jon had "no rights under these agreements." Since part of Appel's suit alleged that Landau had engaged in a "campaign to sabotage the relations between Springsteen and [him]self," Landau—the figure with whom Bruce was most comfortable—had to tread carefully.

In Fein's formal opinion he stated: "The real issue appears to be whether Landau may act as the producer over the plaintiff's objection." But this was true only so long as Springsteen was viewed as merely a "capital generator"—as he would later refer to himself—the maker of a unique product. If Bruce were seen as an artist who was "fighting for [his] life," as he told the judge, the picture would change. In human terms, it

was unconscionable to deny Springsteen the opportunity to work with Landau, who was a key influence on his work and who was the only person he knew who could help him shape it properly. Obviously, this argument is extra-legal; but any assessment of the lawsuit without considering these factors is blinder than justice was ever meant to be.

There was a further factor in Springsteen's motivation in the case, and it is a key to why he was passive for so long (his early depositions were so disastrous that *Appel* released excerpts from them to the press). Bruce was willing to forgive whatever financial wrong-doing might have been done him, but the moment he realized that he did not own his own songs, he realized that he was fighting for his creative life. The notion that

he could be denied rights to *his* work incensed Bruce, and he fought like a tiger to regain control of his career, which he saw slipping away. Everything he had done in contravention of record business formula had been designed to insure the integrity of his songs and his music, and when he saw that the litigation threatened that integrity, he hit back, hard. Although they have never been publicly released, Springsteen's later depositions are said to be as dramatic and pointed as any of his shows. Asked why he refused to go on tour in the circus tent, for instance, Bruce reportedly snapped, "Why don't you try practicing law in a tent for a while? Then I'll think about playing my guitar in one."

Still, Appel was winning the case. He had enough money to wait the situation out, for months or even,

"You talkin' to me? Well, who ya talkin' to then? Ain't nobody else here."

years if necessary. And even if the issues at hand in the State court were settled, the validity of the contracts could not be tested there—those were tied up in Federal court, where it could take more than a year just to get on the docket.

In October, Springsteen switched attorneys, retaining Michael Tannen, who represented the business interests of Paul Simon, John Lennon and the Rolling Stones, among others, and Peter Parcher, a skilled litigation specialist. The new lawyers turned the case around. "The day we hired Michael Tannen was the day we won the case," Bruce says now. Together with Parcher, Springsteen began to roll the record back and rumors of a settlement began to circulate.

In August, to earn some money, Bruce had played a week-long engagement in Red Bank, New Jersey, where he debuted a remarkable new song, "The Promise," as well as a new lighting design by Brickman that was nothing short of breath-taking. And in late September, he headed out on a longer tour, opening in Phoenix, Arizona, where he performed in the Coliseum, a seven-thousand five-hundred-seat leviathan of the variety he had always refused to play; the show was instrumental

in convincing Springsteen that he could go over well in a larger arena. Two dates in Santa Monica made him a major draw in Los Angeles.

But the most important gigs once again came at the end of the tour. In Philadelphia, Bruce was finally convinced to appear in a full-size sports arena, the Spectrum, where the Philadelphia Flyers and 76ers played. "I brought it up to him," says Bell. "I said, Bruce you're gonna have to—for the time in your own mind—*think* about playing the big halls in Philadelphia, the way I put it to him was: 'You're worried about the kids, how they're gonna be affected. But if you were a kid, would you rather sit in the last row of the Spectrum or ask your friend how good he was at the Tower? If I was a kid, I'd rather get in there somehow.'"

Springsteen reached a rapprochement with the huge hall by screening off the back of the stage with a large curtain, and, for insurance, hiring Clare Brothers, the best rock concert sound specialists, to run the P.A. As a triple precaution, he played a four-hour sound check that nearly exhausted the band before there was a patron in the house. But as Bell said, "What he found

all those who have lost.' But the real twist comes during the song's bridge, when he sings the words 'thunder road' and immediately transforms his car into his rock and roll dreams. In 'The Promise,' Springsteen mythologizes himself and compares his struggle to be true to his art to the desperate struggle of the young racer. He sings in 'Thunder Road' that 'tonight's the night all the promises will be broken,' but the dream etched in ''The Promise'' and put into perspective by Springsteen's own experience is clearly a romantic notion that is not easily shattered. Despite a landscape filled with losers—the singer eventually sells his car when he needs money—it's clear that in Springsteen's heart the Challenger's potential will never die.''

When Milward refers to ''Springsteen's own experience,'' he is clearly alluding to the lawsuit, but Milward is canny enough to know that the lawsuit itself is only a symbol of what Bruce had undergone since *Born to Run* catapaulted him to fame. (''I don't write songs about lawsuits,'' Bruce says tersely, and the fact that people might think that ''The Promise'' was concerned only with legalities kept it off his fourth album.) ''The Promise'' is rather about the price everyone pays for success—and the dangers of settling for anything less.

out was that you could get good sound in a big hall—if you were willing to make the effort.''

Even without a new record, the '76 tour was a triumph. ''He was becoming a major star even with a legal problem,'' says Bell. And as if to confirm it, the tour ended with six sold-out shows at the Palladium Theatre, a two-thousand eight-hundred-seat opera house in Manhattan.

Springsteen's prolific writing was also beginning to slip back into gear. The sets opened with ''Rendezvous,'' a new rocker that evoked the spirit of the Manfred Mann and Searchers' Sixties hits that Springsteen loved to sing. And the shows featured two new ballads, ''Something in the Night,'' a tale of pure desolation, and ''The Promise'' a ballad written very much in the romantic spirit epitomized by the Beach Boys' ''Don't Worry Baby.''

''The Promise'' represented a crucial turning point in Bruce's career, and a new kind of maturity in his lyrical perspective. When he heard the song for the first time at a concert in South Bend, Indiana, *The Chicago Reader* critic John Milward was moved to write: ''The song's metaphor is 'The Challenger,' a race car that the singer has built by hand 'to carry the broken dreams of

The weirdest anomaly of success is that it requires compromises never demanded of failure. It isn't just the minor infringements on one's humanity—such as signing autographs at meals, which reduces the very act of eating to a promotional event. It's also the expectation, and the possibility, that one will do *anything* to keep from losing what's been gained. And this, of course, is antithetical to the rock and roll dream, which says that the only way to possess anything of true importance is to risk losing all. "We were gonna take it all . . . and throw it all away," says Springsteen at the end of "The Promise"—which puts a fine point on rock's version of succeeding.

Rock and roll is about promises—covenants between the audience and the star (and vice versa, since the latter is only an idealized version of the former). This is a central tenet of *Mystery Train*, Greil Marcus' great critical study of the music, which in fact may have served as

the inspiration for "The Promise." For Marcus, such promises are an inherent part of America itself; they are at least as old as the Mayflower Compact, and their centrality to the Declaration of Independence and the Constitution is likewise clear. For Bruce, these promises are simply the foundation of the world he knows, and of the life for which he thirsts; compromise such things and you *are* "like an animal." And so when he sings, "When the promise is broken/You go right on living/But it takes something from down in your soul/Like when the truth is spoken/And it don't make no difference/And something in your heart grows cold," he has assessed the price of every syllable.

These are emotions far outside the scope of the punks on *Born to Run*—the feeling is definitely adult, although it certainly does not lack anything in the way of rock spirit. (Which recalls Christgau's line that grown-up rockers wish not to preserve their youth but only

their rebellion.) Still, Springsteen was not quite ready to adopt this dour perspective completely. On the 1976 tour, introducing "Growin' Up," Bruce made light of the pressure: "I went in and did my audition with this song. I remember I went up to the record building, you know ... All these lawyers. Everybody had one but me." Then he broke up in a fit of giggles, as Roy Bittan began to play the tinkling introduction. "Awwww, *so what!*" Springsteen shouted as he began to sing the verses.

But in the middle of the song, the music fell away again, and Bruce stepped forward to tell a fairy tale about fame. Only a pinging electronic sound came from the guitar, while the piano and Danny Federici's glockenspiel tinkle away in the background.

"There we was," Bruce said, punctuating the drama with giggles. "It was me, and the Big Man, and Miami. We were drivin' down this old dark road. All of a sudden (bang!) we got a flat. We were in a '63 Impala, absolutely nothing done to it; a real piece o' shit my old man gave me. It was the only thing we had to get around with, screamin' down the back road, doin' alla fifty-five. Boom! Flat tire.

"We pull over. Course, we ain't got no spare; this is a budget operation. So we try to convince Miami to run with it, while we got to a gas station. But we didn't know where we was. It was dark; it was so dark; there was no moon out. Everybody was hidin' that night. There was trees, a deep dark forest, we couldn't see nothin'.

"And we looked, looked way off, and deep in the forest we saw this light just sorta shinin' there. And we said, somebody must live there, we oughta go find out, get some help, y'know. So we stomped back through the woods—got mud all over us, right? And there in the middle of the forest was this old gypsy lady, sittin' around this fire.

"So we walked up to her and she looked at us and said, 'Got a flat tire, huh?' We felt a little nervous there, you know, how'd she know we have a flat tire, you know? It's like, we were waaay out there on the road. We said, 'Yeah.' She said, 'What'd they send you suckers back here for? Whaddya want? You just tell the gypsy lady—she'll straighten you out right now.'

" 'First of all,' she sez, 'you look like a buncha bums.' This is about six years ago, right? 'First, you cats are not presentable, you know, to do *anything*.' So like, she waved this stick and ... BAM! Miami's standin' there in a red suit in the middle of the woods. She waved it again ... BOOM! The Big Man's standin' there in a white suit, right in the middle of the woods. She waved it again, in front of me. Boom! Nothin' happened.

"She says, 'Don't work alla time. Some people gotta work at bein' bums. Others are born that way.' So I say, 'Hey, gypsy lady, you owe me one—you owe me one now.' She said, 'All right, all right. What can I do for ya?' So I thought real hard, said, 'Well ...' Thought

about a new transmission. Naw, ain't nothin' gonna help that old car— the thing's a goner. I thought about uh ...

"She said, 'Well you gotta just tell me, man. You wanna be a king? You wanna be an emperor? You wanna own your own Pizza Hut? Just tell me, tell the gypsy lady, I'm right here.'

"I said, 'Well. Well, to be honest with ya ... not to pull any punches ... what I really had in mind ... I think I could dig ... I think I wanna be, I think I wanna be, I think I wanna be ... A Rock and Roll Star!' Max's drums explode like tympani, as the band rushes back into the song, playing hard and fast. As Bruce hits the last lines, he looks out at the crowd. For a moment, only a moment, he seems caught up, really that cosmic kid he sang about. "Then I hit 'em with my guitar," he exults. And everything is just right.

The legal maneuvering proceeded throughout the winter months. Bruce's depositions had helped, although at one point, he became so bellicose, peppering his aggressive statements with obscenities, that Appel's lawyers had him hauled before Judge Arnold Fein, who asked him to cool it. But even that worked out for the best—Bruce was able to clarify his personal position to Judge Fein (whose children were reportedly mighty impressed at whose trial he was overseeing), and the incident conveyed to Appel's attorneys the impression that a man so carried away was not about to give in easily. For his part, Mike Appel was anything but a quitter; he, too, was willing to carry the fight to the bitter end.

But the true test of the case was in the legal trenchwork of motions and countermotions. In his initial decision, Fein hadn't flatly refused to hear a case that would resolve the "underlying issue"—which was nothing less than the validity of the contracts, the grounds on which Springsteen initiated his complaint. Therefore, on November 18, Peter Parcher submitted an affidavit asking that the federal and state cases be joined. Parcher's affidavit was bolstered by supporting ones from Jim Cretecos, Appel's former partner, and Robert Spitz, a former Appel employee, both of whom claimed that Appel had reneged on verbal promises made to Springsteen at the beginning of their relationship. "On numerous occasions," said Spitz, "Appel stated to me that he hoped Springsteen never became aware of those agreements. Appel also expressed to me on a number of occasions that he was aware that a court of law would find them unconscionable." Why, then, had Appel instigated an action that would encourage Bruce to investigate the nature of his contracts?

On December 8, Springsteen submitted a key document, in which he requested permission to record an album with Landau producing and CBS advancing the recording costs, the tapes from which would be kept by the court until the suit was resolved. Fein denied this request. But in making his plea, Springsteen also out-

Jackson Browne filters a few tips from Bruce, backstage at the Main Point, in Philadelphia, 1974.
Below: Bagman Ron Delsener tries to rescue the receipts from Springsteen's show at Avery Fisher Hall
Who paid for the stage that collapsed?

lined the potential damage that the delay was causing.

In closing, Springsteen pointed out that, while Appel's interest in the case was strictly financial, his own was his career, which until then had held the promise of making a significant contribution to "an entire generation of music. No amount of money could compensate me if I were to lose this opportunity," Springsteen concluded. This was lawyer talk—but highly persuasive and emotional stuff of its kind. This affidavit was the turning point in making Fein see that the issue of record production was unavoidably linked to the other issues in the case.

On March 22nd, 1977, Springsteen won a motion to submit an amended answer to Appel's state court complaint. That opened the door for resolution of almost

all the federal issues in one trial. It also allowed him to assert as a defense Appel's breach of fiduciary obligation—his conflicts of interest, failure to provide proper accountings and the like. Once more, Springsteen was on the offensive. Bruce was clearly in a position to win if the case came to trial, and since Judge Fein had issued a "speedy trial" order, it was possible to push ahead toward one. It was at this point that a settlement became a genuine possibility, since Appel could not afford a trial he was likely to lose anyway, and since Springsteen, Landau and CBS, for their part, were more interested in getting back to making records.

A final settlement was reached at three A.M. on May 28th, 1977. The details of the settlement were never officially released—the final document in the case file simple says that an amicable settlement had been reached and that the parties could not sue one another again. Both sides claimed victory, of course. Appel said he won because he had gotten some cash (reportedly as much as $1 million), retained some share of the profits from the first three albums and obtained a five-year production deal for Laurel Canyon with CBS. On the other hand, Appel had lost a better artist than he was likely to find again, and the production deal may not have been terribly significant: Appel's first post-Springsteen production client, Arlyn Gale (who looks, but doesn't sound like Bruce) was released through ABC not CBS.

Springsteen felt he had won because he'd gained his freedom. He controlled his music again, in terms of both production and publishing, and he was able to work with Jon Landau. In fact, the pair entered Atlantic Studios in New York with the E Street Band only five days after the settlement, on June 1. The recording contract with Columbia had been renegotiated, with the rate adjusted upward, if not to superstar terms, at least to ones reasonable for a successful performer.

Confident that Landau and Springsteen could record together quickly, CBS laid plans for a Christmas-time release of Springsteen's fourth LP.

Bruce gets a few pointers from his mother, onstage at Madison Square Garden, 1978. (She wanted another encore.)

15
Raising Cain

Entering the studio that June, Springsteen felt prepared. The sessions were being held in Atlantic Records' new studio in Manhattan, running from early evening to about midnight, after which the Rolling Stones came to mix *Love You Live*. (Typically, it was not Bruce but Miami Steve who struck up a quick friendship with Keith Richards; Keith admired Steve's soul-style songwriting, which he'd heard on the Jukes albums.)

The first evening was spent laying down demos of about twenty songs Bruce had written and more-or-less completed during the lawsuit. They included ''Rendezvous,'' ''The Promise,'' ''Frankie'' and ''Something in the Night'' from the live shows of the previous year, and several of the numbers that eventually wound up on *Darkness On The Edge Of Town*, including the title song, plus some still-unreleased numbers such as the screaming rocker, ''Don't Look Back.''

At first things seemed to be progressing smoothly. Landau had gained a great deal of confidence while working with Los Angeles studio professionals on the Jackson Browne album; Jimmy Iovine had engineered and produced a number of acts since *Born To Run*. The E Street Band surprised both of them, however. ''The amazing thing about those guys is how much energy they have,'' Landau told a friend. ''With sessionmen, you almost always get the song done in two or three takes, and after that, it's time to move on to something different; the enthusiasm doesn't last. But with this band, the more takes you do, the better they get.'' Of course, the difference is that the E Street Band knows it is not playing a song for the final time when it is recorded; they still have a few hundred performances onstage left in them.

After a few weeks at Atlantic, though, it became obvious that something was wrong. No one was happy with the drum sound, and the studio wasn't terribly liveable, the latter an important consideration since the recording would inevitably drag on for several months. So the sessions were moved back to the Record Plant, where *Born To Run* was made.

Had Bruce been satisfied with the material he'd written before the recording started, the sessions might have progressed as quickly as planned. But Bruce wanted more than a set of listenable, craftsmanlike songs. One of his goals was to create a set of songs consciously linked, perhaps as a continuation of the story begun with *Born To Run*. Aided by Landau's insight, he now saw threads of continuity in all of his work. ''There's a progression that goes through the records,'' Springsteen later told Walter Dawson of The Memphis *Commercial-Appeal*. ''The first album, that was sort of out of my control, except for the material . . . And on *The Wild, The Innocent And The E Street Shuffle*, I brought my band in and that had real warm songs and a lot of characters, and there was more of an in-society type feeling. Even if it was low-rent, it was more involvement in groups of people.

"And then on *Born To Run*, it sort of gets cut down to usually a guy and a girl. And for me, *Born To Run* maintains some warmth, but there was a certain element, a certain fear that starts to come in. I don't know why.

"And on this record, I think it's less romantic—it's got more, a little more, isolation. It's sort of like I said, 'Well, listen, I'm twenty-eight years old and the people in the album are around my age.' I perceive 'em to be that old. And they don't know what to do. . . There's less of a sense of a free ride than there is on *Born To Run*. There's more of a sense of: If you wanna ride, you're gonna pay. And you'd better keep riding."

It was more difficult for Springsteen to conceptualize his fourth album because it really should have been his fifth; the lawsuit had kept him from making an album the year before, and in the early days of recording *Darkness On The Edge Of Town*, he must have been torn between making the record he would have made in the previous year, and the one he was ready to do now. Eventually, he opted to discard the past and push forward. It was the only sane choice, but it slowed things considerably.

Among the influences that helped shape Springsteen's ideas during this time were the kind of movies Landau had loved as a film critic—the Italian Westerns of Sergio Leone (*For A Fistful Of Dollars, Once Upon a Time In The West*), and John Ford classics like *The Searchers*. *East of Eden*, with James Dean, inspired "Adam Raised a Cain." Bruce came to understand himself and his songs better by viewing the work of film-makers who could depict almost identical situations a dozen times and yet make each of them different. In any event, Ford and Leone are examples Bruce uses in explaining what he was trying to do.

Intrigued by the hero others saw in him, Bruce also took a closer look at his own role models. In July, soon after moving to the Record Plant, Bruce and the band found some advance copies of *Elvis: What Happened?*, Steve Dunleavy's muck-raking book about Presley, in a bookshop around the corner. The influence of the King clicked back in, and for several weeks, the studio took on the look of an Elvis shrine. Bruce identified with Elvis's career, the way it seemed totally in the artist's control at one moment, and careening without guidance the next. "He was an artist, and he wanted to be an artist," Bruce said soon after Presley died, which also summed up Bruce's feelings about himself. But he wasn't about to allow himself to be caught up in anyone's expectations, as Elvis had done. "Mike Appel thought he would be Colonel Parker and I'd be Elvis," Springsteen would later say. "Only he wasn't the Colonel, and I wasn't Elvis."

The lessons of hype, the law suit, the failures of his idol, Elvis, and the natural maturity that came with simply being twenty-eight worked a transformation in Springsteen and his music. If he had sometimes been

passive about the way others were exploiting his work, he now saw such apathy as the gravest irresponsibility. In "The Promised Land," Springsteen says proudly: "*Mister I ain't a boy/ No I'm a man.*" So *Darkness on the Edge of Town* evolved into a statement of what had transpired, not in the court-room or the recording studio, but in Springsteen's life, and the lives of the sort of people he knew.

Eventually, the album sifted down into thirteen songs—the ten that finally appeared on *Darkness on the Edge of Town* plus "The Promise," "Independence Day," and "Don't Look Back." "The trouble was that any way you sequenced them, it came out being a different record," Landau remembered. Not willing to overlook any possibility, Bruce shuffled the songs back and forth for weeks. Eventually, ''The Promise'' was eliminated, because too many reviewers of the live show had construed it as being ''about'' the lawsuit and because Springsteen saw it as too desolate for the message he meant to convey. ''Don't Look Back'' was not selected because it made Side Two sound too harsh. ''Independence Day,'' Bruce thought, really belonged in the next chapter of the story—what happened to the character after he had survived being cut off from society.

Springsteen threw away songs around which others would build albums. He gave ''Fire'' (a rockabilly-style ballad written in the manner of Doc Pomus and Mort Shuman's early Sixties Elvis hits such as ''Marie's Her Name,'' ''Little Sister,'' and ''Viva Las Vegas!'') to Robert Gordon, a young New York rockabilly singer he'd met through Garry Tallent. After Jimmy Iovine took a demo for ''Because the Night'' to the studio next door, where he was producing a record for Patti

Smith, Springsteen let Smith finish the lyric (although he does not sing her version onstage) and the song gave Smith a Top Twenty hit in 1978.

Mixing began in early 1978, with Landau, Springsteen, Iovine and Miami Steve acting as collective midwife. But Landau soon placed a call to Charles Plotkin, who was head of Elektra/Asylum's A&R and with whom Jon had become friendly while Landau was making *The Pretender* in Los Angeles. They respected one another's ideas about production, and Landau asked Plotkin to visit the mix sessions when Chuck came to New York to produce a Harry Chapin record soon afterward. Plotkin immediately grasped the mixture of West Coast clarity and hard rock density Springsteen was after, and his intense, joking personality proved a catalyst that pushed Bruce toward making decisions about the mix much more quickly than he would have otherwise.

The mixing was complete by early spring; this time,

Above and right, Bruce with New Wave rockabilly singer Robert Gordon, for whom he wrote ''Fire,'' and rockabilly legend, Link Wray.

the mastering was done in Los Angeles, and it went much more smoothly. But there were other difficulties. Perhaps the most important was the album cover art. Bruce had selected a photograph by a virtually unknown New Jersey photographer, Frank Stefanko, that he felt reflected the starkness and energy of the record. But Stefanko's picture was not easy to reproduce; Columbia's art director John Berg insisted he could do the job, but after several cover proofs were submitted to Berg, it became clear to Springsteen that there had been a breakdown in communication. He turned to his product manager, Dick Wingate, for help.

About the same age as Bruce, Wingate had been a Springsteen fan since his days as an FM disc jockey in Rhode Island in the early Seventies. He was one of the few people at the record company Bruce felt he could trust. As product manager, Wingate was principally responsible for marketing the album, but in this situation he became involved as *de facto* art director as well.

Dick was in Minneapolis, where he had just seen the

Bruce onstage with Patti Smith, another Jersey kid, during her show at the Bottom Line.

opening date of an Elvis Costello tour, when he received a one-thirty A.M. call from Landau and Springsteen, who were then in Los Angeles. Jon and Bruce had just received another cover proof, with no improvement. In fact, it was so far from what they wanted that Springsteen was on the verge of chucking the whole concept and going to a simpler black-and-white picture. The record release date of mid-May was imperative, because the national tour was set to start then. The album delays had forced the tour to be pushed back several times already, and it was felt that postponing it further would cost too much credibility with local promoters. The next morning, Wingate was on a plane to Los Angeles.

"I went out for the specific purpose of taking Bruce to the engraver, L.A. Color Service, which he had heard was the best. So we went to the place, and spent a couple of hours with these people, going through every fine step of how a cover is made. We wound up going out there two or three times. So the cover proof was finally done to his satisfaction.

"Then the whole scene shifts to New York. And we're down to a matter of days, if we want to get this album out in advance of the tour. After a lot of hassles and delays, it is finally decided that the cover will be printed at Ivy Hill lithographers, because they can do it fastest and supposedly they'll do it as well as anybody. So the day comes for Bruce to do something that no artist in the history of Columbia Records has ever done. Usually, you know, artists approve proofs of their cover, and then it's printed. But Bruce actually wants to go to the place where they print the cover.

"So the morning arrives, around the middle of May—the tour starts the 23rd of May. We jump into a limo with the Ivy Hill people and head out to their printing plant. Bruce is jovial. And we get to Ivy Hill, spend quite a bit of time on the printing press, adjusting the color to exactly how Bruce wants it. It's the kind of art that's very sensitive to the slightest color changes. And you could see it right on the printing

Above: Miami Steve in a serious moment.

Reviewing the printing process for the Darkness cover. Dick Wingate is at Bruce's right.

press. But Bruce finally says, 'This is it. Let's go.' We're all very happy; for me a six week trauma had come to an end.

"On the way back in the car, Bruce is telling stories, really opening up in front of a lot of people. I drop him off at the hotel. An hour later, I'm on the phone with Landau, saying, 'Jon, Bruce just approved the cover. We're smokin'; it looks like the album's gonna be out before the tour.' And Jon says, 'Dick, I couldn't tell you this this morning, but I got some bad news for ya. Bruce and I are going back to L.A. at six o'clock tonight to remix ''The Promised Land.'' ' They were going to put Springsteen's guitar solo back in. I couldn't believe it.

"But what really killed me was Bruce. He'd been obsessed with making this record for eleven months; it must have been gnawing at him all day, that he had to go back to L.A. and remix this song. Because that meant that the whole side would have to be remastered, and there was no way the album would be out for the first week of the tour. But he never rushed us; we took our time to get back to New York; he was in a joking mood, as if he had no place to go. And he had to make

that plane. It was unbelievable."

Wingate had one final problem to solve. "Bruce didn't want any advertising for the album at first. What he conceived of, if he could have had it his way, was that the record would just appear one day in the stores, as if by magic."

Springsteen had had enough of hype; as far as he was concerned, *Darkness on the Edge of Town* would rise and fall completely on its own merits. But he was ultimately concerned with something else. The key factor was that each of his other records had slipped from his personal control. *Darkness* would be different; this album would be his responsibility, start to finish. That way, if anything went wrong, he'd know why. Wingate finally prevailed about advertising by using exactly that rationale; there would be local advertising for the record in every town where Springsteen appeared in concert. If Bruce didn't design an ad, he was going to be seeing a lot of ads he hated. It was the kind of thinking Springsteen appreciated.

"He wanted to come back in total control of his career," Wingate says. "He became totally involved in his career as it related to the record company."

16
Darkness

Darkness on the Edge of Town is one of the most complex rock records ever made, a cycle of songs that continually turns back upon itself in obsessive pursuit of the Big Secrets. But the record's themes might be understood even without lyrics. The sound is pounding and relentless; the guitar screams, the organ howls, the vocals roar, the drums crash. The music lets up only grudgingly, and then not for long. All of it points toward something—not the darkness *per se*, but what might be concealed there, discoverable only by those with immense vision and will.

You could say that this music is about survival, but not the easy kind that pop musicians and consciousness cults like to talk about. This sort of survival isn't about being "happy" or having "fun," or resolving the dilemmas of being sensually satiated. In this context, that kind of "survival"—in which demons are neither conquered nor conquering, but simply ignored—is far more meaningless than death itself could ever be. For Springsteen, survival is a matter of facing up to everything that saps psychic and physical strength; it means taking life on its own terms, and never giving in. "When Bruce Springsteen sings on his new album, that's not about 'fun,'" said Pete Townshend, "That's fucking *triumph*, man."

The price for living to the hilt is paid in the currency of eternal vigilance. It costs something to beat back the slack moments and refuse the petty terrors of the everyday. "I wanna go out tonight," Springsteen sings on "Badlands," the song that opens the record. "I want to find out what I got."

At the end of the album, a man stands alone at the bottom of a hill. He has never had much in a material way; by now, he has been stripped of what little he once possessed. Around him is little but wreckage and the temptation to join it. And in the face of this, this man raises his chin and sings:

Tonight I'll be on that hill, cause I can't stop

Left: Charles Plotkin, Bruce, Jon Landau, Jimmy Iovine—the Darkness production team, minus Miami Steve.
Above: Jon Landau moments after seeing Bruce without shades for the first time!

I'll be on that hill with everything I got
I'll be there on time and I'll pay the cost
Of wanting things that can only be found
In the darkness on the edge of town

The singing now becomes a wordless moan, symbolic not of pain but of effort, the labor of a man trying to raise himself above his circumstances. There is not a hint of defeat. And the music continues, as we watch this man climb his hill, until he simply fades away, leaving us to wonder what's at the top, desperate to know, convinced that it's all been worth it.

But the violence of Darkness is far different from the stylized fighting of "Incident on Fifty-Seventh Street" or the ritualized battles of "Jungleland." This time, the grappling is clumsy, brutal, ugly—not the romantic violence Springsteen imagined when roaming city streets, but the real-life variety he saw in small towns back home. "You can just tell some of these guys are looking for trouble," Springsteen said, recalling the faces in working-class bars in New Jersey. "But they're not looking to punch anybody out. They want to BE punched."

For Springsteen, the most striking part of *The Grapes of Wrath* is the early scene where the Dust Bowl farmer is trying to find out who has evicted him from his land and is confronted with only images of faceless corporations. Similarly, a vague, disembodied "they" creeps into songs like "Something in the Night," "Prove It All Night" and "Streets of Fire" to deny people their most full-blooded possibilities.

Yet, for all the cars, the violence and the searching, the dominant image of *Darkness on the Edge of Town* is labor. There are lines about working in "Badlands," "Adam Raised a Cain," "Racing in the Streets," "The Promised Land," "Factory," and "Prove It All Night" and in three of the other four songs, there are references to wealth or the lack of it. But Springsteen's art is not social realism; he speaks so much of working because jobs are the overwhelming concern of the lives he writes about.

"I know what it's like not to be able to do what you want to do, because when I go home, that's what I see. It's not fun, it's no joke," Bruce has told Robert Duncan. "I see some of my best friends. They're

living the lives of my parents in a certain kind of way. They got kids; they're working hard. These are people, you can see something in their eyes. . . I asked my friend, 'What do you do for fun?' 'I don't have any fun,' she says. She wasn't kidding.''

So when Springsteen wants to compare those who are still alive to those who are just waiting to die, he expresses it in terms of what people do when work is done:

Some guys they just give up living
And start dying little by little, piece by piece
Some guys come home from work and wash up
And go racing in the streets

To me, those lines explain everything about *Darkness on the Edge of Town*, including its seeming obsession with auto imagery. But in the verse that follows, Springsteen makes a fine distinction that would probably occur only to someone who had lived among such people. The singer finds a girl, and loves her, but she can't share his vision. At the end of the song, she is staring off ''into the night with the eyes of one who hates for just being born.'' Springsteen does not desert her, though he sings lines of utter compassion, lines that reveal his knowledge of just how hard it is to keep from being swallowed up by such niggardly existence:

For all the shutdown strangers and hot rod angels
Rumblin' through this promised land
Tonight my baby and me are gonna drive to the sea
And wash these sins off our hands

There's love in those words, and understanding, for precisely those people who are ordinarily shut out of American life: commonplace, anonymous Americans, undistinguished by ethnicity or other cultural memory. These are the sort of people who are romanticized, depicted as the backbone of democracy, but almost never allowed to speak for themselves. *Darkness on the Edge of Town* is an album about such people. It's not an accident that the end of ''Racing in the Streets,'' where Danny Federici's organ blends with Roy Bittan's piano in a fugue-like cry, is the warmest, most affectionate moment on this stark album.

Springsteen had spent most of his young lifetime trying to escape working-class America, only to discover that he remained a product of that society. As Thomas Massey wrote in a *Washington Monthly* article published around the time that *Darkness on the Edge of Town* was being completed, the differences in class life in this country ''can be defined in terms of income . . . culture . . . education and occupation and prestige. But the single clearest class difference, the sum of all the other parts, is the feeling of *control*.'' It was precisely this feeling that he did not run his own life that had spurred Springsteen toward rock and roll; it was his realization that he had lost control of his music that incited his wrath during the lawsuit.

Darkness on the Edge of Town is the fruit of Springsteen's growing awareness of these facts. And in a way, its most remarkable accomplishment is its spirit of com-

passion and reconciliation for everyone and everything that had ever been falsely blamed. The apex of that spirit is ''Adam Raised a Cain,'' in which Springsteen sees himself not only as a product of a specific social situation, but literally as his father's heir:

In the Bible Cain slew Abel and East of Eden he was
    cast
You're born into this life payin' for the sins of
    somebody else's past
Well Daddy worked his whole life for nothin' but the
    pain
Now he walks these empty rooms lookin' for some-
    thin' to blame
You inherit the sins, you inherit the flames
Adam raised a Cain

Like ''It's My Life,'' this is the story of all sons, all fathers. And by telling it in terms of murder—the first murder, a fratricide—Springsteen makes all generations brothers, understanding once and for all that if there is an enemy, its face is not necessarily human. The fractured chords that lead into the song render the guitar a torture device and establish the motivation of the entire album: determination to break out of the vicious circle of pain and futility that robs people of the best parts of their lives.

The fact that music released him from this environment is why Bruce holds onto rock and roll so religiously. ''If you grow up in a home where the concept of art is like 20 minutes in school every day that you *hate*, the lift of rock is just incredible,'' he once told Paul Nelson. ''There's a little barrier that gets broken down, a consciousness barrier. Rock and roll reached down into all those homes where there was no music or books or anything. And it infiltrated that whole thing. That's what happened in my house.''

Perhaps, then, it is not surprising that rock critics (who for the most part have lived middle-class lives where such cultural poverty is unknown) found *Darkness on the Edge of Town* depressing. On the contrary, Springsteen isn't only describing working-class lives at their bleakest, he is writing about people who are breaking through these barriers. ''The characters ain't kids,'' Bruce once told Tony Parsons of *New Musical Express*. ''they're older—you been beat, you been hurt. But there's still hope, there's always hope. They throw dirt on you all your life, and some people get buried so deep in the dirt that they'll never get out. The album's about people who will never admit that they're buried that deep.''

And so the final verse of the record's first song, ''Badlands,'' is both an invocation and a benediction, Bruce Springsteen attempting to do for every listener what rock and roll had done for him:

For the ones who had a notion
A notion deep inside
That it ain't no sin to be glad you're alive
Anyone who finds that depressing ought to pack it
in—or listen a little closer.

17
The Promise

Bruce Springsteen returned to the stage—and a life sealed off by neither lawsuits nor recording hassles—on May 23, 1978, at Shea's Buffalo Theatre. It was the first stop on a tour that would last until January 1, 1979—with only one lengthy break, from October 1 to November 1—and that would see Springsteen and the E Street Band play one hundred and nine shows in eighty-six cities, more than twice as many as they had ever done on a single tour. It was a triumphal tour, selling out even in some places where Bruce had never played before; the best shows came in the biggest halls, too, proving that Springsteen had broken through that final barrier, on his own terms.

But the world in which *Darkness On The Edge Of Town* appeared in 1978 was drastically different to the one that *Born to Run* had conquered. The earlier album had signified the reemergence of rock's underclass, dividing rock and roll between those who were perpetuating an entertainment aristocracy and those who still believed in the fundamental ideals of the music's early days. By 1978, that challenge to the hegemony of rock's show business interests had been picked up by a self-conscious third wave of performers called "punks," who made the threat much more explicit, literally spitting on the conventional values of big-time rock.

The punk movement began in New York, with performers like the poet and sometime-rock-critic Patti Smith and a strange band called the Ramones. Both Smith and the Ramones developed a sound based on inspired amateurism. Their music had a sameness that bordered on monotony, but the energy of the revved-up guitars and unsyncopated drumming could not be denied. When the Ramones toured England in 1976, they left in their wake dozens of kids determined to emulate their raw, crude sound. In fact, the punks' strongest impact was felt in Britain.

American punk was never a unified movement. The Ramones were deliberate satirists of pop-song conventions; songs like "I Wanna Sniff Some Glue" and "I Don't Wanna Walk Around With You" ridi-

culed the druggy romanticism of rock's previous generation. Smith was herself a product of that generation, and while her music blasted with less delicacy and craftsmanship than American rock of the Sixties and early Seventies, her mystical lyrics had specific roots in the work of the Doors, the Velvet Underground and Jimi Hendrix. The other American "punks" believed with Richard Hell of the group Television that they were part of a "Blank Generation," and they cultivated an apolitical, amoral apathy that flattered itself with pretensions to nihilism. Their attitude reflected their roots in bohemian dilettantism; most of the so-called "new wave" in New York—and later, Boston, San Francisco and Los Angeles—was in fact much closer spiritually to the pretensions of Seventies British art-rock performers like Brian Eno and Robert

Fripp than to the basic rock and roll of Smith and the Ramones—much less the Sixties punks.

However, in Britain, (where rock has the status of a major industry) the reaction to the punk possibility was decidedly political; if not always committed to leftist idealism, the punks certainly rejected the rock establishment's aristocratic pretensions. As the most revolutionary band since the MC5, the Clash took this to the furthest extreme. In general, English punk was not a matter of groups—in rejecting the rock aristocrats, the punks denied careerism most explicitly. Punk made rock once more a music of one-shot hits. The perfect example of this is the Sex Pistols, who were to the English outlaw rockers what the New York Dolls had been to Americans in the early Seventies. Threading a fine line between populist outrage and cult decadence, the Sex Pistols mocked such British institutions as the

Queen's Silver Jubilee and threatened not apathy but "Anarchy in the U.K.," all with a wink and a grin that did nothing to belie the seriousness of their intent. Living up to their own beliefs, after recording a half dozen singles and one album, the Pistols broke up. Punk also produced its fair share of exploiters, frauds and morons: Sham 69, who did for the revolutionary Clash what Alice Cooper did for Iggy Pop's sexual ambiguity; the Stranglers, whose sexism was perhaps more offensive than any of the traditional macho men of rock; the Damned, who had all the crudeness and none of the imagination of original punk greats like Count Five. But punk's best moments came on the kind of one shots (Chelsea's "Right to Work," Magazine's "Shot by Both Sides") that the rock establishment could never have created: British punk also inspired a host of small record companies to challenge the marketing abilities of the major corporations—these labels were mostly short-lived or soon bought off in distribution pacts with the majors, but they contributed to an atmosphere of freedom and experimentation. So did the so-called New Wave—artists whose philosophy was somehow linked with the punks but whose music was more carefully crafted or less outrageous: Elvis Costello, Graham Parker and Ian Dury, all affiliated with the Stiff Records' combine, were perhaps the most significant.

Parker and Costello had ties to a new group of

American and British artists who had emerged in the wake of *Born to Run*; these included Bob Seger, Thin Lizzy (an Irish band featuring Phil Lynott), the Boomtown Rats (another Irish group, led by Bob Geldoff), Joe Jackson, and, on the West Coast, Warren Zevon. It would be a mistake to say that all of these performers were inspired by the success of *Born to Run* although Seger's hit, "Night Moves," and Thin Lizzy's "The Boys Are Back in Town" certainly were—but it is clear that without Springsteen's breakthrough, record companies would have been considerably less eager to sign up this kind of tough-but-tender, relatively non-conformist performer. There were also a variety of attempts to create synthetic Springsteens during Bruce's long absence from the studio: Appel's Arlyn Gale, for instance, Johnny Cougar and Billy Falcon. The most commercially successful of the lot was Meatloaf, a three hundred-pound actor/singer whose *Showboat* vocal style and cynically teen-tailored lyrics were redeemed only slightly by the appearance of Roy Bittan and Max Weinberg on his debut album.

If rock had changed enormously in three years, the pop industry had changed even more. Part of the reason was the emergence of a new form of black dance music, disco, as a potent commercial force. Some lamented the virtual disappearance of the old soul crooning style, regarding disco as a mechanical dance machine that stripped singers of their personality. While this is clearly true in some cases, it is also true that some of the best pop records of the late Seventies have been done in that format.

More importantly from a business perspective, the punk and disco movements loosened the power structure's stranglehold on popular music. Punk and disco records could be made quickly and cheaply, meaning that it was now once again feasible to make music that did not conform to the narrow requirements of the Establishment's tastes. (That punk and disco are themselves artistically narrow is a problem yet to be faced.) The major record companies were easily able to attach themselves to the most profitable performers in both idioms, but at least they had to recognize the blacks and gays who originated disco, the uncouth youths who spawned punk.

Sadly, the older rock performers seemed more bankrupt than ever. When Linda Ronstadt recorded Elvis Costello's "Alison" and the Rolling Stones scored a disco hit with "Miss You," the results seemed less acts of rapprochement than products of a desperate cynicism. Ronstadt and the Stones were at a loss for a formula to replace their old one, which had begun to fall apart in the face of the new divisions among the audience.

Springsteen decided to change booking agencies, moving from William Morris to Frank Barsalona's Premiere Talent in early 1977. In 1976, Barsalona had signed the Asbury Jukes, and Springsteen first met him through Miami Steve, but their alliance seemed natural. More than any other Rock Establishment figure, Barsalone had greeted the changes of the preceding years openly, signing Patti Smith, the Ramones, the Sex Pistols and Graham Parker. Barsalona's taste also ran more heavily to hard rock than that of almost any other music executive, and he was canny enough to understand Springsteen's need to determine his own style as a performer. (He was also shrewd enough to hire Barry Bell away from William Morris late in 1977, in time for Bell to work on the *Darkness* tour.)

Of course, attaching himself to Columbia Records and Premier Talent was not a particularly radical position for Bruce to assume. But he had resolved his conflicts about the business world; as he explained to interviewers, after having worked so hard to make the best record possible, he would have been stupid not to attempt to reach as many listeners as possible. Besides, with the aid of Jon Landau (who became Springsteen's manager officially in July, 1978), he was confident he could effectively manipulate the system, always a dangerous presumption, of course, but Springsteen is so single-minded that it seemed likely that he could make it work without any undue compromises. Certainly, by playing sports arenas so successfully Springsteen proved that he could have both quality and quantity; in fact, he got a clearer, more powerful sound in Madison Square Garden than many acts have at the Palladium or the Bottom Line.

To both old wave and new, Springsteen remained an outsider. Rock aristocrats mistrusted his high level of commitment to his fans, which sharply contrast with the way the others kept their distance from their own fans. When Mick Jagger wished to get close to his audience at Madison Square Garden, he teased them by swinging overhead on a rope, just out of reach. When Bruce Springsteen wanted to be with his fans, he climbed offstage and sang from their midst, confident that he would not be ripped to shreds. Such things did nothing to endear him to the more insecure stars of old-line rock.

Oddly, Springsteen was threatening to the punks in much the same way. Because punk ideology was absolutely anti-sentimental, the humanism of *Darkness On The Edge Of Town* seemed old-fashioned to many New Wave ideologues. And Springsteen's devotion to the needs of his audience, and his willingness to go much further than half way to meet those stood in stark contrast to the icy isolation of Elvis Costello, the Sex Pistols and the Clash, all of whom viewed their listeners with at least as much suspicion as they regarded their corporate sponsors. Actually, the comparison is unfair—with the exception of the Pistols' Johnny Rotten, punk has not produced a figure with a fraction of Bruce's charisma. Despite the legitimate claims of others to be taken seriously, Bruce Springsteen often seems like the last rock star, or at least the last one innocent of cynicism.

To anyone witnessing a single show, Springsteen's 1978 tour was reassuring; there was still plenty of vitality in rock and roll. For those lucky enough to follow the progress of the tour, though, it was epochal. Dick Wingate remembers trying to schedule filming a concert for a TV commercial. Someone suggested that Bruce could pick a town where the camera crew's interference on-stage really wouldn't matter. "There's no such place," Springsteen immediately replied. And that was the way the tour went, night after night, three- and four-hour shows back-to-back, then a couple of hours of interviews backstage. After singing all of *Darkness*, all of *Born To Run*, selections from the first two albums, and a few oldies, Bruce was almost always the very last person to leave the auditorium. But if there were any kids still hanging around the backstage door, he'd remain there until every last one of them had a fragment of what he wanted—a couple of moments of conversation, an autograph, just recognition.

The *Darkness* songs went over well, but that didn't prevent Bruce from introducing new material into the show. He did "The Promise" once in a while and "Independence Day" about as often; by early July, he already was performing a newly written song called "Point Blank," a ballad that extended the *Darkness* story into its next phase.

The rockabilly listening of the past year paid off, too, with versions of Buddy Holly's "Not Fade Away," Eddie Cochran's "Summertime Blues," Jerry Lewis's "High School Confidential" and Elvis's "Heartbreak Hotel." But the greatest rockabilly moment came one night at Madison Square Garden: "I hear you got a newspaper strike in town," Bruce said as he stepped to the mike for the first song. "Well, have you heard the news?" The band roared nto Elvis's milestone "Good Rockin' Tonight' that could have lifted the roof.

There was much more; too much to absorb. For every moment cited, there would be another begging for inclusion. That's the way it's supposed to be. The very best moments of the tour were the ones when you could see how far Springsteen had come—they were the times when he'd simply lean forward and smile, laugh, shake his head at a band member as if to say that it was alll too good to be true. "You know," said Max Weinberg, "when I was twelve years old, this is *exactly* what I wanted to be doing." Trying to explain that would really be like trying to tell a stranger about rock and roll.

If Bruce Springsteen's story has a central issue, it's whether dawning maturity is compatible with the rock-and-roll spirit. During the 1978 tour Bruce told a story similar to the one he told in 1976 about the Gypsy Lady. It has the ring of truth, though just how much only Bruce himself can say. In the middle of "Growin' Up," Bruce would step forward with a smile:

"When I was growing up, there were two things that were unpopular in my house. One was me and the other was my guitar. We had this grate, like the heat

was supposed to come through, except it wasn't hooked up to any heating ducts; it was just open straight down to the kitchen, and there was a gas stove right underneath it. When I used to start playing, my pop used to turn on the gas jets and try to smoke me outta my room. And I had to go hide out on the roof or something.

"He always used to call the guitar, never Fender guitar or Gibson guitar, it was always the *God-damned* guitar. Every time he'd knock on my door, that was all I'd hear: 'Turn down that *God-damn* guitar.' He musta thought everything in my room was the same brand: God-damn guitar, God-damn stereo, God-damn radio.

"Anyway, one day my mom and pop, they come to me and say, 'Bruce, it's time to get serious with your life. This guitar thing . . . it's okay as a hobby but you need something to fall back on.' My father, he said, 'You should be a lawyer'—which I coulda used later on in my career. He says, 'Lawyers, they run the world.' But I didn't think that they did—and I still don't.

"But my mother used to say, 'No, no, no, he should be an author, he should write books; that's a good life. You can get a little something for yourself.' But me, I wanted to play the guitar.

"Now my mother, she's real Italian, and my father, he's Irish. So they say, 'This is a big thing. You should go see the priest. Tell him we want you to be a lawyer or an author. Bu don't say *nothin'* about that God-damn guitar.'

"So I went to the rectory and knocked on the door. 'Hi, Father Ray, I'm Mr. Springsteen's son.' I tell him, 'I got this problem. My father, he thinks I should be a lawyer, and my mother wants me to be an author. But me, I got this guitar.'

"Father Ray says, 'This is too big a deal for me. You got to talk to God,' who I didn't know too well at the time. 'Tell him about the lawyer and the author,' Father Ray says, 'but don't say *nothin'* about that guitar.'

"Now I was worried. Where was I gonna find God, right? So I go find Clarence—he knows everybody. Clarence says, 'No sweat. I know right where he is.' So I show up at Clarence's house in my mother's car—an old Nash Rambler. Clarence looks at me. He says, 'You gonna go visit God in that? Man, he's got like, people in Cadillacs, you know. He ain't gonna pay attention to anybody shows up in a Nash Rambler.' But it's all I got.

"So we drive way out of town, along this old dark road. We drive a long ways, and I say to Clarence, 'Man, you sure you know where we're goin'?' Clarence says, 'Sure, I just took a guy out here the other day.' So we finally come to this little house, way out in the woods, nothing around, but all the lights are on inside. There's music blasting out and a little hole in the door.

"I knock and this eye peeps out. I say, 'Uh, Clarence sent me.' So they let me in. And there's God, behind the drums. On the bass drum it says: 'G-O-D.' So I said, 'God, I got this problem. My father, he wants me to be a lawyer, cause he says lawyers rule the world. And my mother, she wants me to be an author, get a little something for myself. But they just don't understand— I got this guitar.'

"God looks at me. He says, 'I know, I know. See, what they don't understand is, Moses screwed up. There was supposed to be an Eleventh Commandment. Actually, Moses was so scared after ten—it was a great show, the burning bush, the thunder, lightning, you shoulda seen it—he went back down the mountain. You see, what those guys don't understand is that there was *supposed* to be an Eleventh Commandment. And all it said was:

LET IT ROCK!''

The Songs

PART ONE

This is a listing of more than one hundred songs written by Bruce Springsteen—a half dozen of them in collaboration with others, including a pair written with George Theiss for the Castiles in 1966. There are about a dozen written with Steel Mill or the Bruce Springsteen Band, but most have been conceived since Springsteen signed with Columbia Records—a prolific pace by any standard. I have noted only official releases, (not bootlegs) here, whether by Springteen or by someone else.

Action In The Streets
Unreleased; title given by fans to untitled, soul-style song from 1976 tours, which featured the line ''Are you alive?'' Possibly recorded for *Darkness On The Edge Of Town* and not used.

Adam Raised A Cain
released on *Darkness On The Edge Of Town*

All I Wanna Do Is Dance
Unreleased; probably unrecorded; written for Bruce Springsteen Band.

American Tune
Unreleased; included on early acetates of *Greetings From Asbury Park, New Jersey*, but replaced by ''It's Hard To Be A Saint In The City''

And The Band Played
Unreleased; from around 1974; recording history uncertain.

The Angel
Released on *Greetings From Asbury Park, New Jersey* and B side of ''Blinded By The Light'' single.

Arabian Nights
Recorded for May, 1973, John Hammond demo tape. Unreleased.

Baby I
Written with George Theiss for unreleased Castiles single, May 1966.

Backstreets
Released on *Born To Run*

Badlands
Released on *Darkness On The Edge Of Town* and later as a single, backed with ''Streets Of Fire.''

Ballad Of The Self-Loading Pistol
Known only from Laurel Canyon lyric sheet circa 1974-5. Recording history unknown.

The Band's Just Boppin' The Blues
Unrecorded; written for Bruce Springsteen Band. (Miami Steve says this may have been the song known to the musicians as ''Funk Says 'Right On' ''—Funk being Garry Tallent, of course.)

Because The Night
Written for *Darkness On The Edge Of Town*; unissued, but oft-bootlegged. Became a top-twenty hit, 1978 in rewritten version by Patti Smith Group which was produced by Jimmy Iovine and smuggled out of Springsteen session into Smith session next door.

Bishop Dance
Unreleased; recording history uncertain, probably from around time of second album.

Blinded By The Light
Released on *Greetings From Asbury Park, New Jersey*, and as first Columbia single with ''The Angel'' as B side. No. 1 hit single for Manfred Mann in 1977 in mangled interpretation. Also recorded by former Hollies singer Allan Clarke.

Born To Run
Released as title track of third Springsteen album; also as single which made No. 18 in 1975. Also recorded by Allan Clarke of the Hollies.

Candy's Room
Released on *Darkness On The Edge Of Town*.

Contessa
Unreleased; probably written between first and second albums; recording history unknown.

Cowboys Of The Sun
Written for Bruce Springsteen Band; recorded for Hammond demos; unissued.

Darkness On The Edge Of Town
Released as title track of fourth Springsteen LP, 1978.

Does This Bus Stop at Eighty-Second Street?
Released on *Greetings From Asbury Park, New Jersey*. Included on Hammond demo.

Don't Look Back
Recorded for *Darkness On The Edge Of Town*; unissued.

Down To Mexico
Written for Bruce Springsteen Band; never recorded.

The E Street Shuffle
Released on *The Wild, The Innocent And The E Street Shuffle*, 1973.

Factory
Released on *Darkness On The Edge Of Town* and as B side of ''Prove It All Night'' single, 1978.

The Fever
Released to radio stations only in tape copy, 1974. Recorded by Southside Johnny on first album, 1976, and in 1977 by obscure UK singer, Dean Ford, as EMI single. Also by Alan Rich (son of C&W star Charlie Rich) on 1975 Epic LP.

Fire
Recorded for *Darkness On The Edge Of Town*; unreleased. Recorded by Robert Gordon and by the Pointer Sisters, both 1978. Pointers made it a Top Three hit, 1979.

For You
Released on *Greetings From Asbury Park, New Jersey* and as B side of ''Spirit In The Night'' 45. Also recorded by Greg Kihn on Beserkeley Records.

Fourth Of July, Asbury Park (Sandy)
Released on *The Wild, The Innocent And The E Street Shuffle*. Also recorded by the Hollies, who enjoyed some European success with a slick single version.

Frankie
Recorded for *Darkness On The Edge Of Town*; unreleased.

Garden State Parkway Blues
Written for Steel Mill; never recorded.

Goin' Back To Georgia
Written for Steel Mill; unrecorded.

Growin' Up
Recorded as part of Hammond demo tape; released on *Greetings From Asbury Park, New Jersey*. Also as part of promotional EP with "Spirit In The Night," and "Rosalita."

Hearts Of Stone
Written and recorded for *Darkness On The Edge Of Town*; unreleased. Issued as title track of Southside Johnny's third album, 1978.

Henry Boy
From Laura Canyon lyric sheet circa 1974-75. Recording history unknown.

Hey Santa Ana
History uncertain—frequent live performances, 1973-74. (Has been bootlegged as "Guns Of Kid Cole.")

I Am The Doctor
Unrecorded; written for Steel Mill.

If I Was The Priest
Done as part of Hammond demo, 1973. Recorded on solo album by former Hollies singer Allan Clarke, 1975.

I Just Can't Change
Written for Bruce Springsteen band; unrecorded.

I'll Be Your Savior
Unrecorded Steel Mill song.

Incident On Fifty-Seventh Street
Released on *The Wild, The Innocent And The E Street Shuffle*.

Independence Day
Written July 1977, recorded for *Darkness On The Edge Of Town* but not included there. Springsteen has mentioned this as a possibility for the fifth album.

I Remember
Bruce Springsteen Band song; unrecorded.

It's Hard To Be A Saint In The City
Released on *Greetings From Asbury Park, New Jersey*.

Janey Needs A Shooter
From 1974-75 Laurel Canyon lyric sheet; recording history unknown.

Jazz Musician
From Hammond demos; unreleased.

Jungleland
Released on *Born To Run*.

Kitty's Back
Released on *The Wild, The Innocent And The E Street Shuffle*.

Like A Stranger
Unrecorded tune for Bruce Springsteen Band.

Little Girl So Fine
Written with Miami Steve Van Zandt for second Asbury Jukes' LP, *This Time It's For Real*, (1977).

Lost In The Flood
Released on *Greetings From Asbury Park, New Jersey*.

Love Is A Crazy Thing
Unrecorded song for Bruce Springsteen Band.

Love On The Wrong Side Of Town
Co-written with Miami Steve Van Zandt for Jukes' *This Time It's For Real* LP.

Magic Kind Of Lovin'
Written for Bruce Springsteen Band; never recorded.

Make Up Your Mind
Bruce Springsteen Band; unrecorded.

Marie
History uncertain—Laurel Canyon lyric sheet.

Mary, Queen Of Arkansas
Recorded on Hammond demo tape; released on *Greetings From Asbury Park, New Jersey*.

Meeting Across The River
Released on *Born to Run* and as B side of title single.

New York City Serenade
Released on *Greetings From Asbury Park, New Jersey*.

New York Song
Frequent performance piece, circa 1974; recording history unknown.

Night
Released on *Born To Run*.

Paradise By The Sea
Instrumental which opened second half of 1978 tour's sets. Issued on a limited basis to radio stations, 1978, in tape form in live version recorded at Berkeley Community Theatre.

The Promised Land
Released on *Darkness On The Edge Of Town*

Prove It All Night
Released on *Darkness On The Edge Of Town*, and as a 45 backed with "Factory." Also issued, on limited basis, as live tape (with "Paradise By The Sea") to radio stations in version taped at Berkeley Community Theatre, 1978.

Point Blank
Written during 1978 summer tour; unreleased.

The Promise
Written between third and fourth albums; recorded for *Darkness on the Edge of Town*, but left off it at last minute in favor of the title track. (Reason: Springsteen was concerned that the lyrics would be interpreted as being about his lawsuit. In fact, the song may have been inspired by Greil Marcus' book, *Mystery Train*.)

Racing In The Street
Recorded in a variety of different versions for *Darkness On The Edge Of Town*, on which it was released.

Rendezvous
Written 1976, recorded for *Darkness On The Edge Of Town*; unreleased, issue elsewhere possible before publication.

Resurrection
Steel Mill; group's last song, with exception of "Sister Theresa"; unrecorded.

Rosalita (Come Out Tonight)

Released on *The Wild, The Innocent And The E Street Shuffle*. Mysteriously, never issued as a single, although it was issued as part of promo EP with "Spirit In The Night" and "Growin' Up." Live version issued on CBS promo disc.

Seaside Bar Song
Recorded for but not released on *The Wild, The Innocent and The E Street Shuffle*, 1973.

Secret To The Blues
Bruce Springsteen band number? History uncertain.

Send That Boy To Jail
Unrecorded Steel Mill song.

Sherry Darlin'
"Frat rock" song, written—but apparently not recorded—during *Darkness On The Edge Of Town*.

She's The One
Released on *Born To Run*, and a B side of "Tenth Avenue Freezeout" 45.

Sister Theresa
Steel Mill's best song; unrecorded.

Something In The Night
Released on *Darkness On The Edge Of Town*. The live version done on winter '76 tour was considerably different, featuring muted trumpets in the background and a different lyric narrative.

Southern Son
From Hammond demos; unissued.

Spirit In The Night
From *Greetings From Asbury Park, New Jersey*. Issued as single with "For You," May 1973 and on promo EP with "Rosalita" and "Growin' Up," same year. Later recorded by Manfred Mann, who released it as attempted follow-up single to "Blinded By The Light," 1977—made the Top Fifty.

Street Queen
Unissued Hammond demo.

Streets Of Fire
Released on *Darkness On The Edge Of Town* and as "Badlands" B side.

Sweet Melinda
Unrecorded song from Steel Mill.

Talk To Me
Written and recorded for *Darkness On The Edge Of Town*; issued 1978 on Southside Johnny's *Hearts Of Stone*.

Tenth Avenue Freezeout.
Issued on *Born To Run*, and as a single backed with "She's The One," 1975.

That's What You Get
Written with George Theiss for unreleased Castiles' single, May 1966.

Thundercrack.
1974 performance piece, oft bootlegged; recording history uncertain.

Thunder Road
Released on *Born To Run*.

The Ties That Bind
Written near end of 1978 tour; may turn up on fifth album. (May not, too.)

Trapped Again
Written with Miami Steve Van Zandt and Southside Johnny Lyon for Jukes' *Hearts Of Stone* LP. Issued as a single, 1978.

Two Hearts
Unissued song from Hammond demo.

Walking In The Street.
History uncertain—has been bootlegged, but not known from live performances. Possibly recorded for second album?

The War Is Over
Unrecorded Steel Mill song.

The Way
Recorded for *Darkness On The Edge Of Town*; unreleased

We'll All Man The Guns
Steel Mill; unrecorded.

When You Dance
Written for Bruce Springsteen Band, resurrected by Southside Johnny for second album.

Why'd You Do That
Unrecorded; Steel Mill.

Wild Billy's Circus Story
Released on *The Wild, The Innocent And The E Street Shuffle*. and on CBS "Playback" promo EP, in live version from company convention, 1974.

Wings For Wheels
Alternate version/title for "Thunder Road," circa 1974.

The Wind And The Rain
Unrecorded Steel Mill song.

You Mean So Much to Me Baby
Written about 1974, not recorded until 1976, on Asbury Jukes' first LP, *I Don't Want To Go Home*, as duet between Southside Johnny and Ronnie Spector.

Zero And Blind Terry
Written between first and second album; recording history uncertain; never released.

PART TWO

Songs Written By Others

(Bruce obviously doesn't do all of these every night, and some he does very rarely, but taken together, they give a sense of the range of his historical influences. I've noted the original artist and/or the songwriter in parentheses.)

A Love So Fine (Chiffons, 1963).
Recorded for *Born To Run*, but never released.

A Fine Fine Girl (Darlene Love, prod. by Phil Spector, 1963)

Ain't Too Proud To Beg (Temptations, 1965)

Around and Around (Chuck Berry/The Rolling Stones)

Baby I Love You (Ronettes, prod. by Phil Spector, 1964)

Back In The U.S.A. (Chuck Berry, 1959)

Be My Baby (Ronettes, 1963)

Carol (Chuck Berry, 1958; Rolling Stones, 1965)

Chimes Of Freedom (Written by Bob Dylan, 1964, also recorded by the Byrds, 1965)

Cry To Me (Solomon Burke, 1962)

Cupid (Sam Cooke, 1961)

Dear Lady Twist (Gary 'U.S.' Bonds, 1961)

Detroit Medley: "Devil With A Blue Dress/Good Golly Miss Molly" and "Jenny Take A Ride" (Mitch Ryder and the Detroit Wheels, 1965–66)

Double Shot (Of My Baby's Love) (Swingin' Medallions, 1966)

Gloria (Written by Van Morrison for Them, 1965)

Goin' Back (Written by Carole King for The Byrds, 1967)

Good Rockin' Tonight (Elvis Presley, 1954)

Heartbreak Hotel (Elvis Presley, 1956)

High School Confidential (Jerry Lee Lewis, 1958)
The first song Bruce played at Madison Square Garden, '78.

I Don't Want To Hang Up My Rock And Roll Shoes (Chuck Willis, 1958)

I Fought The Law (Bobby Fuller Four, 1966)

I'm Ready (Muddy Waters, 1954)

I Sold My Heart To The Junkman (Patti Labelle and the Bluebelles, 1962)

It's Gonna Work Out Fine (Ike and Tina Turner, 1961)

It's My Life (The Animals, 1965)

I Want You (Bob Dylan, 1966)

Higher And Higher (Jackie Wilson, 1967)

Knock On Wood (Eddie Floyd, 1966)
Performed with Floyd, in Memphis 1976.

Let The Four Winds Blow (Fats Domino, 1961)

Little Latin Lupe Lu (Righteous Bros., 1963; Kingsmen, 1964; Mitch Ryder and the Detroit Wheels, 1966)

Little Queenie (Chuck Berry, 1959; Jerry Lee Lewis, the Rolling Stones)

Louie Louie (Kingsmen, 1963, 1966)

Lucille (Little Richard 1957)

Macho Man (The Village People, 1978)
As sung by Clarence Clemons

Mona (Bo Diddley, circa 1956–7)

Mountain Of Love (Harold Dorman, 1960; Johnny Rivers, 1964)

Needles And Pins (Written by Jackie DeShannon, 1963; a hit for The Searchers, 1964)

Night Train (Viscounts, 1960; James Brown, 1962)

No Money Down (Chuck Berry, 1956)

Not Fade Away (Buddy Holly, 1957; Rolling Stones, 1964)

Oh Boy (Buddy Holly, 1957)

Pretty Flamingo (Manfred Mann, 1966)

Quarter To Three (Gary "U.S." Bonds, 1961)
Every night.

Raise Your Hand (Eddie Floyd, 1967)

Rave On (Buddy Holly, 1957)

Ring Of Fire (Johnny Cash, 1963)

Santa Claus Is Coming To Town (Produced by Phil Spector for The Crystals, 1964)
Recorded live in 1976, and sent to radio stations, although never officially released.

Sha La La (Manfred Mann, 1964)

634-5789 (Wilson Pickett, 1966)

Something You Got (Chris Kenner, 1964; Alvin Robinson, 1964; Chuck Jackson and Maxine Brown, 1965)

Soothe Me (Sims Twins, 1961; Sam and Dave, 1967; written by Sam Cooke)

Spanish Harlem (Ben E. King, 1961; Phil Spector and Jerry Leiber wrote the song, which was produced by Leiber and Mike Stoller)

Summertime Blues (Eddie Cochran, 1958; The Who, 1969)

Sweet Little Sixteen (Chuck Berry, 1958)

Then She Kissed Me (Produced by Phil Spector for the Crystals, 1963)

Twist And Shout (Isley Bros, 1962; Beatles, 1964)

Walking The Dog (Rufus Thomas, 1963)

We Gotta Get Out Of This Place (Animals, 1965)

Wear My Ring (Around Your Neck) (Written by Leiber and Stoller for Elvis Presley, 1958)

When You Walk In The Room (Written by Jackie DeShannon; recorded by her and by the Searchers, both 1964)

You Can't Sit Down (Dovells, 1963)

You Never Can Tell (Chuck Berry, 1964)

You Really Got Me (Kinks, 1964)

THE SHOWS

(This list, based on information from the Springsteen / Appel lawsuit and from the CBS Records files, includes the shows Bruce performed from the time when he signed with Laurel Canyon—Appel's company—through Jan. 1, 1979, when he closed the second phase of his *Darkness On The Edge Of Town* tour in Cleveland. Special thanks to Dick Wingate at CBS.

1972

Nov. 12	York, Pa.	————
Dec. 29	Dayton, Ohio	————
Dec.30	Columbus, Ohio	————

1973

Jan. 3	Bryn Mawr, Pa.	Main Point
Jan. 8	Boston, Mass.	Paul's Mall
Jan. 16	Villanova, Pa.	Villanova University
Jan. 24	Chicago, Ill.	The Quiet Knight
Jan. 31	New York, N.Y.	(The Gaslight??)
Feb. 10	Asbury Park, N.J.	(Student Prince?)
Feb. 11	S. Orange, N.J.	(Seton Hall University?)
Feb. 14	Richmond, Va.	————
Feb. 16	Long Branch, N.J.	(Monmouth College?)
Feb. 28	Stockton, Calif.	————
March 2	Berkeley, Calif.	————
March 3	Santa Monica, Calif.	————
March 12	Boston, Mass.	Oliver's
March 18	Kingston, R.I.	————
March 23	Providence, R.I.	————
March 24	Niagara, N.Y.	————
March 29	Kutztown, Pa.	————
April 1	Brunswick, N.J.	————
April 7	Norfolk, Va.	————
April 11	Atlanta, Ga.	(Poor Richard's?)
April 13	Villanova, Pa.	Villanova University
April 18	Lincroft, N.J.	————
April 23	Hartford, Ct.	————
April 24	Bryn Mawr, Pa.	The Main Point
April 27	Athens, Ohio	————
April 28	College Park, Md.	————
May 1	University Park, Pa.	————
May 5	Providence, R.I.	————
May 6	Amherst, Mass.	————
May 11	Columbus, Ohio	————
May 12	Niagara, N.Y.	————
May 24-26	Washington, D.C.	(The Cellar Door?)
May 30	Fayetteville, N.C.	————

(This seems to be the beginning of the Chicago tour)

May 31	Richmond, Va.	————
June 1	Hampton, Va.	————
June 2	Baltimore, Md.	————
June 3	New Haven, Ct.	Arena
June 6	Philadelphia, Pa.	Spectrum
June 8-9	Boston, Mass.	Boston Gardens
June 10	Springfield, Mass.	————
June 13	Binghampton, N.Y.	————
June 14-15	New York, N.Y.	Madison Square Garden

(End of Chicago tour)

June 22-24	Seaside Heights, N.J.	Fat City
July 5-9	Bryn Mawr, Pa.	The Main Point
July 18-23	New York, N.Y.	(Max's Kansas City?)
July 31	Roslyn, N.Y.	My Father's Place
Aug. 1-2, 4	Asbury Park, N.J.	Convention Center
Aug. 14	Cherry Hill, N.J.	Erlton Lounge
Aug. 16	East Paterson, N.J.	Mr. D's
Aug. 20-26	Boston, Mass.	Oliver's
Aug. 31, Sept. 1-2	Seaside Heights, N.J.	Fat City
Sept. 6	Franklin, Mass.	Dean Jr. College
Sept. 7	University Park, Pa.	Penn State University
Sept. 8	Pittsburgh, Pa.	University of Pittsburgh
Sept. 14-16	Syracuse, N.Y.	Jabberwocky Club
Sept. 22	Miami Beach, Fla.	Jai Alai Fronton
Sept. 28	Hampden-Sydney, Va.	Hampden-Sydney College
Sept. 29	Waynesburg, Va.	Waynesburg College
Sept. 30	Stony Brook, N.Y.	SUNY
Oct. 6	Villanova, Pa.	University of Villanova
Oct. 13	Washington, D.C.	Kennedy Center
Oct. 15-16	Boston, Mass.	Oliver's
Oct. 20	Rindge, N.H.	Franklin Pierce College
Oct. 26	Geneva, N.Y.	Hobart College
Oct. 29-31	Bryn Mawr, Pa.	The Main Point
Nov. 3	Houlton, Maine	Rickler College
Nov. 6-10	New York, N.Y.	Max's Kansas City
Nov. 11	Trenton, N.J.	Trenton State College
Nov. 14-16	Roslyn, N.Y.	My Father's Place
Nov. 17	Manayunk, Pa.	Roxy Theatre
Nov. 25	Amherst, Mass.	(Amherst College?)
Nov. 30	Richmond, Va.	————
Dec. 1	Hamden, Ct.	Quinnipiac College
Dec. 6-8	Washington, D.C.	Childe Harold
Dec. 14	New Haven, Ct.	Pine Crest
Dec. 15	Garden City, N.Y.	Nassau Community College
Dec. 16	Hartford, Ct.	Shaboo
Dec. 17-18	Asbury Park, N.J.	Student Prince
Dec. 20	Providence, R.I.	Roger Williams College
Dec. 21-22	Cherry Hill, N.J.	(Erlton Lounge?)
Dec. 27-30	Bryn Mawr, Pa.	The Main Point

1974

Jan. 12	Parsippany, N.J.	Joint in the Woods
Jan. 16	Nashville, Tenn.	————
Jan. 19	Kent, Ohio	Kent State University
Jan. 25	Richmond, Va.	Mosque
Jan. 26	Norfolk, Va.	Chrysler Theatre
Feb. 1	Cleveland, Ohio	Allen Theatre
Feb. 2	Springfield, Mass.	Springfield College
Feb. 7-9	Atlanta, Ga.	Richard's
Feb. 12	Lexington, Ky.	University of Kentucky
Feb. 15	Toledo, Ohio	University of Toledo
Feb. 17	Columbus, Ohio	The Agora
Feb. 18	Cleveland, Ohio	The Agora
Feb. 23	Cookstown, N.J.	Satellite Lounge

*first gig with Boom Carter

Feb. 24-25	Bryn Mawr, Pa.	The Main Point
March 1	New Brunswick, N.J.	State Theatre
March 2	Parsippany, N.J.	Joint in the Woods
March 3	Washington, D.C.	Georgetown University
March 7-10	Houston, Tex.	Liberty Hall
March 15-16	Austin, Tex.	Armadillo World
March 18-21	Dallas, Tex.	Mother Blues
March 24	Phoenix, Ariz.	Celebrity Theatre
April 5	Chester, Pa.	Widener College
April 6	Pemberton, N.J.	Burlington County College
April 7	S. Orange, N.J.	Seton Hall University
April 9-11	Cambridge, Mass.	Joe's Place*

*actually held at Charlie's Bar, since Joe's had burned down. B.S. met Jon Landau April 10.

April 13	Richmond, Va.	Coliseum
April 18	W. Long Branch, N.J.	Monmouth College
April 19	New Brunswick, N.J.	State Theatre
April 20	Collegeville, Pa.	Ursinus College
April 26	Providence, R.I.	Brown University

April 27	Stoors, Ct.	University of Connecticut
April 28	Swarthmore, Pa.	Swarthmore College
April 29	Allentown, Pa.	Roxy Theatre
May 4	Upper Montclair, N.J.	Montclair State College
May 5	Kent, Ohio	Kent State University
May 6	Newtown, Pa.	Bucks County Community College
May 9	Boston, Mass.	Harvard Square Theatre*

*opened for Bonnie Raitt; this show inspired Jon Landau's notorious quote

May 10	Providence, R.I.	Palace Theatre
May 11	Rutherford, N.J.	Fairleigh Dickenson University
May 12	Glassboro, N.J.	Glassboro State College
May 14	Greenville, Tenn.	Tusculum College
May 24	Trenton, N.J.	War Memorial
May 25	Radnor, Pa.	Archbishop High School
May 31	Columbus, Ohio	The Agora
June 1	Kent, Ohio	Kent State University
June 2	Toledo, Ohio	The Agora
June 3	Cleveland, Ohio	The Agora
June 13	Oklahoma City, Okla.	————
June 14	Arlington, Tex.	Texas Hall
June 15	Austin, Tex.	Armadillo World Headquarters
June 16	Houston, Tex.	Music Hall
June 19	Kansas City, Mo.	Cowtown Ballroom
June 26-30	Memphis, Tenn.	Lafayette's
July 5	St. Louis, Mo.	Ambassador Theatre
July 12-14	New York, N.Y.	Bottom Line*

*live broadcast?

July 16	Newark, Del.	Stone Ballroom
July 19	Sedalia, Mo.	Outdoor Concert
July 25	Santa Monica, Calif.	Civic Center
July 26	San Diego, Calif.	————
July 27	Phoenix, Ariz.	Celebrity Theatre
July 28	Tucson, Ariz.	Raceway
Aug. 3	New York, N.Y.	Schaefer Music Festival*

*opened for Anne Murray (see *Thundercrack*)

Aug. 9	Lenox, Mass.	Tanglewood Music Festival
Aug. 10	Portchester, N.Y.	Capitol Theatre
Aug. 12	Boston, Mass.	Performance Center
Aug. 13	Wilmington, Del.	————
Aug. 14	Red Bank, N.J.	Carlton Theatre
Sept. 19	Bryn Mawr, Pa.	The Main Point
Sept. 20	Upper Darby, Pa.	Tower Theatre
Sept. 21	Oneonta, N.Y.	SUNY
Sept. 22	Union, N.J.	————
Oct. 4	New York, N.Y.	Avery Fisher Hall*

*stage collapsed

Oct. 5	Reading, Pa.	Albright College
Oct. 6	Worcester, Mass.	Clark University
Oct. 11	Gaithersburg, Md.	Shady Grove Music Fair
Oct. 12	Princeton, N.J.	McCarter Theatre
Oct. 18	Passaic, N.J.	Capitol Theatre
Oct. 19	Schenectady, N.Y.	Union College
Oct. 20	Carlisle, Pa.	Dickenson College
Oct. 25	Hanover, N.H.	Dartmouth College
Oct. 26	Springfield, Mass.	Springfield College
Oct. 27	Millersville, Pa.	State College
Oct. 29	Boston, Mass.	Music Hall
Nov. 1-2	Upper Darby, Pa.	Tower Theatre
Nov. 6-7	Austin, Tex.	Armadillo World Headquarters
Nov. 8	Corpus Christi, Tex.	Riz Music Hall
Nov. 9	Houston, Tex.	Liberty Hall
Nov. 10	Dallas, Tex.	Lone Star Opera House
Nov. 15	Eaton, Pa.	————
Nov. 16	Washington, D.C.	————
Nov. 17	Charlottesville, Va.	————
Nov. 21	Blackwood, N.J.	Camden Community College
Nov. 22	West Chester, Pa.	College
Nov. 23	Salem, Mass.	Salem State College
Nov. 29-30	Trenton, N.J.	War Memorial
Dec. 6	New Brunswick, N.J.	State Theatre
Dec. 7	Geneva, N.Y.	Hobart College
Dec. 8	Burlington, Vt.	University of Vermont

1975

Feb. 5	Bryn Mawr, Pa.	The Main Point
Feb. 6-7	Westchester, Pa.	Widener College
Feb. 18	Cleveland, Ohio	John Carroll University
Feb. 19	University Park, Pa.	Penn State University
Feb. 20	Pittsburgh, Pa.	University of Pittsburgh
Feb. 23	Westbury, N.Y.	Westbury Music Fair
March 1	Syracuse, N.Y.	Syracuse University
March 2	Plattsburgh, N.Y.	SUNY
March 7	Baltimore, Md.	Painter's Mill
March 8-9	Washington, D.C.	Constitution Hall
July 20	Providence, R.I.	Palace Theatre*

*first gig with Miami Steve.

July 22	Geneva, N.Y.	Geneva Theatre
July 23	Lenox, Mass.	Music Inn
July 25-26	Kutztown, Pa.	Kutztown College
July 28-30	Washington, D.C.	Carter Baron Theatre
Aug. 1	Richmond, Va.	Mosque
Aug. 2	Norfolk, Va.	————
Aug. 8	Akron, Ohio	Civic Theatre
Aug. 9	Pittsburgh, Pa.	Syria Mosque
Aug. 10	Cleveland, Ohio	Allen Theatre
Aug. 13-17	New York, N.Y.	Bottom Line*

*live broadcast

Aug. 21-23	Atlanta, Ga.	Electric Ballroom
Sept. 6	New Orleans, La.	Performing Arts Center
Sept. 11	Arlington, Tex.	Texas Hall
Sept. 12	Austin, Tex.	Municipal Auditorium
Sept. 13-14	Houston, Tex.	Music Hall
Sept. 16	Dallas, Tex.	————
Sept. 17	Oklahoma City, Okla.	Music Hall
Sept. 20	Grinnell, Iowa	Grinnell University
Sept. 21	Minneapolis, Minn.	Tyrone Guthrie Theatre
Sept. 23	Ann Arbor, Mich.	University of Michigan
Sept. 25	Chicago, Ill.	Auditorium Theatre
Sept. 26	Iowa City, Iowa	University of Iowa
Sept. 27	St. Louis, Mo.	Ambassador Theatre
Sept. 28	Kansas City, Mo.	Memorial Hall
Sept. 30	Omaha, Neb.	University of Nebraska
Oct. 2	Milwaukee, Wisc.	Uptown Theatre*

*show delayed by bomb scare

Oct. 4	Detroit, Mich.	Michigan Palace
Oct. 10	Red Bank, N.J.	Carlton Theatre
Oct. 16-19	Los Angeles, Calif.	The Roxy*

*live broadcast

Oct. 25	Portland, Ore.	Paramount
Oct. 26	Seattle, Wash.	Paramount
Oct. 29	Sacramento, Calif.	Memorial Auditorium
Oct. 30	Oakland, Calif.	Paramount
Nov. 1	Santa Barbara, Calif.	University of California
Nov. 3-4, 6	Phoenix, Ariz.	Arizona State University
Nov. 9	Tampa, Fla.	Jai Alai Pavilion
Nov. 11	Miami, Fla.	Jai Alai Pavilion
Nov. 18	London, England	Hammersmith Odeon
Nov. 21	Stockholm, Sweden	————
Nov. 23	Amsterdam, Holland	————
Nov. 24	London, England	Hammersmith Odeon
Dec. 2-3	Boston, Mass.	Music Hall
Dec. 5-7	Washington, D.C.	Georgetown University
Dec. 10	Lewisburg, Pa.	Bucknell Auditorium

Dec. 11	S. Orange, N.J.	Seton Hall University
Dec. 12	Greenvale, N.Y.	C.W. Post College*

*recorded live

Dec. 16	Oswego, N.Y.	SUNY
Dec. 17	Buffalo, N.Y.	Kleinhaus Music Hall
Dec. 19	Montreal, Canada	———————
Dec. 20	Ottawa, Canada	National Arts Center
Dec. 21	Toronto, Canada	Ryerson Theatre
Dec. 27-31	Philadelphia, Pa.	Tower Theatre*

*Born To Run tour ends

1976

March 25	Columbia, S.C.	Township Auditorium
March 26	Atlanta, Ga.	Fox Theatre
March 28	Durham, N.C.	Duke University
March 29	Charlotte, N.C.	Oven's Auditorium
April 1	Athens, Ohio	University of Ohio
April 2	Louisville, Ky.	Macally Theatre
April 4	E. Lansing, Mich.	Michigan State University
April 5	Columbus, Ohio	Ohio Theatre
April 7-8	Cleveland, Ohio	Allen Theatre
April 9	Hamilton, N.Y.	Colgate University
April 10	Wallingford, Ct.	Choate School*

*benefit performance played at request of John Hammond

April 12	Johnstown, Pa.	Memorial Auditorium
April 13	University Park, Pa.	Penn State University
April 15	Pittsburgh, Pa.	Syria Mosque
April 16	Meadville, Pa.	Allegheny College
April 17	Rochester, N.Y.	University of Rochester
April 20	Johnson City, Tenn.	Freedom Hall
April 21	Knoxville, Tenn.	Auditorium
April 22	Blacksburg, Va.	Virginia Polytechnic
April 24	Boone, N.C.	Appalachian State College
April 26	Chattanooga, Tenn.	Tivoli Theatre
April 28	Nashville, Tenn.	Grand Ol' Opry
April 29	Memphis, Tenn.	Ellis Auditorium*

*Bruce tries to visit Elvis Presley after show

April 30	Birmingham, Ala.	Municipal Auditorium
May 3	Little Rock, Ark.	Robinson Auditorium
May 4	Jackson, Miss.	Municipal Auditorium
May 6	Shreveport, La.	Municipal Auditorium
May 8	Baton Rouge, La.	Assembly Center
May 9-10	Mobile, Ala.	Municipal Auditorium
May 11	Auburn, Ala.	Auburn University
May 13	New Orleans, La.	Municipal Auditorium
Aug. 1-3, 5-7	Red Bank, N.J.	Carlton Theatre
Sept. 26	Phoenix, Ariz.	Coliseum
Sept. 29-30	Santa Monica, Calif.	Civic Auditorium
Oct. 2	Oakland, Calif.	Paramount
Oct. 3	Santa Clara, Calif.	Santa Clara University
Oct. 5	Santa Barbara, Calif.	County Bowl
Oct. 9	South Bend, Ind.	Notre Dame University
Oct. 10	Miami, Ohio	Miami University
Oct. 12	New Brunswick, N.J.	Rutgers University
Oct. 13	Union, N.J.	Kean College
Oct. 16	Williamsburg, Va.	William and Mary University
Oct. 17-18	Washington, D.C.	Georgetown University
Oct. 25-26	Philadelphia, Pa.	Spectrum*

*first date in sports arena

Oct. 28-30, Nov. 2-4	New York, N.Y.	Palladium

1977

Feb. 7	Albany, N.Y.	Palace Theatre
Feb. 8	Rochester, N.Y.	Auditorium Theatre
Feb. 9	Buffalo, N.Y.	Kleinhaus Auditorium
Feb. 10	Utica, N.Y.	Memorial Auditorium
Feb. 12	Ottawa, Canada	Civic Center
Feb. 13	Toronto, Canada	Concert Bowl Forum
Feb. 15	Detroit, Mich.	Masonic Auditorium
Feb. 16	Columbus, Ohio	Vets Memorial Auditorium
Feb. 17	Ridgefield, Ohio	Coliseum
Feb. 19	St. Paul, Minn.	Civic Center
Feb. 20	Madison, Wisc.	Dane County Coliseum
Feb. 22	Milwaukee, Wisc.	Auditorium
Feb. 23	Chicago, Ill.	Auditorium Theatre
Feb. 25	Lafayette, Ind.	Purdue University
Feb. 26	Indianapolis, Ind.	Convention Center
Feb. 27	Cincinnati, Ohio	Riverfront Coliseum
Feb. 28	St. Louis, Mo.	Fox Theatre
March 2	Atlanta, Ga.	Civic Center
March 4	Jacksonville, Fla.	———————
March 5	Orlando, Fla.	Jai Alai Fronton
March 6	Miami, Fla.	Jai Alai Fronton
March 10	Toledo, Ohio	Sports Arena
March 11	Latrobe, Pa.	St. Vincent's College
March 13	Baltimore, Md.	Towson State College
March 14	Poughkeepsie, N.Y.	Mid-Hudson Civic Center
March 15	Binghamton, N.Y.	Community Arena
March 18	New Haven, Ct.	Coliseum
March 19	Lewiston, Maine	Central Maine Youth Center
March 20	Providence, R.I.	Providence College
March 22-25	Boston, Mass.	Music Hall*

*last date before recording Darkness On The Edge Of Town.

1978

May 23	Buffalo, N.Y.	Shea's Buffalo Theatre
May 24	Albany, N.Y.	Palace Theatre
May 26-27	Philadelphia, Pa.	Spectrum
May 29-31	Boston, Mass.	Music Hall
June 2	Annapolis, Md	U.S. Naval Academy
June 3	Uniondale, N.Y.	Nassau Coliseum
June 5	Toledo, Ohio	Sports Arena
June 6	Indianapolis, Ind.	Convention Center
June 8	Madison, Wisc.	Dane County Coliseum
June 9	Milwaukee, Wisc.	Arena
June 10	Minneapolis, Minn.	Arena
June 13	Iowa City, Iowa	University of Iowa
June 14	Omaha, Neb.	Music Hall
June 16	Kansas City, Mo.	Municipal Auditorium
June 17	St. Louis, Mo.	Kiel Auditorium
June 20	Denver, Colo.	Red Rocks
June 24	Portland, Ore.	Paramount
June 25	Seattle, Wash.	Paramount
June 26	Vancouver, Canada	Queen Elizabeth Theatre
June 29	San Jose, Calif.	Performing Arts Center
June 30-July 1	Berkeley, Calif.	Community Theatre
July 5	Los Angeles, Calif.	The Forum
July 7	Los Angeles, Calif.	The Roxy*

*live broadcast

July 8	Phoenix, Ariz.	Coliseum*

*concert filmed for TV commercial; ''Rosalita'' later used in Heroes Of Rock And Roll TV Special and an Old Grey Whistle Test on BBC.

July 9	San Diego, Calif.	Sports Arena *
July 12	Dallas, Tex.	Convention Center
July 14	San Antonio, Tex.	Memorial Auditorium
July 15	Houston, Tex.	Coliseum
July 16	New Orleans, La.	Auditorium*

*Clarence Clemons sings ''Macho Man''

July 18	Jackson, Miss.	Civic Center
July 19	Memphis, Tenn.	Ellis Auditorium
July 21	Nashville, Tenn.	Municipal Auditorium
July 28	Miami, Fla.	Jai Alai Fronton
July 29	St. Petersburg, Fla.	Bay Front Center
July 31	Columbia, S.C.	Auditorium
Aug. 1	Charleston, S.C.	Municipal Auditorium
Aug. 2	Charlotte, N.C.	Coliseum
Aug. 4	Charleston, W.Va.	Civic Center
Aug. 5	Louisville, Ky.	Gardens
Aug. 7	Kalamazoo, Mich.	Wings Auditorium
Aug. 8	Toronto, Canada	Ryerson Theatre
Aug. 9	Cleveland, Ohio	The Agora

Aug. 10	Rochester, N.Y.	War Memorial	Nov. 12	Troy, N.Y.	Rensselaer Polytechnic University
Aug. 12	Augusta, Maine	Civic Center	Nov. 14	Utica, N.Y.	Memorial Auditorium
Aug. 14	Hampton, Va.	Coliseum	Nov. 16	Toronto, Canada	Maple Leaf Gardens
Aug. 15	Largo, Md.	Capitol Center	Nov. 17	E. Lansing, Mich.	Michigan State University
Aug. 18-19	Philadelphia, Pa.	The Spectrum			
Aug. 21-23	New York N.Y.	Madison Square Garden	Nov. 18	Oxford, Ohio	Miami University
Aug. 25	New Haven, Ct.	Coliseum	Nov. 20	Champaign, Ill.	University of Illinois
Aug. 26	Providence, R.I.	Civic Center	Nov. 21	Evanston, Ill.	Northwestern University
Aug. 28-29	Pittsburgh, Pa.	Stanley Theatre	Nov. 25	St. Louis, Mo.	Kiel Opera House
Aug. 30	Cleveland, Ohio	Richfield College	Nov. 27	Milwaukee, Wisc.	Milwaukee Arena
Sept. 1	Detroit, Mich.	Masonic Auditorium	Nov. 28	Madison, Wisc.	Dane County Coliseum
Sept. 3	Saginaw, Mich.	Civic Center	Nov. 29	St. Paul, Minn.	St. Paul Arena
Sept. 5	Columbus, Ohio	Veteran's Auditorium	Dec. 1	Norman, Okla.	University of Oklahoma
Sept. 6	Chicago, Ill.	Uptown Theatre	Dec. 3	Carbondale, Ill.	Southern Illinois University
Sept. 9	South Bend, Ind.	Notre Dame University			
Sept. 10	Cincinnati, Ohio.	Riverfront Coliseum	Dec. 5	Baton Rouge, La.	Louisiana State University
Sept. 12	Syracuse, N.Y.	War Memorial			
Sept. 13	Springfield, Mass.	Civic Center	Dec. 7	Austin, Tex.	University of Texas
Sept. 15-17	New York, N.Y.	Palladium	Dec. 8	Houston, Tex.	The Summit
Sept. 19-21	Passaic, N.J.	Capitol Theatre	Dec. 9	Dallas, Tex.	Convention Centre
*Sept. 20 show broadcast live			Dec. 11	Boulder, Colo.	University of Colorado
Sept. 25	Boston, Mass.	Boston Gardens	Dec. 13	Tucson, Ariz.	Community Center Arena
Sept. 29	Birmingham, Ala.	Auditorium			
Sept. 30-	Atlanta, Ga.	Fox Theatre*	Dec. 15-16	San Francisco, Calif.	Winterland*
*first night broadcast live			*(live broadcast first night.)		
Nov. 1	Princeton, N.J.	Princeton University	Dec. 18	Portland, Ore.	Paramount
Nov. 2	Largo, Md.	Capitol Center	Dec. 20	Seattle, Wash.	Seattle Arena
Nov. 4	Burlington, Vt.	University of Vermont	Dec. 27-28	Pittsburgh, Pa.	Stanley Theatre
Nov. 5	Durham, N.H.	University of New Hampshire	Dec. 30	Detroit, Mich.	Cobo Hall
			Dec. 31	Cleveland, Ohio	Richfield Coliseum
Nov. 7	Ithaca, N.Y.	Cornell University		1979	
Nov. 8	Montreal, Canada	Montreal Forum			
Nov. 10	St. Bonaventure, N.Y.	St. Bonaventure U	Jan. 1	Cleveland, Ohio	Richfield Coliseum

Acknowledgments

In 1975, writing a piece about what he called the Rock Critic Establishment, my friend and colleague Robert Christgau was generous enough to remark that my "quickie" paperback on Bruce Springsteen might lend new dignity to that benighted form. But I don't think he thought that my method was going to mean delaying publication for four years. It certainly wasn't what I had in mind.

For me, this project has been worth every minute—and I stole lots of them from other things in order to scheme and dream about it. There is a great deal left out, a thousand hilarious stories that just didn't fit. But mostly, I valued this book so much because writing it meant making so many friends.

To start with, there was Ron Oberman, who convinced me to listen to Bruce's first album and wooed me to my first Springsteen show. That I didn't adequately appreciate either wasn't his fault.

Jon Landau dragged me away from a TV set in Cambridge one night in 1974, and changed both our lives. I remember his exact words—"If I can't watch Kojak, neither can you. Now get down here." As he tells it, I introduced him to Bruce, but what I remember about the show at Charley's Bar is a blur, and the two of us looking at each other from time to time to make sure that what we were seeing was real. I also had the good fortune to edit Jon's *Real Paper* column about Bruce, in which he uttered the sentence heard round the world, and to see a lot of Springsteen shows, listen to a lot of records and talk about the man and the music for hours with Jon. So I know why they call him the King.

Glen Brunman was more than just a Columbia Records publicist to me. He is one of my best friends, and the nights we stayed up till dawn sorting out the past and the future were some of the best of my life. When I did the initial research in 1975, he was indispensable; when I thought I'd never be lucky enough to be typing the final sentences of this manuscript, the Brahma was always there to encourage me. But I remember more than anything our hours on the phone and sitting around the house—there's lots more of that guy in this book than his quotes.

Obie Dziedzic is a miracle worker. She brought me much closer to my own feelings, not just about Bruce but about rock and roll in general. In a funny way, I've always thought that rock and roll is more about the audience than the performer, and Obie is the best fan any rock and roller could ever hope to have. That such a person could actually become a friend of mine is as much as I have ever hoped for.

There were other fans, too. Hundreds of them wrote me letters asking about Bruce and the book during the period when it lay in limbo; it sustained me to know that so many people were interested in seeing this book come to life. I wish I could thank each of them in person. A few of them, however, I got to know, and they are the faces I saw as ideal readers. Barry Bell and Dick Wingate appear in the text; I thank them again for letting me share their experiences and insights. Dave McGee, who generously shared his file on the lawsuit, Barry Singer and Wayne King all contributed a great deal to the research. In a different way, so did Lou Cohan, who put it all on the line.

My colleagues Jim Henke, John Milward, Paul Nelson, Jay Cocks, Kit Rachlis and especially Dave McGee and Greil Marcus also provided invaluable advice, comments and assistance. My editor at *Rolling Stone*, Barbara Downey, did not work on this book—but she has been the single most important factor in improving my writing in the past three years; for that I thank her.

Miami Steve Van Zandt, Garry Tallent, Max Weinberg, Clarence Clemons, Danny Federici and Roy Bittan—the E Street Band—gave me companionship and stories as good as their music. There isn't anything better than that. Jim McHale, Bob Chirmside, Mark Brickman, Bruce Jackson, Mike Batlan and Doug Sutphin of Bruce's road crew all went out of their way to make me comfortable. They ought to be celebrities in their own right.

Rock and roll is supposed to be something closed to all except the youngest. John Hammond helps prove that a lie every day of his life. So do Tex and Marion Vinyard, who showed me a great deal, not just about Bruce, but about courtesy and dignity.

Debts of gratitude are also owed to Stephanie Bennett and all at Delilah; Mick Rock, Ernie Thormahlen and T.R.A. Studios; Gerry Helferich at Doubleday; and especially Mike Mayer and Ted Nussbaum, who took this book far more seriously than they were obliged to do.

Among the others who contributed to making the book possible are Debbie Gold, Southside Johnny, Kevin Kavanaugh, Ed Sciaky, Kevin Stein, Jimmy Iovine, Mike Pillot, Kathy Heavey, Gary Baker, Marianne Partridge, Susan Ginsberg, Phil Ceccola, Dave Gahr, and the people who first proposed that I write it, Josh Feigenbaum and Bob Zenowich.

Barbara Carr lived through it all without complaining, understanding my obsession even when it got in the way of normal living; for the three A.M. noise and for helping me believe—my thanks and my love. And more of the same for Sasha and Kristen, who are still young enough to know what it will mean to look back on the funny side of all this someday.

Finally, thanks to Bruce, who contributed much more than comments on the text. Rock and roll has given me the best moments of my life, and my best moments in rock and roll have come from him. Knowing the guy has been more than I needed; the real inspiration is watching him make dreams come true every night. To Bruce, from all of us, thanks for the lift.

Photo Credits

Richard Aaron: 107, 120, 123

Mary Alfieri: 92, 109

Rob Brown: 38

CBS: 1 Eric Meola, 36, 40 Chris Gulker, 59 Chris Gulker, 157 73 Chris Gulker, 88, 98, 108, 124 Michael Putland, 164 Chris Gulker

Phil A. Ceccola: 31, 32, 47, 48, 49, 50, 52, 53, 62, 63, 64, 65, 67, 68, 74, 75, 81, 82, 83, 84, 93, 94, 101, 102, 105, 128, 142

David Gahr: 19, 39, 45, 61, 76, 77, 86, 87, 89, 90, 104, 110, 113, 114, 115, 116, 118, 122, 127, 131, 132, 133, 139, 175 161, 163, 165, 176

Lynn Goldsmith: 5, 12, 15, 17, 20, 22 27, 35, 41, 42, 58, 136, 147, 154, 156, 158, 159, 165

Bob Gruen: 137, 143

Bob Leafe: 57, 99

Paul Natkin: 39

New Haven Journal Courier: 83, 162, 173

Peter Jay Philbin: 85, 91, 97, 111, 121

Chuck Pulin: 8, 10, 11, 35, 37, 46, 51, 54, 55, 56, 57, 60, 66, 69, 66, 69, 71, 78, 80, 93, 100, 129, 142, 148, 149

Michael Putland: 9, 14, 23, 144

Kate Simon: 125, 158

Frank Stefanko: 3, 13, 28, 34, 135, 138, 139, 140, 146, 150, 152, 153, 169

Allen Tannenbaum: 26, 33

Belinda Taylor: 30

Tex Vinyard Collection: 24, 25

Doug Yule: 151

175